GLOBAL DIASPORAS

In a perceptive and arresting analysis, Robin Cohen introduces his distinctive approach to the study of the world's diasporas. The book investigates the changing meanings of the concept and the contemporary diasporic condition, including case studies of Jews, Armenians, Africans, Chinese, British, Indians, Lebanese and Caribbean peoples.

The first edition of this book had a major impact on diaspora studies and was the foundational text in an emerging research and teaching field. This second edition extends and clarifies Cohen's argument, addresses some critiques and outlines new perspectives for the study of diasporas. The book has also been made more student-friendly with illustrations, guided readings and suggested essay questions.

Reviews of the first edition

"Cohen's erudition is vast … his interpretations are solid and well informed. By and large one can only marvel at the scope of Cohen's learning and the richness of his vocabulary." – *Mark J. Miller, University of Delaware, Journal of World History, Fall 1999.*

"Cohen's book offers a timely overview of diasporas. The book is also engagingly written, with Cohen's personal anecdotes adding zing rather than self-indulgence to the analysis." – *Robert C. Smith, Columbia University, Political Studies Quaterly, Spring 1999.*

"Reading this book I thought 'Cohen is doing for diaspora what Weber did for religion'." – *Fran Markowiz, Ben Gurion University, American Anthropologist, June 1999.*

"A succinct but satisfying book … as Cohen convincingly demonstrates here, the diaspora wave is well and truly upon us." – *Sarah Ansari, Royal Holloway College, Times Higher Educational Supplement, 6 March 1998.*

Robin Cohen is Professorial Fellow at Queen Elizabeth House, University of Oxford. He taught for many years at Warwick and has also held appointments at the Universities of Ibadan, the West Indies and Cape Town. His other books include *The New Helots* (2003), *The Cambridge Survey of World Migration* (edited, 1995), *Frontiers of Identity* (1994), *Migration and its Enemies* (2006) and *Global Sociology* with Paul Kennedy (rev. 2007).

GLOBAL DIASPORAS
Series editor: Robin Cohen

The assumption that minorities and migrants will demonstrate an exclusive loyalty to the nation-state is now questionable. Scholars of nationalism, international migration and ethnic relations need new conceptual maps and fresh case studies to understand the growth of complex transnational identities. The old idea of "diaspora" may provide this framework. Though often conceived in terms of a catastrophic dispersion, widening the notion of diaspora to include trade, imperial, labour and cultural diasporas can provide a more nuanced understanding of the often positive relationships between migrants' homelands and their places of work and settlement.

This book forms part of an ambitious and interlinked series of volumes trying to capture the new relationships between home and abroad. Historians, political scientists, sociologists and anthropologists from a number of countries have collaborated on this forward-looking project. The series includes two books which provide the defining, comparative and synoptic aspects of diasporas. Further titles focus on particular communities, both traditionally recognized diasporas and those newer claimants who define their collective experiences and aspirations in terms of diasporic identity.

This series is associated with the Transnational Communities Programme at the University of Oxford funded by the UK's Economic and Social Research Council.

Published titles:

New Diasporas
Nicholas Van Hear

The Sikh Diaspora
Darshan Singh Tatla

Italy's Many Diasporas
Donna R. Gabaccia

**The Hindu Diaspora:
Comparative Patterns**
Steven Vertovec

The Israeli Diaspora
Steven J. Gold

The Ukrainian Diapora
Vic Satzewich

New African Diasporas
Edited by Khalid Koser

The Palestinian Diaspora
Helena Lindholm Schulz

**Global Diasporas:
An introduction (second edition)**
Robin Cohen

GLOBAL DIASPORAS

An introduction

Second edition

Robin Cohen

LONDON AND NEW YORK

First published 2008
by Routledge
2 Park Square, Milton Park, Abingdon, Oxon OX14 4RN

Simultaneously published in the USA and Canada
by Routledge
270 Madison Avenue, New York, NY 10016

*Routledge is an imprint of the Taylor & Francis Group,
an informa business*

© 2008 Robin Cohen

Typeset in Bembo by Keyword Group Ltd
Printed and bound in Great Britain by TJ International Ltd,
Padstow, Cornwall

British Library Cataloguing in Publication Data
A catalogue record for this book is available
from the British Library

Library of Congress Cataloging in Publication Data
A catalog record for this book has been requested

ISBN 10: 0-415-43550-1 (hbk)
ISBN 10: 0-415-43551-X (pbk)
ISBN 10: 0-203-92894-6 (ebk)

ISBN 13: 978-0-415-43550-5 (hbk)
ISBN 13: 978-0-415-43551-2 (pbk)
ISBN 13: 978-0-203-92894-3 (ebk)

TO
AMELIA RACHEL TICKNER AND
LOUIS SETH TICKNER

CONTENTS

CONTENTS

TABLES

FIGURES

ACKNOWLEDGEMENTS

The new edition of this book has been delayed by various other pressing commitments. I have sorely tried the patience of Gerhard Boomgaarden at Routledge, who has been a helpful and supportive editor since he assumed the responsibility for this title and the remaining ten titles in the Global Diasporas series. My apologies go to his assistant, Ann Carter, for my evasive emails about progress.

Over the years I have been lucky enough to meet many of the leading scholars in diaspora studies, some of whom have been instrumental in forcing me to clarify, reaffirm or reshape my ideas (though, of course, I cannot hold them in any way responsible for the revisions contained in this text). Khachig Tölöyan remains the supreme interpreter of diasporic phenomena and the most diligent of journal editors. Many scholars have benefited from his lengthy and learned comments. I met two pioneers of the field, James Clifford and Gabriel Sheffer, at Poitiers, where three major French scholars of diaspora were also present – William Berthomière, Christine Chivallon and Stéphane Dufoix. I also enjoyed talking to Chantal Bordes-Benayoun in my ridiculously bad French. All have greatly influenced me. Gloria Totoricagüena kindly invited me to a conference in Reno centred on the Basque diaspora, where I finally could shake hands with William ('Bill') Safran, whose work I had long admired.

I have worked closely with the authors and editors of my series on Global Diasporas, including Nicholas Van Hear, Darshan Singh Tatla, Donna G. Gabaccia, Steven J. Gold, Vic Satzewich, Khalid Koser, Edward Alpers, Helena Lindholm Schulz and Steven Vertovec. Steven Vertovec and Alisdair Rogers have been close colleagues over the years. We have co-operated in so many ways it would take a lengthy panegyric to thank them.

I have been lucky to have supervised many wonderful doctoral students, four of whom have written innovatively on diasporas – Ravi Thiara (on Indians in South Africa), Östen Wahlbeck (on Kurds), David Griffiths (on Kurds and Somalis) and Dominic Pasura (on Zimbabweans).

Other colleagues, including Stephen Castles, Jeff Crisp, Josh DeWind, Robert Fine, Barbara Harriss-White, Electra Petracou, Annie Phizacklea, Peter Ratcliffe and Paola Toninato have always 'been there' when I needed them.

ACKNOWLEDGEMENTS

The copyrighted photographs used in this book have been purchased from iStockphoto International and used within the terms of the company's licence.

Finally, I have to thank Selina Molteno Cohen for her companionship and editorial help. At last, Selina, I have learned the difference between a defining and non-defining adverbial pronoun.

PREFACE TO THE SECOND
EDITION

Like many ideas, the idea of a book on Global diasporas arrived serendipitously. On study leave late in the early 1990s, I was trying to find some creative way of understanding emerging patterns of international migration, which looked very different from conventional depictions of one-way flows from source country A to destination country B. 'Labour migration', 'family migration' and 'brain drain migration' were the main descriptive categories deployed at the time, though later 'unauthorized' and 'refugee migration' become much more central. What I intuited was that none of these descriptions adequately captured the complex transversal and circular flows that joined 'home' and 'away'. It even was questionable whether starting with this binary divide was particularly helpful.

For a while, I experienced brain drain of a more personal sort, probably arising from my onerous responsibilities directing the Centre for Research in Ethnic Relations at Warwick. Looking meditatively (or was that vegetatively?) at the garden out of my window, I suddenly thought how migration scholars were increasingly using gardening terms like 'uprooting', 'scattering', 'transplanting' and the then newly-fashionable word 'hybridity'. My interest mounted when I found that 'diaspora' was derived from the Greek work *speiro* ('to sow' or 'to disperse'). Could refashioning the old idea of diaspora provide a means to understand new and revived forms of transnational and transtatal movements? How were these movements mapping onto, and changing, the accepted ways of understanding global migration, emerging identities, complex oscillating flows and unexpected patterns of settlement and integration?

'Discoveries' are rarely the happy lot of the individual social scientist because, of course, many other people had got there before me or were rapidly to supersede my initially simple ideas. Stuart Hall, James Clifford and Paul Gilroy had written pioneering work. An even greater sign that a revitalized concept of diaspora had arrived was the launch of a new journal called *Diaspora: a Journal of Transnational Studies* in 1991 under the editorship of the Armenian scholar, Khachig Tölöyan. In the first issue of the journal a path-breaking article by William Safran well and truly got the ball rolling.

The first edition of *Global diasporas: an introduction* caught this *zeitgeist*. It was initially published in the UK in 1997 by a newly-founded and creative university press, UCL Press, then by the University of Washington Press and, finally by the current publishers, Routledge. It has been reprinted many times, translated into a number of languages and cited in hundreds of scholarly articles. It would be nice to believe this attention was due to the brilliance and originality of the arguments I advanced but, without false modesty, I must acknowledge that I had simply written the right book at the right time. If this is indeed the case, what justifications are there to produce a revised edition a decade later?

- First, there is a considerable conceptual literature that has built up since 1997, much in support of my propositions, some in criticism. It is an act of arrogance not to respond to critics at all, though to get the tone right is rather difficult. It is all too easy to be defensive, or appear to be addressing issues with a closed mind. Again, to speak to every comment in detail would be intolerable to the reader. I have tried therefore to enter a dialogue with a few critics, where I wanted to acknowledge the validity of a comment, defend my position, extend my argument or, at the very least, clarify it.
- Second, the sheer volume of research on the comparative and theoretical study of diasporas in the social sciences and, increasingly the humanities, over the last decade has been truly astonishing. Accessing Google in August 2007 yielded an impressive 14,100,000 hits from the word 'diaspora', while the more delimited 'global diaspora' generated 2,100,000 hits. Using Google Scholar, there were 81,900 hits for the first term and 31,800 for the second. When I consulted the Library of Congress in the mid-1990s, the entries included a few hundred titles on diasporas, overwhelmingly concerning Jewish, Greek, Armenian and African experiences. By August 2007, the keyword entry 'diaspora' produced 2,503 results covering a multitude of ethnic groups and, much more rarely, other social formations not defined by ethnicity or religion. I have sampled, but by no means covered, this budding literature in the new edition.
- Third, as with so much else after 9/11, the discussion of diasporas has been drawn into the security agenda. Does a diasporic identity imply potential disloyalty to the state of residence and with what possible consequences? Although 'homeland politics' was discussed in the first edition, this rather limited formulation now needs further consideration (see Chapters 6 and 9).
- Fourth, in many cases, diasporic communities have shown a continuing or newly asserted attachment to places of origin. This has generated many attempts at using diasporas for the purposes of homeland economic and social development, sometimes in co-operation with international development agencies and the governments of rich countries (Chapter 9). At the same time, the idea that 'homeland' and 'home' are intrinsic to the diasporic condition has been questioned.

- Finally, a number of similar or related terms – notably transnationalism, hybridity cosmopolitanism and creolization – addressing complex flows, diversity and multi-locality in different ways have become current, sometimes causing considerable conceptual confusion, particularly on the part of students. All four of these terms have been used more consistently in this edition.

In all, I have tried to maintain a balance between retaining the original vision of the book, updating sources and data, making the book more student-friendly and responding to new debates.

Figure 1.1 A Hispanic migrant in the USA symbolically chains herself to the Stars and Stripes. Is she an 'immigrant', a member of a 'minority' or part of a diaspora of her country of origin? Similarly vexed definitional issues are discussed in this chapter. © iStockphoto.com/Robin Cohen

1

FOUR PHASES OF DIASPORA STUDIES

Arguably, diaspora studies have gone through four phases, which I specify below, then explore in greater detail:

- First, the classical use of the term, usually capitalized as Diaspora and used only in the singular, was mainly confined to the study of the Jewish experience. The Greek diaspora made an off-stage appearance. Excluding some earlier casual references, from the 1960s and 1970s the classical meaning was systematically extended, becoming more common as a description of the dispersion of Africans, Armenians and the Irish. With the Jews, these peoples conceived their scattering as arising from a cataclysmic event that had traumatized the group as a whole, thereby creating the central historical experience of victimhood at the hands of a cruel oppressor. Retrospectively and without complete consensus, the Palestinians were later added to this group.
- In the second phase, in the 1980s and onwards, as Safran notably argued, diaspora was deployed as 'a metaphoric designation' to describe *different categories* of people – 'expatriates, expellees, political refugees, alien residents, immigrants and ethnic and racial minorities *tout court*'.[1] Moreover, a point again made by Safran, the term now designated a vast array of *different peoples* who either applied the term to themselves or had the label conferred upon them. Given their number (certainly now over one hundred), their historical experiences, collective narratives and differing relationships to homelands and hostlands, they were bound to be a more varied cluster of diasporas than the groups designated in phase one.[2]
- The third phase, from the mid-1990s, was marked by social constructionist critiques of 'second phase' theorists who, despite their recognition of the proliferation of groups newly designated as diasporas and the evolution of new ways of studying them, were still seen as holding back the full force of the concept.[3] Influenced by postmodernist readings, social construction-ists sought to decompose two of the major building blocks previously delimiting and demarcating the diasporic idea, namely 'homeland' and

'ethnic/religious community'. In the postmodern world, it was further argued, identities have become deterritorialized and constructed and deconstructed in a flexible and situational way; accordingly, concepts of diaspora had to be radically reordered in response to this complexity.

• By the turn of the century, the current phase of consolidation set in. The social constructionist critiques were partially accommodated, but were seen as in danger of emptying the notion of diaspora of much of its analytical and descriptive power. While the increased complexity and deterritorialization of identities are valid phenomena and constitutive of a small minority of diasporas (generally those that had been doubly or multiply displaced over time), ideas of home and often the stronger inflection of homeland remain powerful discourses and ones which, if anything, have been more strongly asserted in key examples (see Chapter 7). The phase of consolidation is marked by a modified reaffirmation of the diasporic idea, including its core elements, common features and ideal types.

THE PROTOTYPICAL DIASPORA

Let me elaborate on each of these four phases, starting with one of the key features of the classical, victim diaspora – the idea of dispersal following a traumatic event in the homeland, to two or more foreign destinations. Migration scholars often find it remarkably difficult to separate the compelling from the voluntary elements in the motivation to move. However, when we talk of a trauma afflicting a group collectively, it is perhaps possible to isolate a class of events characterized by their brutality, scale and intensity so as unambiguously to compel emigration or flight. Being shackled in manacles, being expelled by a tyrannical leader, or being coerced to leave by force of arms, mass riots or the threat of 'ethnic cleansing' appear qualitatively different phenomena from the general pressures of over-population, land hunger, poverty or a generally unsympathetic political environment.

Although Jews often allude to their earlier period as slaves in ancient Egypt, particularly in the Passover rituals that recount the story of the Exodus, it was the destruction of Solomon's laboriously-constructed temple in 586 BC by the Mesopotamian Empire that is evoked as the central folk memory of trauma. The Jewish leader of the time, Zedekiah, vacillated for a decade, and then impulsively sanctioned a rebellion against the powerful Mesopotamian Empire. The Babylonian king, Nebuchadnezzar, brutally suppressed the revolt and dragged Zedekiah and the key military, civic and religious personnel in chains to Babylon.[4] Jews had been compelled to desert the land 'promised' to them by God to Moses and thereafter, the tradition suggests, forever became dispersed.

As I shall argue in Chapter 2, the catastrophic origins of the Jewish diaspora have been unduly emphasized in their collective consciousness – though I by no means wish to minimize some of the calamities that afflicted diasporic Jews over the centuries. The remaining four prototypical diasporas have also had unambiguously shocking episodes in their history that led to their original or further dispersion. Let me turn, for example, to the 'first' African diaspora set into motion by the African slave trade. (Twentieth-century, post-colonial African emigration prompted by civil war, famine, economic failure and political instability can be thought of as generating a 'second', incipient, set of 'new' African diasporas.[5]) The horror of the slave trade has been exposed so many times that justifiably hyperbolic language begins to lose its force. The under-researched Indian Ocean African slave trade to Asia and the Middle East was enormous − perhaps as many as four million were involved − but it was the forcible transhipment of ten million people across the Atlantic for mass slavery and coerced plantation labour in the Americas that provided the defining misfortune that constituted the African diaspora.

There were early expulsions of Armenians by a Byzantine emperor in the sixth century AD and many Armenians were involved in long-distance commerce and trade. However, the crucial historical events that led Armenians to be characterized as a victim diaspora followed the massacres of the late nineteenth century and their forced displacement during 1915–16, when the Turks deported two-thirds of their number (1.75 million people) to Syria and Palestine. Many Armenians subsequently landed up in France and the USA. It is now widely accepted (though still implausibly disputed by Turkish sources) that a million Armenians were either killed or died of starvation during this mass displacement, the twentieth century's first major example of what has come to be known as 'ethnic cleansing'.

The migration of the Irish over the period 1845 to 1852, following the famine, can be regarded as a comparable tragedy. To be sure, there have been ups and downs by Irish historians of migration in seeking to assess just how salient the famine was in propelling the vast and continuous transatlantic migrations of the nineteenth century. However, in her powerfully argued and scholarly account, Kinealy suggests that there was much more deliberation in the British response to the potato blight than had previously been adduced. She argues that, far from *laissez-faire* attitudes governing policy, the British government had a hidden agenda of population control, the modernization of agriculture and land reform.[6] This gives the Irish events a greater similarity to those that propelled the Jewish, African and Armenian diasporas.

When Britain withdrew from Palestine on 14 May 1948, the Israeli army occupied the vacuum and the ethnically-based state of Israel was proclaimed. Initially out of prudence, then out of panic, two-thirds of the Arab population of Palestine left their homes and became refugees, at first in neighbouring countries, then all over the Middle East and beyond. As Schultz recounts, 'To the Palestinians, the birth of Israel is thus remembered as the catastrophe, *al-nakba*, [serving] to imprint the suffering caused by dispersal, exile, alienation and denial.'[7] The 3.9 million-strong Palestinian diaspora had been born.

Ironically and tragically, its midwife was the homecoming of the Jewish diaspora.

These scarring historical calamities – Babylon for the Jews, slavery for the Africans, massacres and forced displacement for the Armenians, famine for the Irish and the formation of the state of Israel for the Palestinians – lend a particular colouring to these five diasporas. They are, above all, victim diasporas in their vital historical experiences. This does not mean that they do not also exhibit features characteristic of other diasporas, including voluntary migration for the purposes of trade or work or for other reasons. Rather, their victim origin is either self-affirmed or accepted by outside observers as determining their *predominant* character. Again, there are many contemporary examples of forced displacement that have created incipient victim diasporas, which over time may create sufficient social cohesion to separate particular groups from their surrounding context in their countries of settlement. In both established and embryonic victim diasporas the wrench from home must survive so powerfully in the folk memories of these groups that restoring the homeland or even returning there becomes an important focus for social mobilization, and the mould in which their popular cultures and political attitudes are formed. At the end of this chapter I shall build up a consolidated list of the common features of a diaspora, but for the meantime let me draw two elements from the prototypical cases discussed above: *the traumatic dispersal from an original homeland* and *the salience of the homeland in the collective memory of a forcibly dispersed group.*

THE EXPANDED CONCEPT OF DIASPORA

One of the most influential statements marking the beginning of contemporary diaspora studies was Safran's article in the opening issue of the then new journal, *Diaspora*.[8] Safran was strongly influenced by the underlying paradigmatic case of the Jewish diaspora, but correctly perceived that many other ethnic groups were experiencing analogous circumstances due perhaps to the difficult circumstances surrounding their departure from their places of origin and/or as a result of their limited acceptance in their places of settlement. Safran was, of course, not alone in recognizing the expanded use of the concept of diaspora, but he was crucial in seeking to give some social scientific contour to the new claims rather than allow a journalistic free-for-all to develop. The Jewish experience continued to influence Safran's view of the vital importance of homeland in defining one of the essential characteristics of diaspora. For him, members of a diaspora retained a collective memory of 'their original homeland'; they idealized their 'ancestral home', were committed to the restoration of 'the original homeland' and continued in various ways to 'relate to that homeland'.[9]

The violent wrench from home determined these attitudes. By contrast, while there may have been compelling elements in the history of other diasporas, these either may have involved less cruelty or may have had less impact on the natal society. Let me take, for example, the nineteenth-century system of indentured labour abroad, which affected many Indians, Japanese and Chinese. It does not minimize the oppressive aspects involved in this system of labour recruitment and control to say that in some crucial respects they differed from those of the victim diasporas. In all three Asian cases, the numbers involved in indenture were a very small fraction of the total population, the migrants had the legal right to return and the recruitment process and work conditions were legally regulated, however badly. Again the indentured labourers were augmented by subsequent much larger migration from India, China and Japan for the purpose of work, trade or business.

In allowing such cases (and many others) to shelter under the increasingly broader circumference of the diasporic umbrella, we need *both* to draw generalized inferences from the Jewish tradition *and* to be sensitive to the inevitable dilutions, changes and expansions of the meaning of the term diaspora as it comes to be more widely applied. In addition to the groups already mentioned, Safran lists Cubans and Mexicans in the USA, Pakistanis in Britain, Maghrebis in France, Turks in Germany, Poles, blacks in the North America and Corsicans in Marseilles. We can immediately think of others. Ukrainians, Italians, Afghans, Lebanese, Vietnamese, Iranians, Tibetans, Russians, Germans, Tamils, Sikhs, Hindus, Somalis or Kurds all have at least as strong a claim to inclusion as diasporas and have been so described. There are also many more ambiguous cases – the Japanese, the Roma, the Hungarians, the Croatians, the Serbs, the British, and Caribbean peoples[10] either call themselves, or could be called 'diasporas' (to name but some possibilities).

In short, it is difficult to decide where to draw the line. However, social scientists do have at least four important tools to help in this task:

1   We can distinguish between emic and etic claims (the participants' view versus the observers' view) and discuss how these claims map onto the history and social structure of the group concerned.
2   We can add a time dimension looking at how a putative social formation, in the case of a diaspora, comes into being, how it develops in various countries of settlement and how it changes in response to subsequent events in hostlands and homelands.
3   We can list the most important features that seem to apply (or partly apply) to some, most or all of the cases we consider are part of the phenomenon we are investigating.
4   Finally, we can create a typology, classifying phenomena and their subtypes using the measures of consistency, objectivity, pattern recognition and dimensionality with a view to evolving an agreed and controlled vocabulary. In social science, Weber's 'ideal types' (explained briefly below and then in Chapter 9) is a widely used method, which I also adopt.

Though I will explain my reservations shortly, Safran made a huge step in the right direction in his first list of the main characteristics of diasporas. He is properly relaxed in allowing that no contemporary diaspora will meet all the desiderata. However, he maintained that the concept of a diaspora can be applied when members of an 'expatriate minority community' share several of the following features:

- They, or their ancestors, have been dispersed from an original 'centre' to two or more foreign regions;
- they retain a collective memory, vision or myth about their original homeland including its location, history and achievements;
- they believe they are not – and perhaps can never be – fully accepted in their host societies and so remain partly separate;
- their ancestral home is idealized and it is thought that, when conditions are favourable, either they, or their descendants should return;
- they believe all members of the diaspora should be committed to the maintenance or restoration of the original homeland and to its safety and prosperity; and
- they continue in various ways to relate to that homeland and their ethnocommunal consciousness and solidarity are in an important way defined by the existence of such a relationship.[11]

In response to the normal canons of social scientific debate initiated by this author and others Safran has amended and extended his list to one that will command considerable consensus among diaspora scholars.[12] In his first list, four of the six features mentioned were concerned with the relationship of the diasporic group to its homeland. Though this aspect is clearly of crucial importance, there was some degree of repetition of the argument. I suggested that two features should be 'tweaked', while four other features needed to be added, mainly concerning the evolution and character of the diasporic groups in their countries of exile. I amended the first stated feature by adding that dispersal from an original centre is often accompanied by the memory of a single traumatic event that provides the folk memory of the great historic injustice that binds the group together. I adapted the penultimate characteristic to allow the case not only of the 'maintenance or restoration' of a homeland, but its very creation. This covers the cases of an 'imagined homeland' that only resembles the original history and geography of the diaspora's natality in the remotest way. (In some cases – the Kurds or Sikhs come to mind – a homeland is clearly an *ex post facto* construction.)

Now let us move on to the four additional features. The first is that we may wish to include in the category diaspora, *groups that disperse for colonial or voluntarist reasons*. This is probably the most controversial departure from the prototypical Jewish diasporic tradition, but one that can be justified, as we shall see in Chapter 2, by the compelled *and* voluntary elements of the Jews' own migration patterns. It also conforms to the use of the word to describe trading and commercial networks (the Lebanese, for example, have been so described), to those seeking work abroad and to imperial or colonial settlers. As you now may have spotted, we have begun a process of sub-categorization. The defining feature of the Indian indentured migrants was that they were recruited for their labour to be used in the tropical plantations. They could therefore, with some justification, be called a 'labour diaspora'. In the example of the Chinese, at least as many traders as indentured labourers had begun to spill outside the Chinese mainland to the rest of Southeast Asia. Moreover, the merchants' long-term influence was far greater. It therefore seems more appropriate to describe the Chinese as primarily a 'trade diaspora'. To the original prototypical *victim* diaspora we have added other qualifying adjectives identifying three subtypes – *labour, trade* and *imperial* diasporas (see below).

I also thought there should be more recognition of *the positive virtues of retaining a diasporic identity* than is implied in Safran's original list. The tension between an ethnic, a national and a transnational identity is often a creative, enriching one. Take again the paradigmatic case of the diasporic Jews. Jews in Babylon, the Islamic world and in early modern Spain were responsible for many advances – in medicine, theology, art, music, philosophy, literature, science, industry and commerce. Though one must be careful to distinguish hagiography from history, it is difficult to discount the achievements of diasporic Jews in such diverse areas of settlement as Bombay, Baghdad or Vienna.[13] Even if there is a degree of subterranean anxiety in the diaspora, it may be possible to argue that this is precisely what motivates the need for achievement. If life is too comfortable, Neusner convincingly argues, creativity may dry up.[14] One – admittedly crude – index of the continuing successes of Western diasporic Jews is the extraordinary number of Nobel prizes won in the arts, medicine and the sciences.[15] The virtues, rather than the dangers and traumas, of a diasporic existence are also emphasized by Werbner who alludes to 'the positive dimensions of transnational existence and cosmopolitan consciousness'.[16]

Another feature I would add to Safran's list is that diasporas often *mobilize a collective identity*, not only a place of settlement or only in respect of an imagined, putative or real homeland, but also *in solidarity with co-ethnic members in other countries*. Bonds of language, religion, culture and a sense of a common fate impregnate such a transnational relationship and give to it an affective, intimate quality that formal citizenship or long settlement frequently lack. A useful description of this sentiment is 'co-responsibility'.[17] There is sometimes considerable tension in the relationship between scattered co-ethnic communities. A bond of loyalty to the country of refuge/settlement competes with co-responsibility, while those who have achieved national social mobility are often reluctant to accept too close a link with a despised or low-status ethnic group abroad, even if it happens to be their own.

Finally, I depart more radically from Safran's list by suggesting that in some limited circumstances the term *'diaspora' can be used to describe transnational bonds*

7

of co-responsibility even where historically exclusive territorial claims are not strongly articulated. As I explain in Chapter 7, this applies particularly to groups that have been multiply displaced, to those whose homelands are for all practical purposes lost to them, and to some religious communities. Besides, in a global age where space itself has become reinscribed by cyberspace a diaspora can, to some degree, be cemented or recreated through the mind, through artefacts and popular culture, and through a shared imagination. To cover such examples, I use the expression *deterritorialized diaspora.*[18]

SOCIAL CONSTRUCTIONIST CRITIQUES OF DIASPORA

To return to the opening section of this chapter, we now have a clear idea of phases 1 and 2 in the evolution of diaspora studies, the first marked by an analysis of the prototypical victim diaspora, the second by a gradually more sophisticated listing of key features and a grouping into subtypes. This process of analytical refinement is a routine part of social science, but the already brisk pace of conceptual progress was suddenly disrupted by what, in its little way, became nothing less than a diaspora craze. From the mid-1990s diaspora was chic and, it seemed, nearly everybody who was anybody wanted to be part of one. Dufoix opens the US edition of his book *Diasporas*, with a droll blog penned by a frustrated Nigerian:

> I have been away from Nigeria for 30 years ... In all these 30 years I have been convinced that I was living abroad and, at a push, overseas. It now turns out, however, that I have actually been living in the diaspora. This sounds like a very lovely place, with flora and fauna, nubile virgins, blue skies and a certain *je ne sais quoi.* The sort of place where you can tiptoe through the tulips, stopping every so often to smell Rose, her friends Chantel, Angel, Tiffany and any other delicacies that take your fancy ... All this time I have been 'abroad' studying and working my ass off, sitting in dull offices, with dull people, doing dull things to pay off dull bills, when I could have been in the diaspora with nubile virgins with understanding ways. I am so mad.[19]

As Dufoix avers, the word 'diaspora' seems to have escaped its conceptual cage and was used now to describe, among many examples, scientists, intellectuals, engineers and football players.[20] An internet search yielded even more exotic examples. In January 2007, Taiwanese architects undertook the task of turning a living space into a hyperreal diaspora. In February 2007, a Dutch non-governmental organization advertised for a person from the Dutch–Somali diaspora who had expertise in accountancy and auditing. Two months later a touring company in the USA called 'A Journey through two diasporas' presented a first-half act, Curry Tales, which explored identity, nationalism, fertility, love, hunger and globalization. More conventionally, the second-half act, called Griots t'Garage, celebrated 500 years of music in the African diaspora.

This is all great fun and a long way from the melancholic sentiments of displacement, alienation and exile associated with the prototypical diaspora. Academics also wanted to come to the party. For example, Gopinath explored how 'queer diasporas' challenged both the hegemonic discourses of 'Gay International' and the male-dominated diaspora discourse of South Asia.[21] As part of a five-year programme based at the University of Leeds on 'diasporas, migration and identities' funded by the Arts and Humanities Research Council, the programme leader promised to examine questions like: 'Can there be diasporas without migration, for example the gay diaspora, anti-capitalist or terror networks as diaspora?'[22]

We can perhaps immediately spot the problem in this process of invention, creative as it might be. There is a serious danger of emptying out the diasporic baby with an increasing volume of bathwater. In his very astute contribution, Brubaker warned that 'if everyone is diasporic, then no one is distinctively so'.[23] Like the original phenomenon, he continued, the concept had itself become dispersed:

> As the term has proliferated its meaning has been stretched to accommodate the various intellectual, cultural and political agendas in the service of which it has been enlisted. This has resulted in what one might call a 'diaspora' diaspora – a dispersion of the meaning of the term in semantic, conceptual and disciplinary space.[24]

One can hardly do anything about the spread of the expression in popular discourse, but perhaps it is appropriate to show how, in servicing their own agendas and adopting an unchallenging social constructivist position, some academics unduly privileged the emic over the etic and showed scant respect for the etymology, history, limits, meaning and evolution of the concept of diaspora.[25] In particular, they sought to deconstruct the two core building blocks of diaspora, home/homeland and ethnic/religious community. 'Home' became increasingly vague, even miasmic, while all ethnicities, they suggested, had to be dissolved into their component parts and surrounding context – divided by gender, class and race and other segments and enveloped by a world of intersectionality, multiculturality and fluidity.

While a degree of decoupling of diaspora from homeland was signalled in the first edition of this book, this rupture had taken a more insistent turn in Brah,[26] who sought to dethrone the foundational idea of a homeland, arguing instead that her concept of diaspora 'offers a critique of discourses of fixed origins, while taking account of a homing desire, which is not the same thing as a desire for "homeland"'. So, homeland had become a homing desire and soon home itself became transmuted into an essentially placeless, though admittedly lyrical, space. This is how Brah put it:

> Where is home? On the one hand, 'home' is a mythic place of desire in the diasporic imagination. In this sense it is a place of no return, even if it is possible to visit the geographical territory that is seen as the place of 'origin'. On the other hand, home is also the lived experience of a locality. Its sounds and smells, its heat and dust, balmy summer evenings, or the excitement of the first snowfall, shivering winter evenings, sombre grey skies in the middle of the day … all this, as mediated by the historically specific everyday of social relations.[27]

Through this and similar interventions, 'home' became more and more generously interpreted to mean the place of origin, or the place of settlement, or a local, national or transnational place, or an imagined virtual community (linked, for example, through the internet), or a matrix of known experiences and intimate social relations (thus conforming to the popular expression that 'home is where the heart is').

Anthias upped the stakes further by criticizing a number of scholars for using what she described as 'absolutist notions of "origin" and "true belonging"'.[28] For her, diasporic discourse showed insufficient attention to internal divisions with ethnic communities or to the possibilities of selective cultural negotiations between communities:

> the lack of attention given to transethnic solidarities, such as those against racism, of class, of gender, of social movements, is deeply worrying from the perspective of the development of multiculturality, and more inclusive notions of belonging. For a discourse of antiracism and social mobilization of a transethnic (as opposed to a transnational) character, cannot be easily accommodated, within the discourse of the diaspora, where it retains its dependence on 'homeland' and 'origin', however configured.[29]

Two years later Soysal amplified the charge. Despite the fact that notions of diaspora were 'venerated', they inappropriately 'privileg[ed] the nation-state model and nationally-defined formations when conversing about a global process such as immigration'.[30] Postwar developments, she maintained:

> render diaspora untenable as an analytical and normative category, and direct our discussion to new formations of membership, claims-making and belonging – which either remain invisible to the conventional conceptions of diaspora, or are frequently deemed insignificant in the face of its normative weight … In this [erroneous] formulation, the primary orientation and attachment of diasporic populations is to their

homelands and cultures; and their claims and citizenship practices arise from this home-bound ethnic-based orientation.[31]

After her initial critique of diaspora, Soysal attended to her case of European citizenship, but she returned with a vengeance to her dislike of the concept of diaspora in a postscript, maintaining that the idea 'suspends immigrant experience between host and home countries, native and foreign lands, home-bound desires and losses – thus obscuring the new topography and practices of citizenship, which are multi-connected, multi-referential and postnational'.[32]

The crucial effect of these and similar appraisals of what I have called the first and second phases of diaspora studies was to force a larger and larger wedge between 'diaspora' on the one hand, and 'homeland', 'place' and 'ethnic community' on the other. Clearly for some authors – of whom Anthias and Soysal are good representatives – diaspora was irredeemably flawed. It simply could not adequately address their own agendas by doing what they wanted – in Anthias's case, it could not produce a platform for a transethnic, gender-sensitive, anti-racist movement while, in Soysal's case, it could not provide a means of understanding post-national citizenship in Europe.

THE CONSOLIDATION PHASE

One response to such critiques of diaspora might have been to regard them as inappropriate or misplaced as they reflected political agendas that had little to do with the history and meaning of the term, or the phenomena it sought to, and continues to, explain. Diaspora theorists made no claim to explain the full spectrum of immigrant experiences, did not see their task as creating a progressive anti-racist movement (desirable as that may be), and did not seek to describe patterns of sociality and citizenship unrelated to some degree of prior kinship or religious affiliation. In other words, the concept of diaspora is not a magic bullet and cannot be used to slay all enemies.

A more mature and astute response was to find some dialogical possibilities between diaspora scholars and their social constructionist critics. Tölölyan, the leading scholar of diasporas and editor of the journal *Diaspora*, led the way by picking a path carefully through the middle, though still insisting that an attachment to place remained important in understanding the concept:

> Diasporists shaped by globalizing discourse describe genuine erosions of the link between a bounded place and a people, diagnose it as irresistible, and quickly affirm its contribution to a pluralistic, multicultural, hybrid world of which they approve. Diasporists like myself, who want to argue that attachment to place was indispensable to diasporic life and thought until very recently, and that despite its erosion it remains important today, must tread carefully in order to

avoid the charge that we are either imitating discredited nationalist rhetoric about the link between land, people, and culture, or that we remain naive about the global spaces that have opened up in the past several decades.[33]

Brubaker also insisted that, despite the dispersion of its meaning, there remained 'three core elements that remain widely understood to be constitutive of diaspora'.[34] These are *dispersion* (either traumatically or voluntarily and generally across state borders; *homeland orientation* (whether to a real or imagined homeland) and *boundary maintenance* (the processes whereby group solidarity is mobilized and retained, even accepting that there are counter processes of boundary erosion).[35]

Though the social constructionist position was clearly overstated, the productive effect of their intervention was to generate a requestioning and more sophisticated understanding of shifts in the homeland–diaspora relationship, the ways in which a diaspora is mobilized and how diaspora studies connect to post-colonial studies. In the sections below, I describe the recent work of one established and two younger diaspora scholars who, in my judgement, have moved the debate forward in these directions and in so doing have contributed to the current phase of consolidation.

Shifts in the homeland–diaspora nexus: the case of dezionization

My first example summarizes a recent paper by the reputable scholar of diasporas, William Safran, whose work on the necessity of homeland has already been discussed. In his later work he adopts a more flexible use of conventional diasporic theory. Partly on the basis of attitudinal surveys, Safran now argues that in the case of Israel on the one hand, and European and American Jews on the other, the links between hostlands and homeland are becoming more tenuous.[36] Those in the Jewish diaspora experiencing a process of 'dezionization' include groups he designates as secularists, socialists, potential investors in Israel, non-orthodox believers, enlightened Western Jews, left-wing ideologues, academics and others disillusioned with the expressions of Israeli state power. The other side of the coin is that (despite intermittent bursts of anti-Semitism) life in the diaspora is sufficiently attractive and sufficiently emotionally and physically secure not to prompt an invariable identification with Israel.

Intriguingly, proto-Zionists have also promoted summer camps when, in safe rural US settings, virtual *aliya* (migration 'up' to Israel) can take place, complete with Israeli flags, Hebrew lessons, religious rituals, imitations of life on a kibbutz and access to other attractive aspects of Israeli popular culture.[37] As Safran himself recognizes, the harder notion of homeland has now yielded to softer notions of a 'found home' in the diaspora and to a 'virtual home' in a summer camp - perhaps augmented by occasional visits to Israel rather than permanent settlement. I will add that the unexpected but considerable flow of Israelis *to* the USA and Europe (which attracts strong disapprobation by Zionists), has also fundamentally changed the relationship between the Jewish homeland and the Jewish diaspora.[38]

Mobilizing diasporas

My second example arises from the work of a younger scholar, Martin Sökefeld who, somewhat uncritically, acknowledges a number of the unsympathetic comments of the social constructionists, but neatly inverts their purpose.[39] Instead of using intersubjectivity as a means for questioning the concept of diaspora, he uses the same starting point for interrogating how diasporas can come into being and sustain themselves. He considers the formation of diasporas as 'a special case of ethnicity'. They are 'imagined transnational communities which unite segments of people that live in territorially separated locations'. Not all migrants will cohere into communities and not all migrant communities will imagine themselves as transnational, thus it is a fundamental error to allow the use of diaspora as a synonym for all migrants. A diasporic consciousness has, moreover, to be mobilized (that is, socially constructed). A significant number of social actors need to accept their collective self-definition as a transnational community, organize to spread this perception and persuade others to participate in actions designed to cement their diasporic character and status.

Sökefeld then makes his most innovative theoretical intervention. While diasporas cannot simply be equated to social movements, there are sufficient parallels for him to advocate using the social movement literature to gather insights on the formation of diasporas. In particular, diasporas need (a) *opportunity structures* like an enhanced means of communication and a permissive legal and political environment; (b) *mobilizing practices* like neighbourhood associations, demonstrations and fund-raising events; and (c) *frames* that allude to ideas like 'roots' and 'home' and the importance of memory in history, which then feed into the collective imagination of the group concerned. In other words, Sökefeld moves away from assigning particular attributes to particular ethnic groups and instead asks questions like: What events or developments propel a diasporic response? What agents undertake the dissemination of a diasporic discourse and foster a diasporic imaginary? What threats and opportunities unite people in transnational organization? What ideas do opinion formers use in galvanizing a diasporic consciousness? By posing these as research questions, Sökefeld has provided an empirical pathway to establish the form and extent of diasporic mobilization.

Post-colonial diasporas

My final example draws on the work of David Chariandy, who has great expectations of the concept of diaspora.[40] Chariandy has not abandoned hope that it can be used to illuminate contemporary forms of progressive cultural politics. Although he recognizes that we are still 'struggling to develop adequate terms for the profound socio-cultural dislocations resulting from modern colonialism and nation building', he finds in diaspora the potential for showing how 'historically disenfranchised peoples have developed tactics to challenge their subordinate status'. Though initially assigning these aspirations to other scholars, it is clear that he too also sees a rosy future for diaspora studies:

> In the past fifteen years, 'diaspora' has emerged as a highly favored term among scholars whom we might associate with contemporary postcolonial studies; and while there exists within the nebulous field of postcolonial studies no simple agreement on what diaspora is or does, scholars such as Paul Gilroy, Floya Anthias, Stuart Hall, Carole Boyce Davies, Rey Chow, Smaro Kamboureli, Diana Brydon, and Rinaldo Walcott all seem to share these hopes: that diaspora studies will help foreground the cultural practices of both forcefully exiled and voluntarily migrant peoples; that diaspora studies will help challenge certain calcified assumptions about ethnic, racial, and above all, national belonging; and that diaspora studies will help forge new links between emergent critical methodologies and contemporary social justice movements.[41]

In Chariandy's progressive ambitions for post-colonial diaspora studies, formerly designated 'third world' peoples can find some space to express their anti-nationalist and radical political preferences and can even prefigure a utopian future. Yet, he is sufficiently self-critical and dialectical to understand that the cosmopolitan voices of third-world intellectuals may be somewhat self-serving, and that 'the virtues of fluid and border-crossing identities are endorsed not only by radical scholars, but, sometimes, ever more earnestly, by the powers that be'. This last insight links the expression of a diasporic consciousness to the increased density and velocity of the circuits of capital (a process captured partly by the expression 'globalization'), without, however, suggesting that in some crude way diasporic intellectuals or communities are unwitting agents of capital.

Summary

In the examples used, I have shown how the objections raised by the social constructionists can, at least partially, be integrated into the current phase of diaspora studies. Let me consider the implications of the work, of Safran, Sökefeld and Chariandy in turn. If the Jewish diaspora is progressively becoming dezionized, as Safran argues, it is, by the same token, finding links, affinities and shared cultural and political associations in the hostlands that are not solely connected to a homeland. We could, of course, imagine pure enclave societies where diasporic groups were both dezionized *and* cut off from their surrounding communities. However, as is clear from Safran's comments about political participation and the growth of exogamy, many in the diaspora have adapted to a form of dual consciousness – poised between virtual Zionism on the one hand and interculturality or creolization on the other.[42] For Sökefeld, diasporas have to be mobilized so, by inference, there are periods when they are not mobilized or perhaps circumstances when they became demobilized. In these two last cases forms of sociality with other communities are inevitable. Finally, for Chariandy a diasporic consciousness represents but one form of mobilization in a wider struggle to attain global social justice. Again the implication of crossover with other communities is clear and indeed he perhaps goes furthest in meeting Anthias's demand that the diasporic idea should be made compatible with a cross-ethnic cooperative struggle by progressive forces and third world peoples of many different backgrounds. Despite their different intent, all three thinkers are a long way from the notion that a diaspora is a single, endogamous, ethnic group with a fixed origin, a uniform history, a lifestyle cut off from their fellow citizens in their places of settlement and political aspirations wholly focused on their places of origin.

CONCLUSION: THE TOOLS TO DELINEATE A DIASPORA

There is little doubt that the reason why the term diaspora has become so contested is that it has become so popular. Friends, enemies and sceptics at least concur on that. For Soysal, the term has become 'venerated', for Anthias it has become a 'mantra', for Chariandy it is 'fashionable' and 'highly-favoured', for Sökefeld the term is 'hip' and 'in'. One scholar, Donald Akenson, is so annoyed at its popularity that he complains that 'diaspora' has become a 'massive linguistic weed'.[43]

One possible way of dealing with this escalation is to allow self-declaration (the emic view) to prevail. In such a hands-off approach, any group can be a diaspora if it wishes to and a wide range of meanings can be applied to the term. Who are we to object? Another strategy is to follow the tactic adopted by the ancient Greek, Procrustes, who offered hospitality in his iron bed to passers-by. So that they would fit the bed precisely, he stretched short people and cut off the limbs of long people. By analogy, we could espouse an utterly rigid set of criteria to which all newer diaspora claimants would have to conform before we would allow them to lie on our conceptual bed. Rejecting these two strategies, I propose instead to deploy the four tools of social science mentioned earlier (emic/etic claims, the time dimension, common features and ideal types) to help us find a middle path in delineating a diaspora.

Let us start with the emic/etic relationship. Here I can be blunt. Not everyone is a diaspora because they say they are. Social structures, historical experiences, prior conceptual understandings, and the opinions of other social actors (among other factors) also influence whether we can legitimately label a particular group a diaspora. Understanding a social actor's viewpoint is important, but it is not the end of the argument. We would be on stronger ground, however, if we were to argue that diasporas can be formed and mobilized in certain circumstances. The mould (the opportunity structure) will constrain the extent to which this is possible. The clay (the history and experience of the group in question) will act like sedimented silicate, providing the necessary and basic chemical compound. And the potters (the active political, social and cultural leaders of the putative diaspora) will have to organize effective institutions to create and shape diasporic sentiments and galvanize them to a common purpose.

Our second social scientific tool is the rather convenient wisdom of hindsight, the passage of time. This was first strongly emphasized by Marienstras, who argued that 'time has to pass' before we can know that any community that has migrated 'is really a diaspora'.[44] In other words, one does not announce the formation of the diaspora the moment the representatives of a people first alight from a boat or aircraft at Ellis Island, London Heathrow or Chatrapati Shivaji (Bombay). Many members of a particular ethnic group may intend to and be able to merge into the crowd, lose their prior identity and achieve individualized forms of social mobility. (The changing of ethnically identifiable names by new immigrants signals this intention.) Other groups may intermarry with locals, adopt or blend with their religions and other social practices (creolize) and thereby slowly disappear as a separable ethnic group. A strong or renewed tie to the past or a block to assimilation in the present and future must exist to permit a diasporic consciousness to emerge, while the active fraction of the incipient diasporic must have time to mobilize the group concerned.

My third tool is to produce a consolidated list of the 'common features' of a diaspora, drawing on the classical tradition, on Safran's desiderata, his revised list and my own views (Table 1.1).[45] And here comes the first of my two health warnings. I deliberately use the expression *common* features to signify that not every diaspora will exhibit every feature listed, nor will they be present to the same degree over time and in all settings. These are the main strands that go into the making of a diasporic rope (see Chapter 9). The number of strands present and the more tightly coiled they are will provide the descriptive tool needed to delineate any one diaspora.

I turn now to my fourth and final tool to aid in the delineation of a diaspora, the use of Weberian 'ideal types'. By using a qualifying adjective – victim, labour, imperial, trade and deterritorialized – I have evolved a simple means of typologizing and classifying various diasporas, not by ignoring what they share in common, but by highlighting their most important characteristics (Table 1.2). In subsequent chapters of this book I explore these types in detail. But here comes the second, and sterner, health warning. Students who are unfamiliar with Weber's method are understandably annoyed at the adjective

Table 1.1 **Common features of diaspora**

1. Dispersal from an original homeland, often traumatically, to two or more foreign regions;

2. alternatively or additionally, the expansion from a homeland in search of work, in pursuit of trade or to further colonial ambitions;

3. a collective memory and myth about the homeland, including its location, history, suffering and achievements;

4. an idealization of the real or imagined ancestral home and a collective commitment to its maintenance, restoration, safety and prosperity, even to its creation;

5. the frequent development of a return movement to the homeland that gains collective approbation even if many in the group are satisfied with only a vicarious relationship or intermittent visits to the homeland;

6. a strong ethnic group consciousness sustained over a long time and based on a sense of distinctiveness, a common history, the transmission of a common cultural and religious heritage and the belief in a common fate;

7. a troubled relationship with host societies, suggesting a lack of acceptance or the possibility that another calamity might befall the group;

8. a sense of empathy and co-responsibility with co-ethnic members in other countries of settlement even where home has become more vestigial; and

9. the possibility of a distinctive creative, enriching life in host countries with a tolerance for pluralism.

'ideal', thinking that if the group they are examining does not conform, it is less than ideal, imperfect, or even inferior in relation to some gold standard. This is definitely not the case. 'Ideal' is meant to contrast with 'real'. Weber uses a deliberately exaggerated abstraction, which is useful for analytical and comparative purposes. It is normal, general, indeed *expected*, that real diasporas will differ from their prototypical ideal types. The scholar gains purchase on the phenomenon by acknowledging and evaluating the extent of real life deviation from the ideal type.[46]

The above ways of delineating a diaspora should also enable students to understand the diasporic phenomenon in the round, though there are other aspects of diaspora that have not yet been covered. As I explain in the concluding two chapters, the new themes in diaspora studies include looking at their changing role in international politics (particularly in the wake of 9/11) and seeing them as a means of facilitating the development of their home areas. Regrettably, I have insufficient space to cover literature, the visual and performing arts and some other areas of the humanities on which diaspora studies have made a dramatic impact in recent years.

In closing this chapter it might be worth explaining why the concept of diaspora is so attractive to so many groups. I advance the thought that in the

17

Table 1.2 **Ideal types of diaspora, examples and notes**

Main types of diaspora	Main examples in this book	Also mentioned and notes
VICTIM	Jews, Africans, Armenians	Also discussed: Irish and Palestinians.
		Many contemporary refugee groups are incipient victim diasporas but time has to pass to see whether they return to their homelands, assimilate in their hostlands, creolize or mobilize as a diaspora.
LABOUR	Indentured Indians	Also discussed: Chinese and Japanese; Turks, Italians, North Africans.
		Many others could be included. Another synonymous expression is 'proletarian diaspora'.
IMPERIAL	British	Also discussed: Russians, colonial powers other than Britain.
		Other synonymous expressions are 'settler' or 'colonial' diasporas.
TRADE	Lebanese, Chinese	Also discussed: Venetians, business and professional Indians, Chinese, Japanese.
		Note also the auxiliary elements discussed in Chapter 5.
DETERRITORIALIZED	Caribbean peoples, Sindhis, Parsis	Also discussed: Roma, Muslims and other religious diasporas.
		The expressions 'hybrid', 'cultural' and 'post-colonial' also are linked to the idea of deterritorialization without being synonymous.

face of the insecurity, risk and adversity characteristic of our global age, many social groups want to reach in and to reach out, to be simultaneously ethnic and transnational, local and cosmopolitan, to have a comfort zone and a questing impulse. We must thus consider not only whether the concept of diaspora has been appropriately used or improperly abused, *but also* what function it is serving to the many groups that have adopted it. For better or for worse, the ancient Greeks launched this conceptual vessel, and some may want to repel all recent boarders. However, many unexpected passengers are embarking whether we like it or not. Scholars of diaspora need to recognize the potency and ubiquity of the term, and to be open and flexible to new experiences and uses, without neglecting the constraints that the history, meaning and evolution of the term impose. As a casual internet search will show, the sceptics have conspicuously failed to blunt the popularity, rude good health and continuing heuristic value of the concept of diaspora.

FURTHER READING

- For a history and evolution of the term diaspora, see Stéphane Dufoix, *Diasporas* (Berkeley: University of California Press, forthcoming). This short but well-informed book was first published in French and is helpful in drawing attention to non-English sources and uses.
- William Safran 'The Jewish diaspora in a comparative and theoretical perspective', *Israel Studies*, 10 (1) 2005, pp. 37–60, includes an excellent restatement and extension of his original key features.
- Though his principal case study on Alevis is rather specialized, Martin Sökefeld's 'Mobilizing in transnational space: a social movement approach to the formation of diaspora', *Global Networks*, 6 (3) July 2006, pp. 265–84 is an important fresh approach.
- Rogers Brubaker, 'The "diaspora" diaspora', *Ethnic and Racial Studies*, 28 (1) 2005, pp. 1–19 is an essential reference with a light sardonic touch.

QUESTIONS TO THINK ABOUT

- What are the key elements defining the prototypical or classical diaspora?
- Examine the list of 'common features of a diaspora' (Table 1.1). Discuss whether it is useful to gain an insight into a social phenomenon by producing a list of this kind. Are there other features of a diaspora that you think are missing?
- Sökefeld argues that groups need particular *opportunity structures, mobilizing practices* and *frames* if they are to construct themselves as diasporas. What does he mean by these expressions and is he right?

Figure 2.1 A Jewish cameraman prays at the Wailing Wall, the remaining structure that survived the razing the Second Temple by the Romans in AD 70. The wall and the surrounding area was captured by the Israelis in the 1967 war.
© iStockphoto.com/Robin Cohen

2

CLASSICAL NOTIONS OF DIASPORA

Transcending the Jewish tradition

> By the waters of Babylon we sat down and wept:
> when we remembered thee, O Sion.
> As for out harps we hangèd them up:
> upon the trees that are therein.
> For they that led us away captive required of
> us then a song, and melody, in our heaviness:
> Sing us one of the songs of Sion.

The loneliness and sadness of the diasporic experience of the Jews is poignantly evoked in this psalm (reproduced here in the English Prayer Book version). Such evocations are common. Indeed, until a few years ago, most characterizations of diasporas emphasized their catastrophic origins, their mass nature and their disturbing effects. The idea that diaspora implied forcible dispersion was found in Deuteronomy (28: 28) with the addition of a thunderous Old Testament warning to a people who had forsaken the righteous paths and abandoned the old ways:

> If you do not observe and fulfil all the law ... the Lord will scatter you among all peoples from one end of the earth to the other ... Among these nations you will find no peace, no rest for the sole of your foot. Then the Lord will give you an unquiet mind, dim eyes and a failing appetite. Your life will hang continually in suspense, fear will beset you night and day, and you will find no security all your life long.

So closely had diaspora become associated with this biblical use that the origins of the word have been virtually lost. In fact, the term is found in the Greek translation of the Bible and, as Baumann observes, originates in the composite verb *dia* and *speirein*, namely 'to scatter', 'to spread' or 'to disperse'.[1] There are in fact two other Hebrew words, *gôla* and *galût*, signifying 'banishment' and 'exile', but 'diaspora' evolved as the preferred and catch-all expression covering sin, scattering, emigration and the possibilities of repentance and return.[2] Over the centuries the term diaspora assumed a predominantly negative meaning used

21

to capture the various misfortunes that afflicted this group. However, Jewish migratory experiences were much more diverse and more complex than the catastrophic tradition allows.

As we have seen in Chapter 1 the expression has evolved far from its origins. However, even for those who find in the changed meanings of the contemporary concept a fresh and exciting way of understanding cultural difference, new ethnicities and complex migration flows, the classical origins and connotations of the term have to be assimilated and understood before they can be transcended. Thus, James Clifford avers that: 'We should be able to recognize the strong entailment of Jewish history on the language of diaspora without making that history a definitive model. Jewish (and Greek and Armenian) diasporas can be taken as non-normative starting points for a discourse that is travelling in new global conditions.'[3] Similarly, while accepting Clifford's argument that the Jews should not be thought of as the normative model, Kirshenblatt-Gimblett argues that in discussing issues of homelessness, placelessness and statelessness, 'the Jew has served as the oncomouse of social theory.'[4] Finally, Boyarin holds that: 'It is important to insist, not on the *centrality* of Jewish diaspora nor on its *logical priority* within comparative diaspora studies, [but] ... on the need to refer to, and better understand, Jewish diaspora history within the contemporary diasporic rubric.'[5]

'BABYLON' AS A SITE OF OPPRESSION

How then do we interrogate and seek to supersede the Jewish tradition of diaspora? The destruction of Jerusalem and razing of the walls of its Temple in 586 BC created the central folk memory of the pessimistic, victim diaspora tradition – in particular the experience of enslavement, exile and displacement. The Jewish leader of the time, Zedekiah, vacillated for a decade, and then impulsively sanctioned a rebellion against the powerful Mesopotamian Empire. No mercy for his impudence was shown by the Babylonian king, Nebuchadnezzar. His soldiers forced Zedekiah to witness the execution of his sons; the Jewish leader was then blinded and dragged in chains to Babylon. Peasants were left behind in Judah to till the soil, but the key military, civic and religious personnel accompanied Zedekiah to captivity in Babylon.[6] Jews had been compelled to desert the land 'promised' to them by God to Moses and thereafter, the tradition suggests, forever became dispersed.

Babylon subsequently became a codeword among Jews (and, as we shall see in the next chapter, Africans) for the afflictions, isolation and insecurity of living in a foreign place, set adrift, cut off from their roots and their sense of identity, oppressed by an alien ruling class. Since the Babylonian exile, 'the homelessness of Jews has been a leitmotiv in Jewish literature, art, culture, and of course, prayer'.[7] Jewish folklore and its strong oral tradition retold stories of the perceived, or actual, trauma of their historical experiences. The use of the word Babylon alone was enough to evoke a sense of captivity, exile, alienation and isolation. Collectively, Jews were seen as helpless chaff in the wind. At an individual level, diasporic Jews were depicted as pathological half-persons – destined never to realize themselves or to attain completeness, tranquillity or happiness so long as they were in exile.

'BABYLON' AS A SITE OF CREATIVITY

Perhaps the obvious starting point to a revisionist view of Babylon is that the benefits of integration into a rich and diverse alien culture were evident both to many of the first group of Judeans and to their immediate descendants. A substantial number adopted Babylonian names and customs; the group as a whole used the Babylonian calendar and embraced the language of Aramaic.

For those who wished to stay true to their roots, their enforced residence in Babylon provided an opportunity to construct and define their historical experience, to invent their tradition. Myth, folk tales, oral history and legal records were combined into the embryonic Bible, while the earnest discussion groups at the homes of charismatic figures like Jeremiah and Ezekiel ('the prophets') turned into rudimentary synagogues.

It was, however, the stirring prophecies of a figure known as the second Isaiah (not his real name, but subsequent editors of the Bible perpetrated this error) that galvanized a return movement of the exiles. Isaiah (13: 20–22) hurled colourful imprecations at the Babylonians, beseeching 'the remnant of Israel' to rebuild the Temple in Jerusalem before it was too late. If they did, redemption (another great diasporic theme) would surely follow. Some followed Isaiah's pleading, but the purposes of their journeys were neither quite so heroic, nor so spiritually pure, as Isaiah had urged. Cyrus, the Persian king who had conquered Babylon, permitted and even encouraged the return of groups of Judeans as a form of enlightened colonialism. 'It suited him to have an enclave of beholden Jews in Palestine, close to the Egyptian border.'[8]

Moreover, the return was not a triumphant success. The restored Temple (completed in 515 BC) was a paltry affair; the priests were venal and the returnees rubbed raw with the Judeans who had remained. It took a Persian-supported Babylonian priest, Ezra, to implement the law codified in Babylon (the Torah). His reforms led to a much greater ethnic particularism and what we would nowadays call religious fundamentalism. Though previously common, exogenous marriages were now frowned upon, while the highly prescribed purification rituals (including circumcision, atonement, and the stringent dietary laws) also date from Ezra's period. For the next five centuries the evolution of Judaism in Palestine was marked by apocalyptic dreamers, messianic claimants, zealots, revolutionaries and mystics. Unsophisticated attempts by the Greeks to Hellenize the country (a pig was sacrificed on an altar to Zeus set up in the Temple in 167 BC) then to Romanize it, only served to fan the flames of resistance and play into the hands of the zealots.

By contrast, the Jewish communities in Alexandria, Antioch, Damascus, Asia Minor and Babylon became centres of civilization, culture and learning. The Exilarch (the head of the Babylonian Jews) held a position of honour among Jews and non-Jews alike, Jewish academies of learning flourished, while the centrepiece of theological exegesis, the Babylonian Talmud, comprising 2.5 million words, made the religious leaders, the Gaons, the cynosure of Jewish culture until the early eleventh century. Sassanian Persia had tolerated and encouraged a cultural *mélange* of several brands of Christianity, astrology, a Persian literary revival, Zoroastrianism, and Indian and Hellenistic thought. Judaism thrived in this hothouse through engagement, encounter, emulation, competition and the cut and thrust of religious and intellectual debate.

Consequently, though the word Babylon usually connotes captivity and oppression, a rereading of the Babylonian period of exile can be shown to demonstrate the development of a new creative energy in a challenging, pluralistic context outside the natal homeland. When the Romans destroyed the second Temple in AD 70, it was Babylon that remained as the nerve- and brain-centre for Jewish life and thought. Beyond Babylon, there were flourishing Jewish communities all over the Hellenic world. In Alexandria, the Greek translation of the Scriptures was completed (and the word 'diaspora' put into general use among the literate), while under the Egyptian Ptolomies Jews served as administrators and army officers. Despite occasional outbursts of hostility, philo-Semitism was the normal experience of the many Jewish communities scattered around the Greco-Roman world. By the fourth century BC there were already more Jews living outside than inside the land of Israel.[9]

THE JEWISH DIASPORA AND CHRISTIANITY

Accepting that there are positive early historical experiences to record with respect to the most prominent 'victim diaspora' and that a number of the far-flung Jewish communities were *not* forcibly dispersed, we are then faced with the inevitable resulting question. Why is the received wisdom describing the Jewish diaspora generally so tragic and miserable? To explain this, we need to return, if only briefly, to the opening of the Christian era.

Superficially, the crushing of the revolt of the Judeans against the Romans and the destruction of the Second Temple by the Roman general Titus in AD 70 precisely confirmed the catastrophic tradition. Once again, Jews had been unable to sustain a national homeland and were scattered to the far corners of the world. However, numerically and experientially, the exodus of the Jews after Titus's campaign was not that decisive an event. It was, nonetheless, so construed by prominent Christian theologians, who were anxious to demonstrate that God's punishment followed what they regarded as the Jews' heinous crime in acting as accomplices to deicide. The fact that the bulk of the Jewish diaspora long preceded the rise of Christianity, or the destruction of the Second Temple, was conveniently forgotten.

The image of the 'wandering Jew' became part of a continuing Christian myth, a myth often absorbed and perpetuated by Jews themselves. Jews are forced to wander, so the dogma went, because of their part in the killing of Christ. The Son of God is said to have condemned them to eternal restlessness.[10] In this respect, orthodox Jewish and firebrand Christian theologians are curiously yoked together. Both see the dispersion of the Jews as a suitable punishment for their sin, though the sins thought to be committed are different – disobeying God's law in the first case, unforgivable deicide in the second. Beyond the idea of perpetual wandering, the extraordinary longevity of the Jewish people attracted a good deal of convoluted speculation and even backhanded compliments from certain historians, philosophers and Christian dogmatists. The seventeenth century philosopher Pascal, for example, noted that of all the peoples of antiquity only the Jewish people remained intact. (The San of southern Africa, the Parsis and other groups of Asian origin could dispute this claim.) He considered the Jews' endurance to be divinely sanctioned because the suffering of the 'carnal Jews' had to be patently visible to all, in order to demonstrate the veracity of Christianity. The presence of Jews in the Christian world therefore acted as a form of living witness to the truth of biblical claims.

For many in European Christendom this 'living witness' was like a ghastly parade of 'the living dead'. Leon Pinsker, one of the prominent Zionists of the nineteenth century, captured this idea of a zombie-like condition vividly, talking of the

> ghostlike apparition of a people without unity or organization, without land or other form of union, no longer alive, but moving among the living. This eerie form scarcely paralleled in history, unlike anything that preceded or followed it, could not fail to make a strange and peculiar impression upon the imagination of the nations. And if the fear of ghosts is something inborn, and has a certain justification in the psychic life of humanity, is it any wonder that it asserted itself powerfully at the sight of this dead but living nation? Fear of the Jewish ghost has been handed down and strengthened for generations and centuries. It led to a prejudice which in its turn, in connection with other forces ... paved the way for Judeophobia.[11]

These mysterious, eternal, wandering Jews were feared as much as they were despised. Jews had not only mulishly refused to accept the Saviour, but had helped the Romans to crucify Him. (The 'helped to' was discretionary in some circles.) This perception produced a complicated and contradictory set of Christian attitudes to the Jews. By being responsible for the Son of God's death, they were condemned to eternal suffering. Why then did they endure and sometimes even prosper? Perhaps it would be a good Christian's duty to punish them for their unforgivable sin? By murdering Jesus, Jews had murdered life itself. Attempts on their own lives were therefore only to be expected. Equally, they could never be entirely innocent victims. Jewish people, some Christian theologians thought, could neither repent nor be reprieved. They were doomed, forever, to carry a 'death taint stigma'.[12]

Despite the sinister tone of these muddled theological musings, until the eleventh century the degree of discrimination against the Jews in the Roman world was quite modest. This was to change dramatically for the worse with the Crusaders, fired as they were by the desire for vengeance for the blood of Jesus. In the summer of 1096, as they were passing through European towns on their way to Jerusalem, they found it offensive to encounter peaceful, thriving Jewish quarters. Beginning at Rouen, they slaughtered or forcibly converted the majority of Jews in the Rhine Valley, killing 1,000 in Mainz alone. When the Crusaders finally arrived in Jerusalem in 1099 they gathered all the Jews they could find into a convenient synagogue and burned them alive.

The Catholic hierarchy also remained wedded to its hostile position for centuries. Early in the twentieth century, Pius X (1903–14) spelled it out. He told the Zionist leader Teodor Herzl that, so long as the Jews refused to convert, the Church would not recognize the Jewish people, nor would he sanction their remigration to their historic homeland.[13] He warned that 'If you come to Palestine and settle your people there, we shall have churches and priests ready to baptize all of you.'[14] At least, we can agree, baptism was a rather more agreeable prospect than being incinerated by Crusaders. After the foundation of the State of Israel in 1948, the Vatican conspicuously ignored its existence. An agreement to exchange diplomats was made only in 1995, nearly half a century after the *fait accompli*. The delegitimation of the Israeli state is a tradition continued by many Christian pilgrims coming to visit the Holy Sites, who still insist on calling their destination 'The Holy Land', thus desecularizing Israel and doggedly continuing the 2,000 year-old tradition of deterritorializing the Jews.

Other examples of Christian religious intolerance abound. Between 1290 and 1293 the Jewish communities in the Kingdom of Naples were almost entirely destroyed, Dominican monks having led a campaign for their forcible conversion. The fervour of religious zealotry was also behind the most famous example of Catholic hostility towards the Jews – the Spanish Inquisition. It is, of course, important to remember that the Inquisition was directed against Muslims as well as Jews. After the Moorish conquest of Spain in AD 711, Jews and Moors had cooperated for seven centuries in helping to make southern Spain a centre of literacy and enlightenment. Thousands of *Marranos*[15] (Jews and Muslims who pretended to be Christians to avoid persecution) were denounced, tortured and put to the stake. Unsurprisingly, for those who can hazard a guess about the psychology of such matters, the first, most vicious and most dreaded inquisitor-general, Torquemada, was himself of Jewish origin. In the summer of 1492, between 100,000 and 150,000 Jews fled Spain to the sound of 'lively music' ordered by the rabbis.[16]

Fortunately for the Jews in the Protestant parts of Europe, unrelieved theological animosity was seen as being, to some degree, internally inconsistent. After all, Christ had preached forgiveness not punishment. Were not the disciples Jewish? And was not Christ, in his human aspect at least, also a Jew? Protestants in Amsterdam and Puritans in England were both more pragmatic and more open to these contrary religious positions. Amsterdam welcomed *Marrano* traders for the role they could play in enhancing its budding mercantilist empire. In England, the Puritans were genuinely curious about the people of the Old Testament and one of their number, Sir Henry Finch, a lawyer active in James I's reign, advanced the bold theory that the Jews would all soon be converted and their dispersion would be at an end. Even more fancifully, he affirmed that a Jewish king would once again reside in Jerusalem and have dominion over all the peoples of the world. This last idea rather alarmed James I, who promptly had Sir Henry arrested. The king nonetheless allowed the translation of the Hebrew scriptures (the famous King James Bible) to go ahead. The now popularly available Bible fed the convictions of those who found the fire and brimstone of the Old Testament much more to their liking than the milk and water of the New.

The breakthrough in England finally came in Oliver Cromwell's period. A rabbi friend of Rembrandt, Manasseh ben Israel, petitioned Cromwell to allow Jews to return. Amid much hatred, all Jews in England had been expelled in 1290 in the reign of Edward I. Cromwell had to move slowly. Church dignitaries feared that the Jews would proselytize and warned that 'Moloch-worship' would stalk the land. Merchants were alarmed at the thought of new competition. When Cromwell refused to accept his petition, ben Israel returned to Amsterdam to die broken-hearted. However, not long afterwards, a fortuitous legal decision in favour of a Portuguese Jewish merchant, who had had his property seized for being an illegal resident, gave legal force to the idea that Jews already living in England could not be treated differently from other residents. Twenty *Marrano* families 'came out' (as we would say today) and established a synagogue and a Jewish cemetery. One family head was admitted to the Royal Exchange without having to swear a Christian oath. In Amsterdam and London, Jews had finally gained a toehold in Protestant Europe.[17]

THE JEWISH DIASPORA AND ISLAM

Anxious to dispel current images, there is a good deal of special pleading in the literature on behalf of the proposition that Jews were well treated in Islamic societies and accorded respect as 'scripturaries', namely people of the Book. This attempt at a historical corrective is hardly surprising in view of what Edward Said calls 'the almost total absence of any cultural position [in the West] making it possible either to identify with or dispassionately to discuss the Arabs or Islam … The web of racism, cultural stereotypes, political imperialism, dehumanizing ideology holding in the Arab or the Muslim is very strong indeed.'[18]

While diffuse anti-Muslim sentiments were general in many Western societies, wilder notions of an eternal war of hate between Jews and Muslims were given an ample injection of oxygen by the horrific events of 9/11 and their aftermath. We should remember that there were many occasions when the two communities shared a common fate. I have already mentioned that Jews and Moors were both victims to the zeal of the Inquisition and *Reconquista* in the case of fifteenth-century Spain. Many of the expelled Jews were to find refuge in Muslim Africa and the Middle East. What I omitted to say, as I was dealing earlier with Christian attitudes to Jews, was that, like the Jews, the Muslims of Jerusalem were also ruthlessly attacked by the Crusaders four centuries earlier, to the point that 'not a single Muslim was left alive within the city walls'.[19]

At a general level, one can make a good case that until the scale of Zionist settlements in Palestine became apparent Jews were generally well-treated in Islamic societies. Nevertheless, it would be over-egging the historical custard to suggest that there were not tensions between Jews and Muslims right from the start. When Mohammed fled in AD 622 to Medina (a town extensively populated, some sources say founded, by Jewish date growers), it was only the Jews who resisted his message that he was a true prophet in the line of Moses and Abraham. Having won the allegiance of the local Arabs and Bedouin, he was strong enough to expel the Jews from Medina and force those at Khaybar into a tributary relationship. Bernard Lewis maintains that expulsion was not their only fate: 'As soon as the Arabs had attained unity through the agency of Muhammed they attacked and ultimately eliminated the Jews [of Medina].'[20]

Despite the spectacular military success of the Muslim armies over the next century, the caliphs had to evolve a *modus vivendi* with the many religious minorities over whom they presided. Notable among these groups were the Jews and Christians, both groups being known in the Koran as *dhimmi*, the subservient people. Under the Pact of Omar (*c.* AD 800), the *dhimmi* were accorded religious autonomy, security of life and property and exemption from military service. In return, they had to show due deference to Muslims by not bearing arms, riding horses or building new synagogues, churches or houses grander than those of their Muslim neighbours.[21] In AD 850–4, Christians and Jews had to affix wooden images of devils to their houses, wear yellow garb and put yellow spots on the dress of their slaves. The word of a Jew or Christian could not be accepted against that of a Muslim.[22]

While not seeking to minimize these considerable formal restrictions, it is true that many Jews managed to evade their spirit and often attained considerable prestige and prosperity in Muslim societies. Hitti quotes a contemporary traveller to Syria in AD 985 to the effect that 'most of the money–changers and bankers were Jews'. In Baghdad, the traveller continued, the Jews maintained 'a good-sized colony', while the Exilarch

> seems to have lived in affluence and owned gardens, houses and rich plantations. On his way to any audience with the caliph he appeared dressed in embroidered silk, wore a white turban gleaming with gems and was accompanied by a retinue of horsemen. Ahead of him marched a herald calling out 'Make way before our lord, the son of David'.[23]

Though recognizably separate, the Jews were heavily dominated by Muslim culture. The eminent scholar of the Jews of the Arab world, Goitein, concludes the second volume of his massive study of eleventh-century Mediterranean society by suggesting that, although communal life was left to their own initiative, 'Christians and Jews shared with their Muslim compatriots their language, economy, and most of their social notions and habits'.[24] As for the Jews, they tended to write and speak Arabic (though Aramaic and Hebrew were never totally displaced). Freely-made conversions to Islam were relatively common either for personal reasons or on grounds of conviction.

Perhaps the most extraordinary figure to emerge from this nesting of Jewish community life within an overarching Islamic culture was Moses Maimonides (1135–1204). He was born in Cordoba, Spain, which fell to the militant Almohades in the summer of 1148. He and his family were forced into exile. They settled in Fez in 1160 (where there is some speculation that he converted to Islam), then left for Acre, Alexandria and Cairo. Along the way he became a veritable sponge for every fragment of knowledge about medicine, law, philosophy and religion. In Cairo, he was the court physician to the vizier appointed by Saladin, while simultaneously attaining the unquestioned spiritual leadership of the Jewish community. His vast output of theological exegesis included the definitive religious tract, *The recapitulation of the Law*, but he also contributed to general philosophy in his famous book, *Guide to the perplexed*.

The Almohades were eventually to snuff the life from this creative intersection of Judaism and Islam. The centre of Jewish intellectual and spiritual life gradually moved to the Ottoman Empire, then to northern Europe. Before I turn to these experiences, I want to draw one key inference from the period up to the thirteenth century. The Jewish communities in Babylon, North Africa, Spain and the rest of the Mediterranean were *not* primarily defined by their attachment to a lost homeland in Judea. Drawing on Goitein's work cited earlier, Clifford describes the Jews of the Arab world in these terms:

> This sprawling social world was linked through cultural forms, kinship relations, business circuits, and travel trajectories as well as through loyalty to the religious centers of the diaspora (in Babylon, Palestine and Egypt). The attachment to specific cities (sometimes superseding ties of religion and ethnicity) characteristic of Goitein's medieval world

casts doubt on any definition that would 'center' the Jewish diaspora in a single land. Among Sephardim [even] after 1492, the longing for 'home' could be focused on a city in Spain at the same time as the Holy Land.[25]

The position of the Jews under the Ottomans (c. 1300–1918) did not vary a great deal from the earlier Muslim regimes. Jewish (and Christian) communities were accepted as scripturaries, who believed in God, the prophets and judgement, and who belonged to the same spiritual family as Muslims. From the time of the capture of Constantinople, the Great Rabbi received official investiture from the sultan and represented the Jews of the empire to the government.[26] Inside each community spiritual heads were responsible for legal matters, for collecting the poll tax and for maintaining law and order. Individual Jews often attained high office under the Ottomans. For example, there were Jewish bankers, finance ministers and advisers to the district governors of Baghdad, Basra, Damascus and Aleppo.[27] Generally, trade in the Ottoman Empire passed into the hands of oriental Christians and Jews. They often enjoyed consular protection and possessed knowledge of European languages and business methods. The Jews of Damascus, Aleppo and the coastal towns were able to build trading networks to Alexandria, Livorno, Trieste and Marseilles.[28]

Like other empires before it, the Ottoman Empire began to lose control of its marginal lands, including Palestine – an outcome crucial to the fate of the Jewish diaspora. Instead of the established oriental Jews and those who came to study, pray or die, a new sort of Jew from eastern and central Europe began to arrive in Palestine. In contrast to the complex, multi-faceted, multi-located history of Jewish life in the diaspora, the new settlers were infused by Western concepts of the unbreakable link between race, nation and territory. Despite the Ottoman government's opposition and the increasing alarm of the local Arab population, by 1914 Palestine's Jewish population was 85,000, 12 per cent of the total. Moreover, a quarter of them were settled by the Jewish National Fund on land that was deemed by the organization to be the inalienable property of the Jewish people.[29] The clash between those who advocated the territorialization of Jewish identity as a solution to 'the Jewish problem' and those who held that a viable and enriching life in the diaspora was possible, or even preferable, was to be played out with titanic fervour among the Ashkenazi Jews.

ASHKENAZI FATES

Who are the Ashkenazim? Conventional Jewish histories make the perfectly proper trisection between the Jews of the Iberian Peninsula (the Sephardim), those of the Muslim Middle East, and the Ashkenazim[30] of northern Europe. They suggest that, in an attempt to pick up the pieces of the Roman Empire, Charlemagne had encouraged the immigration of Jewish merchants because of their strong economic connections with the Mediterranean and the Middle East. From these pioneer merchants, such accounts continue, there evolved a community life, a distinctive language (Yiddish), and shared customs and religious traditions.

A far more heterodox scenario is advanced by the political commentator, Arthur Koestler. He shows how precisely at the period when Charlemagne was crowned Emperor of the West, the area between the Caucasus and the Volga was dominated by the little discussed, but far from insignificant, Khazar Empire. As Judaism has historically rarely been a proselytizing religion, it is surprising to discover that the ruling classes and much of the citizenry of Khazaria were recently converted Jews. When the empire was crushed by the Russians in AD 985, the Khazars migrated north, retaining their Jewish faith. This group, he suggests, provide the bulk of the Ashkenazim, just as its descendants (in Europe, the Americas and South Africa) make up most of the world's Jews. Koestler concedes readily enough that forcible miscegenation, two-way conversions and intermarriage complicate the picture, but essentially he sees the Turkic Khazars as a wholly different people from the Semitic Sephardim.[31] In the appendix to his account, Koestler vehemently guards himself against accusations that he is against the existence of Israel, saying that it does not really matter whether the chromosomes of its people are of Khazari, Semitic, Roman or Spanish origin. However, there is no doubt that his account punctures many common myths about the Jewish diaspora. It becomes implausible to claim, for example, that Jews are a single people with a single history and identity and, by implication, that there is a continuous claim for an ancient homeland that applies to all Jews. It was little wonder that many Zionists were hopping mad at the publication of Koestler's book.

What then happened to the Khazar–Turkic–Ashkenazi part of the Jewish diaspora? Here, I will have to cut a long story very short. I will use the scholars' shorthand, the device of a case study, taking the Pale of Settlement[32] in the first instance (as the home of most Ashkenazim and the source of the very large emigration flows between 1881 and 1914) and France in the second (as one site where the tensions between integration into the local citizenship and Zionism were sharply posed).

It is no great revelation that the tsarist authorities did not get on well with their Jewish subjects. The Russian rulers had always been hostile to Jewish settlement while they inherited a large Jewish population by accident with the partition of Poland in the eighteenth century. The Jews did not want to be there and the Russian authorities did not know what to do with them. By the 1870s anti-Jewish sentiment was prevalent in official circles and among the Russian population at large. The pogroms of the spring of 1881 affected more than 100 Jewish communities, but far from condemning these outbreaks, the tsar used them as a means to garner populist sentiment in favour of the monarchy. A set of special commissions was established to examine the 'harm' caused by Jewish economic activity on the 'main population'. Jewish schools were shut down because, it was argued, the 'main population' did not have sufficient schooling itself. Quotas were then established (in 1882) restricting the number of Jews who could enter the professions or higher education, while heavy fines were imposed on the families of those who did not report for military service.

The *rekrutchina* (draft) was indeed a fearsome prospect, as the tsar could demand no less than 25 years of military service. The attempts to evade the draft also split the Russian Jews by class. Jewish *khappers* (recruiters) rounded up draft dodgers, but wealthier families could usually bribe them to ignore their own children at the expense of the poorer families.[33] The combination of draft evasion and fear of pogroms (more than 600 were recorded from 1903 to 1906) propelled the major political response of the Jews of the Russian Pale – emigration. In the first national census of the Russian Empire in 1897, 5,189,401 Jews were recorded. Over half of this number emigrated. Some, in response to the earnest pleadings of the Zionist movement, found their way to Palestine and emerged as the creators of the state of Israel and the elite of its political parties, labour movement and social life. Most, however, headed west to other European countries or to the principal magnet, the USA.

Those who stayed in the Pale often sought to preserve community life and their rabbinical traditions. This turned out to be a poor option. The pogroms continued with increasing intensity under the tsars, while there was little respite under the Bolsheviks, who frequently denounced Jews as troublemakers or exploiters. Later, in the 1940s, Jews in the areas that were about to be overrun by the advancing Nazi armies found the local population enthusiastically butchering them before the Nazis arrived and in the certain knowledge that they would approve. A final option, taken by a significant number of intellectuals and workers, was to join the socialist and communist movements, either by assimilating directly to progressive Russian parties or by organizing separately in youth movements or in bodies like the Jewish Bund (which was affiliated to the Social Democratic Workers' Party). Jewish employers, tsarist officials and Zionists alike were angry and frustrated at the attractiveness of socialist internationalism to Jewish activists. The prominent Zionist Chaim Weizmann, for example, lamented that 'The large part of the contemporary younger generation is anti-Zionist, not from a desire to assimilate, as in Western Europe, but through revolutionary conviction.'[34] The relationship between Zionists and the Jewish diaspora in the wake of the formation of the state of Israel is further discussed in Chapter 6.

The tutor to Nicholas II is said to have remarked that the 'Jewish Question' in Russia would be solved by the conversion of one-third of the Jews, the emigration of another third and by the death of the remaining third. Shift these proportions a little and allow that the 'conversion' was to socialism rather than to the Russian Orthodox Church and one has a roughly accurate way of describing the fate of the Russian Jews.

Let me now turn to the second of my case studies, the Jews in France. Like their counterparts in Germany, Hungary and Austria, French Jews stood in marked contrast to the *Ostjuden* of the Russian Pale. They were more urbane, more liberal and more bourgeois. In Berlin, Budapest, Vienna and Paris Jews had made notable contributions to the professions and to intellectual, literary and artistic life. Normally, their primary loyalties were to their countries of settlement rather than to their religion, even less to their ethnicity. In France, legal emancipation had fostered the belief that adherence to the Jewish religion was no barrier to full citizenship and integration into France. However, as Muslims are currently discovering in France, the revolutionary civic tradition in France has compelling and not always comfortable secular implications. As one nineteenth-century French politician bluntly put it: 'To the Jews as Jews, nothing. To the Jews as citizens, everything.'[35]

French Jews who chose to ride both horses – Judaism plus emancipation – were from time to time confronted with significant crises that divided their loyalties. The first major dilemma arose in the 1840s. At the beginning of that decade the Sharif Pasha of Syria had arrested a Jewish barber on the charge of ritual murder after the mysterious disappearance of an Italian friar and his servant. Confessions under duress, the arrest of Jewish children and mob violence followed. Because of the then heated European rivalries in the Middle East, the 'Damascus Affair' commanded much attention. The French government got drawn into supporting the charges, the Austrian and British governments denounced them. French Jews were suddenly confronted with an impossible conundrum. To advance French international ambitions, the state that had emancipated them was prepared to countenance an anti-Semitic libel. After much shilly-shallying, the initiative was seized by Adolphe Crémieux, a Jew and prominent French politician, who cooperated with eminent Jews in Great Britain and Austria (France's enemies) to secure the release of the prisoners in Damascus. The outcome was an apparent victory in humanitarian terms, but was a pyrrhic one.[36] Thereafter, French patriots argued that love of their brethren would always be greater than the love of French Jews for France. Jews would always be Jews. Moreover, their increasing prominence in commerce and banking meant that wealthy and powerful Jews could act against the nation's interest. It was but a small step to convince fellow patriots that Jews were part of an omnipotent global conspiracy. Such a widely held perception was later to fuel nineteenth- and twentieth-century anti-Semitism.

The Damascus Affair was followed by an equally momentous event, the Dreyfus Affair, when in 1894 a French Jewish army officer was falsely accused of spying for the Germans.[37] 'The Affair', as it came to be known, led to a profound change of heart for Teodor Herzl, hitherto an assimilated, bourgeois, Viennese journalist, who had been sent to cover the Dreyfus trial and later became the key advocate of Zionism. More in sadness than in anger, he concluded:

> Everywhere we Jews have tried honestly to assimilate into the nations around us, preserving only the religion of our fathers. We have not been permitted to … We are a nation – the enemy has made us one

33

without our desiring it ... We do have the strength to create a state and, moreover, a model state.[38]

Faced with apparently inevitable outbursts of anti-Semitism, even in a country like France that proclaimed the revolutionary ideals of Liberty, Equality and Fraternity, it was all too easy for Zionist ideologues to promote the idea of creating a national homeland as an alternative to a doomed attempt at assimilation.[39] The partial acceptance of such an aspiration lent further support to the charges of dual loyalty, even if not to the more fanciful notions of an international conspiracy. The apparently persistent belief in France that Jews essentially remained an alien element was given dramatic affirmation in Vichy France where, half a century after the event, disturbing evidence emerged that collaboration with the Nazis to identify and round up Jews for the death camps was widespread.[40]

If I try to summarize the fates of the Ashkenazi emigrants, I would start by insisting on the diversity of outcomes. Though there were often serious outbreaks of anti-Semitism in France, Britain or the USA from time to time, it would be unduly perverse to compare them in scale and intensity with the unremitting pogroms of the Russian Empire or the stunning, virtually incomprehensible horror of the holocaust in Nazi Germany and Nazi-occupied territories. Those parts of the diaspora in the more benign countries of settlement were often beneficiaries of tolerance and acceptance and, like the Jews of Babylon, profited from the stimulus of cosmopolitanism and pluralism. Nonetheless, the Zionists have their strongest argument in stating that the outcome is essentially unpredictable, whatever appearances might suggest. It is virtually unimaginable to construct a scene of state-sponsored genocidal killers or mass anti-Semitism either in contemporary Britain or in the USA. Yet the obvious riposte is that the German Jews of the 1930s could equally not believe this possibility and it was precisely their stubborn lack of prescience that contributed to the scale of their appalling fate. Though the French events of the 1940s were of a lesser magnitude, there was an equal incomprehension that a friendly neighbour, *boulangeur* or *restaurateur* could harbour such a reservoir of hatred that they happily identified Jews to the Nazi authorities.

CONCLUSION

All scholars of diaspora recognize that the dominant Jewish tradition is at the heart of any definition of the concept. Yet, if it is necessary to take full account of this tradition it is also necessary to transcend it. I hope readers will have been patient with my elucidation of Jewish history, for it is crucial to the wider arguments in this book to demonstrate that Jewish diasporic experiences are much more complex and varied than many assume. The Jews are not a single people; they have a multi-faceted, multi-located history with a genetically complex set of roots. At different periods, they looked either to their homeland or to more local links. Like other ethnic groups, their history is socially constructed and selectively interpreted.

One narrative, promoted often by Zionists and religious leaders in the tradition of Ezra and the prophets, depicts the Babylonian and Sephardi experiences as a wholly negative process of deracination. However, such experiences were distinguished by considerable intellectual and spiritual achievements that simply could not have happened in a narrow tribal society like that of ancient Judea. The voluntarist component in the history of Jewish migration should also not be overlooked. Many Jewish communities outside the natal homeland resulted from the proliferation of trade and financial networks, not from forcible dispersal.

The tapestry of Jewish diasporic experiences becomes more nuanced, but more accurate, when we accept a dual model, with the warp of the Jewish diaspora being one of creativity and achievement and its weave being one of anxiety and distrust. However economically or professionally successful, however long-settled in peaceful settings, it was difficult for many Jews in the diaspora not to 'keep their guard up', to be aware of the weight of their history and the cold clammy fear that brings demons in the night reminding them of their murdered ancestors. The sense of unease or difference that members of the diaspora felt in their countries of settlement often resulted in a felt need for protective cover in the bosom of the community or a tendency to identify closely with their imagined homeland and with co-ethnic communities in other countries. Bonds of language, religion, culture and a sense of a common history continued to be stressed by community and religious leaders who sought to deepen the symbolic bonds constructing a sense of community. Such bonds lent credence to the idea that Jews share a common fate and a transnational community with an affective, intimate quality that formal citizenship or even long settlement could not fully match.

We are now long past the stage where the meaning of diaspora can be confined to a description of the forcible dispersal of a people and their subsequent unhappiness, or supposed unhappiness, in their countries of exile. Nowadays, with the increased use of the term to describe many kinds of migrants and other communities, a more relaxed definition seems appropriate, even if some definitional limits have to be set. Moreover, transnational bonds no longer have to be cemented by migration or encased by exclusive spatial claims based on territory and a nation-state. Some scholars, as I have mentioned in Chapter 1, even want to abolish a common ethnicity or a homeland as prerequisites for a diasporic self-description. I resist going all the way down this path, but as we shall see later in this book, in the age of cyberspace a diaspora can, to some degree at least, be held together or re-created through the mind, through popular culture and through a shared imagination.

FURTHER READING

- For a rich account of the Arab world's relationships to the Jewish diaspora, with particularly interesting observations on the Ottoman Empire, see the account by the late and much revered Lebanese scholar Albert Hourani *A history of the Arab peoples* (Cambridge, MA: The Belknap Press of Harvard University Press, 1991).
- Avi Shlaim's *The iron wall: Israel and the Arab world* (Harmondsworth: Penguin, 2001) is excellent on the early Zionist settlements in Palestine, though too wordy later.
- James Clifford's 'Diasporas', *Current Anthropology*, 9(3), (1994), 302–38 is not only a key article in the theoretical exposition of diaspora theory, he also has a sophisticated appreciation of the complexity of Jewish history.
- Martin Baumann's article 'Diaspora: genealogies of semantics and transcultural comparison', *Numen*, 47(3), (2000), 313–37 is an authoritative account of the origins and semantics of the word diaspora.

QUESTIONS TO THINK ABOUT

- Why is it important to understand the multi-faceted nature of the Jewish diasporic experience?
- How did the image of 'the wandering Jew' begin? Does it still persist? If so, why?
- Has the expansion of the term 'diaspora' beyond its common original reference to Jews, now gone 'too far', with the effect that the idea is losing its force?

Figure 3.1 A Rastaman in Kingston, Jamaica. Rastas describe their places of dispersal as 'Babylon' and look to 'Ethiopia' (usually understood as a metaphorical and symbolic place) for redemption. © iStockphoto.com/Robin Cohen

3

VICTIM DIASPORAS

Africans and Armenians

In Chapter 1, I identified the Jewish, Irish, Palestinian, African and Armenian diasporas, which, through self-description or construction by others, can be labelled with the preceding adjective of 'victim'. Writers and political leaders representing these peoples reinforce this classification with their constant cross-references and comparisons to one another. Readers with literary leanings might, for example, remember one of the characters in James Joyce's famous novel *Ulysses* talking of the Irish peasants in the 'black 1847' as being driven out 'in hordes'. 'Twenty-thousand of them died in the coffin ships' (a description frequently used of the African slave ships). 'But', his character continues, 'those who came to the land of the free remember the land of bondage' (a clear reference to the way the biblical Jews conceived ancient Egypt).

Tragically, for Palestinians their 'great calamity' (*Nakba*) was induced by the return of the Jews to Palestine and their formation of the state of Israel. As Bamyeh puts it: 'Since its beginning in the cataclysmic events of 1948, diaspora life itself has signified for Palestinians the essence of their dispossession and one of the most compelling elements of their cause.'[1] The majority of the Palestinians are in diaspora, the majority of these are, in turn, officially registered as refugees. Though some precarious half-beginnings of statehood in Gaza and the West Bank occasionally signal a partial resolution of the Israeli–Palestinian conflict, military interventions, terrorism and the bitter flavour of exile (so near yet so far from their natal homes) soon sours any hopes of peace and reconciliation.

While there was no causal connection, Jews often provided the point of comparison in the case of other victim diasporas. Africans abroad have long felt an affinity with the Jewish diaspora,[2] though the expressions black diaspora or African diaspora were not widely used until the mid-1950s or 1960s. There are potent and obvious parallels between Jewish and African historical experiences. Servitude, forced migration, exile and the development of a return movement are all similarities noted by a number of writers of African descent in the Americas in the nineteenth century as well as by early West African nationalists.[3]

For Armenian commentators, the obvious point of comparison is between the Armenian massacres of 1915–22 and the Jewish holocaust of the Second World War. In contrast to the massacres of earlier historical periods, Dekmejian argues that these two events were characterized by 'supranationalist ruling elites' who were bureaucratically organized and had the technological capacity and ideological imperative to carry out mass extermination. Although the level of technological sophistication is questionable in the Ottoman case, 'the scale, speed, and efficiency of human destruction and its systematic implementation through impersonal bureaucratic rationality ... [were] five characteristics [all] present in the Armenian and Jewish cases'.[4]

In this chapter, I propose to investigate two diasporas, African and Armenian, looking both at how they compare with the victim diaspora narrative and how they conform to the list of common characteristics of all diasporas developed in Chapter 1. However, there is a difference between resemblance and similitude. For example, unlike the Africans, Ashkenazi Jews did not arrive in the New World as slaves. Nor were they that different phenotypically from the majority of immigrants to the Americas. This made it easier for them to be absorbed into, or accepted by, the white populations and thereby become less obvious targets of discrimination. As the rate of social mobility of US Jews accelerated so too did their tendencies to vote Republican, to abandon their old urban haunts and, with them, their progressive social and political attitudes. Those Jews who remained, either as landlords or small businesspeople, or as highly visible followers of religious sects, became the targets of furious hate campaigns by some militant black leaders in the 1980s.

Likewise, we have to remember the fundamental differences between the Armenian and Jewish diasporas. While the holocaust occurred when the Jewish diaspora had already been in existence for over 2,000 years, the massacres of Armenians in the late nineteenth century and again during the First World War constituted the primary trauma events, which occasioned the creation of a significant diaspora for the first time. Dekmejian makes a related point in a different way. Whereas, he reminds us, the Armenians were an indigenous population, the Jews of Germany were a minority. And, he adds, whereas the Nazis regarded the Jews as racially inferior, the Young Turks accused the Armenians of elitism.[5] Again, while Nazi Germany was in an advanced stage of modernization, the Ottoman Empire remained somewhat feudal and considerably decentralized, despite the Young Turks' aspirations to modernity.

ORIGINS OF THE AFRICAN DIASPORA

It is often argued that an oppressive social practice – be it the beheading of murderers, the circumcision of women or the burning of witches – has to be understood in terms of the meaning of such practices to the local actors who were bound by their own time and circumstances. So they must. However, we should also guard against the opposite danger of accepting, under the guise of an actor-directed view of the world, the sort of cultural relativism that leaves the historian and social scientist in a pilotless moral vacuum. The apologia of a different time is, in any case, impossible to mount with respect to African slavery, as there is a wealth of evidence that those who conducted the trade were well aware that they offended *contemporary* standards. Take, for example, the account of one William Bosman, the chief agent of the Dutch West India Company at its main slave trading station in modern-day Ghana:

> When these Slaves come to Fida, they are put in Prison altogether ... they are thoroughly examined, even to the smallest Member, and that naked too both Men and Women, without the least Distinction of Modesty. Those which are approved as good are set on one side; and the lame and faulty are set by as Invalides ... the remainder are numbred, and it is entred who delivered them. In the mean while a burning iron, with the Arms or Name of the Companies, lyes in the Fire; with which ours are marked on the Breast ... *I doubt not but this Trade seems very barbarous to you, but since it is followed by meer necessity it must go on*; but we yet take all possible care that they are not burned too hard, especially the Women, who are more tender than the Men (emphasis added).[6]

For 'necessity' read 'profit'. For the more considerate treatment meted out to women read 'moral humbug'. For the ship captains, merchants (European and African) and, above all, for the plantation owners in the New World, African slaves meant vast profits for a relatively modest outlay. And when there were plenty of slaves to be had, the cruelty was quite profligate. Some slaves were branded several times over – to prove ownership, to demonstrate that export duty had been paid, to show their vassalage to the king of the country concerned or, in a supreme act of double standards, to indicate that they had been baptized. In 1813, branding was replaced by a metal collar or bracelet, but it was restored five years later, this time with a silver branding iron and still with the evident intention of making clear that the slave was a commodity, not a person.[7] The transatlantic trade deposited Africans in the Caribbean, Mexico and Brazil – in each case to work on tropical plantations. Their suffering has been embellished on the consciousness of Europeans and Americans partly because of their historical complicity in owning and exploiting slave labour, but also by the extraordinary success of New World Africans in conveying a sense of their plight through art, literature, music, dance and religious expression.

However momentous and powerful the experience of the Atlantic diaspora, it is important not to overlook the commencement of Africa's experience of a slave trade and forced migration during the Islamic hegemony of the seventh and eighth centuries. As Hunwick contends:

> Beginning some eight centuries before the transatlantic slave trade, and not ending until several decades after the latter was halted, the movement of slaves across the Sahara, up the Nile Valley and the Red Sea, and across the Indian Ocean to the Persian Gulf and India, probably accounted for the uprooting of as many Africans from their societies as did the transatlantic trade.[8]

George Shepperson also fires a useful warning shot across the bows in discussing the comparison of the Jewish and African diasporas. Arguing that the expression 'African diaspora' has been one-sided and drawn only on the catastrophic tradition, he counsels:

> Some knowledge of Jewish history would help students of Africans abroad to realize that, in the expression 'the African diaspora' *diaspora* is being used metaphorically. This would prevent it becoming an over-rigid, ideologized concept, to the detriment of serious and imaginative research. Furthermore, knowledge of Jewish usage enables the appreciation of the voluntary as opposed to the involuntary element in the diaspora of the Jews … Excessive concentration on the western rather than the eastern direction of the African diaspora may be responsible for the concealment of the voluntary element in the dispersal, even in the slave days.[9]

These comments are pertinent, giving us a richer and more complex reading of the origins and destinations of the 'first' African diaspora, based on the slave trade across the Atlantic *and* Indian Oceans. Africans ended up in Asia and the Mediterranean, as well as in the Americas, and some of the non-American migrants were traders rather than slaves. But we must not therefore minimize the element of compulsion and collective trauma that accompanied the creation of the transatlantic African diaspora. Where, clearly, we do need to draw a distinction between the African and some others diasporas is in the prolonged time scale of the African slave trade – from the seventh to at least the nineteenth century. (The website of the Anti-Slavery Society provides the depressing information that the long-distance slave trade continues intermittently.) Whereas the creation of the African diaspora was a prolonged affair, the Palestinians, Armenians and, more arguably, the Irish diaspora were propelled by a single set of events. Although the Jewish diaspora has also been assumed to have been galvanized by a single cataclysmic event, as we have seen in Chapter 2, many early Jewish colonies were the result of trade and voluntary settlement, not forcible dispersal.

THE AFRICAN DIASPORA: HOMELAND AND RETURN

Is there a collective myth about the African homeland, including its location, history and achievements? Is there a desire to return? In fact, the African diaspora in the New World generated a number of myths[10] about its origins. Haiti, for example, provides two contrasting myths. A 'macho' man might have beaten his chest and boasted that he was *neg Ginin* (a black from Guinea). 'Guinea' had come to symbolize the 'mythical origin of valour and virtue'. It referred to 'a mythical place of origin that had become an ideal of resistance to slavery, its suffering, and its humiliation'.[11] By contrast, a Haitian would be insulted to be called *neg Congo* (a black from the Congo). This designation was used to allude to Haitians who had been under Western influence, in particular Christianity, even in Africa. It was imputed that they were docile and used as house slaves – in contrast to the sturdy, solidaristic field hands. The pantheon of spirits was also divided in two. The Guinean spirits, *lwa Ginin*, were bold, strong, helpful and efficient, while the *lwa Congo* were uninterested in the destiny of the people. Their redeeming feature was that they were gentle and encouraged joyful dances expressing good humour and the desire for a happy life. After their lives in exile the dead would return to Guinea: their souls would transmigrate and they would return to their ancestors' shrines.

Other African 'homelands' were constructed from the places where African returnees, or liberated or manumitted slaves, were conveyed by the European and American powers. Perhaps I could elaborate with a personal experience? I once worked on the remote island of St Helena in the south Atlantic – halfway between Angola and Brazil. In the period after 1807, when the British slave trade (as opposed to slavery, which went on far longer) had been abolished, Portuguese slavers had been intercepted on the high seas by the British Navy. Their wretched human cargo had been deposited at a forsaken beach on the island, where a hospital had been established. As I paced alongside the ruins of the hospital, I was overpowered by a sense of the agonies of the many who had died there and, by contrast, felt the half flicker of hope of those who were told they would be taken from the island to Freetown (in Sierra Leone), one of the ports at which the recaptives were landed. Some recaptives actually made their way back from Sierra Leone to their original homes, but most stayed. Those that did stay found in Freetown – so named because of their presence – 400 Westernized Christianized returnees from England (plus others from the USA, Canada and Jamaica) who had been sent to Sierra Leone under the sponsorship of British abolitionists.

The groups congealed to become the core of an educated, Westernized bourgeoisie who reached elite positions in the church, in commerce and in government. In 1879, the son of a recaptive, Gurney Nicol, became the first African graduate of Cambridge University.[12] Returnees from Brazil created a similar creolized bourgeoisie in Lagos and other port cities in West Africa where their substantial, though somewhat dilapidated, houses can still be observed.[13]

'Homeland' also was Liberia. Again the name signified the involvement of abolitionists, this time from the USA. The repatriates to Liberia were from the USA and many had already achieved a modest independent status in America. This meant they came back as settlers rather than impoverished returnees. The Americo-Liberians, as they were called, soon took on the appearance of colonists – refusing to learn the local languages, imposing American-style institutions, acquiring the airs of a social elite and ruthlessly monopolizing political power. In the 1930s a League of Nations investigation found that some Americo-Liberians, including a number holding political office, had reinstituted slavery – this time, however, with the boot on the other foot. In short, Liberia was quite a long way from utopia. Nevertheless, the Liberian constitution committed the country 'to provide a home for the dispersed and oppressed children of Africa' and for many black intellectuals and political leaders in the diaspora it remained an island of optimism in a sea of racial discrimination and colonial domination.

Guinea, Freetown and Liberia were all versions of 'homeland'. But by far the most significant notions of the African homeland were imbricated in 'Ethiopia' – the place, the symbol, the idea and the promise.[14] Ethiopia was seen as the heartland of African civilization, indeed – a claim replicated in a number of self-images of different diasporas – the heartland of *all* civilization. A favourite quote in demonstration of this belief was from the pre-Christian Greek historian, Diodorous Siculus, who wrote:

> The Ethiopians conceived themselves to be of greater antiquity than any other nation, and it is probable that, born under the sun's path, its warmth may have ripened them sooner than other men. They supposed themselves to be the inventors of Worship, of festivals, of solemn assemblies, of sacrifice, and every religious practice. One typical African–American pamphlet, in the style of a Ripley's 'Believe-It-Or-Not' story, claimed that Ethiopia, that is Negroes, gave the world the first idea of right and wrong and this laid the basis of religion and all true culture and civilization.[15]

Just as 'Zion' and 'Israel' were often imagined entities, for many New World Africans 'Ethiopia' was more of a concept of 'blackness' or 'Africanity', only loosely connected with the country of Ethiopia itself.[16] Nonetheless, the fictive community generated social movements that were real enough. For example, in the 1930s the precursor to Rastafarianism in Jamaica was 'Ethiopianism'. The movement made the connection with Jewish history and reinforced the negative version of their experiences in Babylon.

> Generally throughout Jamaican Ethiopianism, the sense of a Negro awakening combined with the feeling of being a scattered and oppressed, but nevertheless 'chosen' people in a way which made it easy to identify 'Babylon' – the white or near-white establishment ... It was thus a feature of Jamaican Ethiopianism as an ideology that it moved from a sense of being a chosen people to the identification of Babylon with the white enslaver, and thence to an interpretation of history which predicated the doom of the oppressor.[17]

The spiritual and mystical forms of Ethiopianism were suddenly given a massive boost after the crowning of Ras (meaning 'prince') Tafari as Emperor Haile Selassie of Ethiopia in November 1930. This led directly to the formation of the Rastafarian movement in Jamaica. Among the Jamaican Rastafarians, the cross-identification with the biblical Jews was complete:

> The Rastas take it from the Bible that they are the true Jews of the prophecy, buried alive in a hostile and godless white society that couldn't care less about the black man down at the bottom of the heap. They never wanted to come here and they don't want to stay. So they take no part. They have disenfranchized themselves ... They have defected body and soul from Jamaican society into an outcast astral identity beyond the law.[18]

The newly-independent government of Jamaica, anxious at the large following the movement was attracting, thought they would prick the balloon by inviting Haile Selassie on a state visit. Far from having the intended effect, seeing the stately figure of the emperor on the steps of an aircraft at Kingston airport propelled an even more fervent belief in Rastafarianism and in his divinity.

The attack on Ethiopia by the Italian Fascists in October 1935 had, however, brought the astral aspects of Ethiopianism down with a thump. Suddenly, the very existence of this potent symbol of black pride and independence was imperilled. In the USA, emotions spilled over in East Harlem, with African-Americans assaulting their Italian neighbours. Joe Louis's boxing triumph over Primo Carnera was seen as a successful attack on the Fascists. Some 20,000 protesters, some bearing Ethiopian flags, marched in a rally to Madison Square. The spirit of the times was well captured by a Cleveland physician, who urged that 'every son and daughter of African descent should render assistance to their blood relatives in Ethiopia. We must not desert our Race in Africa. We must stand, "One for all, All for one" '.[19]

45

Despite this help from the diaspora, and only after a brave fight, Haile Selassie was forced to flee into exile in Britain. In its notorious period of appeasement before the Second World War, the British government at first capitulated to Italy's demands for recognition of its new-found empire, but finally swung to the emperor's side, recognizing that it was impossible to accommodate the Axis powers. Its fear of mass revolt in the British colonies also pushed the British government to a more militant anti-Fascist stance. With the help of the British, but not forgetting the commendable heroism of the Ethiopian patriots, Haile Selassie was finally restored to his throne in 1941.[20]

OTHER ASPECTS OF THE AFRICAN DIASPORA

Notwithstanding the attempt to promote ancient Ethiopia as a major world civilization, one major hurdle for those promoting a positive idea of Africa was that for many African-Americans its image was singularly disheartening. To many, 'Africa' signified enslavement, poverty, denigration, exploitation, white superiority, the loss of language and the loss of self-respect. It is little wonder that the key basis of the appeal of populist leaders like the Jamaican-born Marcus Garvey was to the desperate need to escape this abasement and self-hatred and to express self-esteem and dignity. The African-American writer, Richard Wright, was a perceptive observer of this early movement of black consciousness. To Wright, the Garveyites showed

> a passionate rejection of America, for they sensed with a directness of which only the simple are capable that they had no chance to live a full human life in America ... The Garveyites had embraced a totally racialist outlook which endowed them with a dignity I had never seen before in Negroes. On the walls of their dingy flats were maps of Africa and India and Japan ... the faces of coloured men and women from all parts of the world ... I gave no credence to the ideology of Garveyism; it was, rather, the emotional dynamics of its adherents that evoked my admiration.[21]

Garveyism has normally been analysed as a failed return movement. Certainly, the small colonies sent to Liberia and elsewhere on the continent were ill-fated. However, it is worth remembering that the name of Garvey's movement was the Universal Negro Improvement Association and its immense popularity was closely related to its promotion of self-pride and self-betterment. This could involve continuing to stay in the Americas, while idealizing the homeland and undertaking a commitment to its restoration, safety and prosperity. At the height of his influence, Garvey proclaimed himself provisional president of Africa, but he never visited the continent and died in obscurity in London after his movement was infiltrated, then discredited, by the

American authorities. Garvey created a court of Ethiopia with dukes, duchesses and knight commanders of the Distinguished Order of Ethiopia. By 1921, the organization claimed a membership of four million people, the largest following of African-Americans ever mustered, before or since. Like the prophet Isaiah, Garvey thundered: 'No one knows when the hour of Africa's redemption cometh. It is in the wind. It is coming. One day, like a storm it will be here.'[22]

Another towering leader of the African diaspora was W. E. B. DuBois, whose writings perfectly expressed two desiderata of a diaspora – that there should be a sense of empathy and solidarity with co-ethnic members worldwide and that there should be a sense of distinctiveness, a common history and the belief in a common fate. What was it, DuBois asked, that tied him to Africa so strongly?

> On this vast continent were born and lived a large proportion of my direct ancestors going back a thousand years or more. But one thing is sure and that is the fact that since the fifteenth century these ancestors of mine and their other descendants have had a common history, have suffered a common disaster and have one long memory ... But the physical bond is the least [tie] and [merely] the badge; the real essence of this kinship is its social heritage of slavery, the discrimination and insult; and this heritage binds together not simply the children of Africa but extends through yellow Asia and into the South Seas. It is this Unity that draws me to Africa.[23]

DuBois became a central figure in the early Pan-African movement, a political commitment that also excited visionaries from the black Caribbean. The movement articulated a sense of a common fate, particularly in the New World, and a common purpose to build a powerful, united and wealthy Africa. One of the Caribbean leaders was the formidable Trinidadian Trotskyite C. L. R. James who, though more of an internationalist than an African nationalist, was nonetheless influential in African anti-colonial circles. He was joined by his influential fellow-Trinidadian, the communist George Padmore, who finally made his break with the Comintern (the communist international movement) when it started issuing denunciatory statements about Liberia.[24] These and other Caribbean leaders were partly responsible for convening the watershed Manchester Conference of 1945, when the basic lines of struggle for African self-determination were articulated and agreed. Other manifestations of black solidarity on the part of New World Africans took a more cultural than political appearance. In the francophone Caribbean, Aimé Césaire made his spiritual journey in *Return to my native land* (1956). He was also an important influence on the Négritude movement and, more generally, had a continuing dialogue with Africans and the peoples of African descent in literary and political journals such as *Présence Africaine*.

Reference to the literary talents of a Caribbean writer and politician leads me to the final notable feature of the African diaspora – namely its extraordinary cultural achievements. This is true of dance, literature, architecture, sculpture and fine art. Perhaps the most notable contribution, however, has been in the development of a musical tradition centred in the USA, but now with an appreciative following in most countries. The most inclusive and popular general designation of this musical tradition is 'jazz', but within and alongside that catch-all word are spirituals, the blues (derived from the West African *griot* tradition), ragtime, gospel music and swing. Particular styles also developed – New Orleans, Chicago, bop, bebop, modern jazz, free jazz, and so on. And the music attained a mass following through its commercial derivatives like rhythm and blues, rock,[25] fusion music, pop and Motown (an abbreviation of Motortown, so named by African-Americans working in the Detroit car factories). Nor were other diasporic Africans musically out in the cold. To mention only the obvious, the diaspora in Brazil gave us samba, that in Trinidad the calypso and from Jamaica came ska and reggae – the last dominated by the Rastafarian Bob Marley and full of explicit diasporic themes.[26]

THE CREATION OF THE ARMENIAN DIASPORA

Armenians are a people to whom the appellation 'diaspora' has often been applied both by themselves and by outsiders. They qualify on the criteria set out in Chapter 1 in a number of important ways. The Armenians, for example, share a common myth of origin, centred on the figure of Haik – the derivative word 'Hay' is a name that Armenians apply to themselves.[27] While earlier research suggested that the 'original' peoples of Armenia migrated from central Europe, newer theories suggest conscious ethnogenesis arose in Asia Minor itself. Armenian writers claim that the places and peoples known as Armani, Hayasa, Biainili and Urartu all alluded to Armenia and Armenians. The heroic tradition, moreover, boasts that Urartu ('the land of Ararat') survived its rival nation Assyria by some 300 years.

Rather as Ethiopia was claimed as the source of 'all true culture and civilization' by the nineteenth-century African-American pamphleteer already cited, many Armenian writers claim a primacy for Armenia's contribution to world history. A slightly less modest claim is made by the British scholar of the Caucasian region who, while conceding that the Mesopotamian civilizations and Egypt were 'the main sources of civilized life in the modern sense', nonetheless maintains that 'Armenia too has a claim to rank as one of the cradles of human culture'.[28] Armenian myth invokes biblical authority to sustain this claim. According to the Book of Genesis (8: 4), after 150 days of rain, on the seventeenth day of the seventh month Noah's ark 'grounded on a mountain in Ararat'. Mount Ararat is in the centre of historic Armenia. As the beasts, birds and humans (namely Noah's family) are believed to have issued forth from this place, Armenia can be considered to be at the epicentre of the rebirth, if not the birth, of the earth.

Centre it may have been, but the Armenians subsequently had some difficulty resisting being walked over by intruders from the periphery. One powerful colonizing group were the Medes, who first used the name 'Armini' as a self-description, a name the Greeks later modified to Armenia. Cultural survival in the face of the Hellenist and Persian influences was also difficult, though Artashes I managed to encourage his subjects to retain the Araratian dialect. A brief period of expansion in the period 93–66 BC – when Armenia stretched from the Mediterranean to the Caspian Sea – was halted by the Romans in the latter year. Christianity became ideologically dominant and was adopted as a state religion in AD 301. Next, the Byzantine Emperor Maurice (who is popularly supposed to have been a simple Armenian peasant who made good) exerted his ascendancy by setting an ominous precedent. In AD 578 he transported 10,000 Armenians to Cyprus, 12,000 to Macedonia and 8000 to Pergama – these deportations being the origins of the Armenian diaspora. Maurice was no great lover of his fellow Armenians. As he wrote to the Persian king:

> The Armenians are a knavish and indolent nation. They are situated between us, and are a source of trouble. I am going to gather mine and send them to Thrace; you send yours to the east. If they die there, it will be so many enemies that will die; if, on the contrary, they kill, it will be so many enemies that they kill. As for us, we shall live in peace. But if they remain in their own country there will never be any quiet for us.[29]

Armenia was later subordinated by the force of Islamic arms and turned into 'the Emirate of Armenia'. This was followed by subordination to the Seljuk Turks and the migration west to Cicilia by many Armenians. Tartar, Mongol and Turkoman domination followed. The last significant invaders were the Russians, sweeping down in 1828 and forcing the division of Armenia into Turkish, Persian and Russian Armenia.[30]

Through all these vicissitudes Armenians maintained their distinctive language and two particular brands of Christianity – the Catholic Armenian Church and the Armenian Orthodox Church. The modern disaster and dispersion began in the late nineteenth century when a pan-Armenian nationalist and revolutionary movement trying to reunite the three parts of Armenia was met by the Ottoman Sultan Hamid ('The Red Sultan') with massive violence. Close to 300,000 Armenians were killed in Turkish Armenia between 1894 and 1896. This was, however, merely the prelude to an even greater assault by the Turks during the First World War.

The most traumatic event in Armenian history commenced in 1915 when the Turks initiated the killing of Armenians or their deportation to Syria and

Palestine. On the night of 23 April 1915, political, religious, educational and intellectual leaders were rounded up and murdered. The same fate awaited Armenians who had been serving in the Ottoman army.[31] It is now widely accepted (though still fiercely disputed by Turkish sources) that 'close to one million' people – about half the Armenian population – were either killed or died of starvation during the 1915–16 period.[32] If we add to this figure those who perished in the period up to 1922, 'the number of Armenian dead may safely be put at around 1,500,000'.[33] Much of the documentation recording the shocking events of 1915 was compiled by a young Oxford historian, Arnold Toynbee – subsequently to become one of the greatest scholars of world history. His services were secured by James Viscount Bryce, chairman of the Anglo-Armenian Association, who was determined to provide irrefutable evidence of the Ottomans' wrongdoing. Toynbee's collection of documents was given the imprimatur of the British government and was published in French the next year.[34]

Toynbee's conclusions were both explicit and graphic. He made no bones about accusing the Turks of the perpetration of mass genocide and large-scale atrocities. 'The river Euphrates changed its course for about 100 yards to a barrage of dead bodies', one witness claimed. Another, a German employee of the Baghdad Railway, confirmed that this was not a momentary phenomenon:

> For the last month, corpses have been observed floating down the Euphrates, in twos tied back-to-back, or tied together by the arms in groups of three to eight. A Turkish officer who was posted to Djerablous, was asked why he did not have the corpses buried. He replied that no one had given him any orders to do so, and, in any case, it was impossible to establish whether the corpses were those of Muslims or Christians since their penises had been cut off. (The Muslims would have been buried but not the Christians.) The corpses stranded on the bank are devoured by dogs. Other bodies which had been cast up on the sand banks were the prey of vultures ... About 10,000 have arrived in Der-el-Zor, on the Euphrates, and so far there is no news of the others. It is said that those who have been sent towards Mosul are to be sent to colonize land 25 kilometres from the railway; that means they are to be driven into the desert, where their extermination can be carried out without witnesses.[35]

The Turkish government's response to the mountain of testimony describing its soldiers' genocidal actions was to suggest that the government was merely putting down a revolt and to make the even more implausible charge of Armenian massacres directed against the Turks.[36] Nationalist Turkish politicians and state-sponsored historians still vigorously refute that the genocide ever took place. Internationally, they are joined in this absurd denial only by Pakistan, presumably because of some misplaced sense of Islamic solidarity.

Naturally, the Armenians who survived the massacres and forcible deportations consider themselves to have been victims of a uniquely appalling crime. So it was. However, with the benefit of hindsight, we can also see that 1915–16 provided a rehearsal for the Nazi holocaust with which it has indeed been systematically compared.[37] The events of 1915–16 also bear some comparison with later examples of mass displacements of peoples in the face of intolerant nationalisms and ethnic particularisms. Though the genocidal intentions are normally absent, there is a clear moral, if not causal, connection between the Armenian deportations and events like the mass displacements of the Palestinians by the Israelis in 1948, the population swaps between India and Pakistan in 1947, the tit-for-tat expulsions between Nigerians and Ghanaians, and the 'ethnic cleansing' of inconvenient groups in the micro-states that emerged following the disintegration of Yugoslavia and parts of the former Soviet Union.

AFTER THE MASSACRES: ARMENIANS AT HOME AND ABROAD

What happened to Armenia itself after the 1915–16 massacres? To explain this outcome I briefly need to set the scene. The Turkish government had been allied to Germany in the First World War, but had made a poor showing against the Russians in the first six months of 1916 when the tsarist armies had overrun Turkish Armenia. Normally, this would have been a cause for Armenian celebration, but the Armenian volunteer units had been disbanded as a nationalist threat to the Russian Empire, and the Armenians scattered in the victorious tsarist army found little but corpses and skeletons to greet them.[38] In a secret Anglo-Russian deal, the tsar had secured British agreement to annex Turkish Armenia after the war. But all such calculations were rendered nugatory by the extraordinary events in Russia.

The Menshevik revolution in the spring of 1917 had allowed Armenians to seize a measure of self-determination and a precarious liberal-democratic state was born. However, the increasing demoralization of the Russian soldiers and the lure of the revolution led to mass desertions, while the Treaty of Brest-Litovsk, signed by Trotsky, left the Caucasian peoples to the mercies of the Germans and Turks. Bloody battles between the ultimately successful Turkish army and the desperately defending Armenians ensued, with considerable atrocities on both sides. Amid starvation, famine and deprivation, the Armenians hung on for 'grim death', but by the end of 1920 all that was left of their 'independent state' was Soviet Armenia, one-tenth of the imagined 'Great Armenia'.

The Armenians who survived the atrocities joined earlier communities in the Middle East, particularly in Lebanon, Syria, Palestine and Iran. Significant numbers were scattered further afield – to Ethiopia, the Far East, Latin America (particularly Argentina), Greece, Italy and England. But very large and most well-established Armenian diasporic communities emerged in France and the USA. There is a confusing plethora of population statistics to choose from, but various counts of the distribution of the Armenians worldwide are shown in Table 3.1.

The discrepancies between the columns are partly accounted for by population increases, but also by the difference in sources, with a tendency for some sources to count every last Armenian, however far they may have strayed from their grandparents' more indelible identity – forged as it was in the fire of the genocide. Also creating anomalies are the movements of population from the Middle East and from the former Soviet Union after the fall of official communism in 1989. Whatever the exact numbers may be, the proportions are likely to be roughly accurate. As can readily be observed, considerable numbers

Table 3.1 **Armenians worldwide**

Country	1966	1976	1985	Latest (date of data)
Armenia (Soviet Socialist Republic until 1991)	2,000,000	2,600,000	3,000,000	2,971,650 (2007)
Azerbaijan (SSR until 1991)	560,000	n.a	560,000	580,000–690,000 displaced from Nagorno-Karabakh (2006)
Georgia (SSR until 1991)	550,000	n.a	550,000	264,822 (2007)
Russia (SFSR until 1991)	330,000	n.a	360,000	1,109,000
Others	60,000	n.a	n.a	n.a
USSR minus Armenia SSR	n.a	1,400,000	1,610,000	–
TOTAL USSR	3,500,000	4,000,000	4,610,000	–
USA and Canada	450,000	500,000	800,000	945,615
Turkey	250,000	n.a	70,000	115,000
Iran	200,000	n.a	200,000	202,000
France	200,000	n.a	300,000	273,000
Lebanon	180,000	n.a	200,000	260,000
Syria	150,000	n.a	100,000	200,000 (contested figure)
Argentina	n.a	n.a	100,000	132,000
Others	570,000	n.a	233,000	n.a
Total (rest of the world)	2,000,000	n.a	2,003,000	n.a
TOTAL worldwide	5,500,000	n.a	6,613,000	7,580,000

Source: For 1966 figures, Lang and Walker, *The Armenians*, p.12; for 1976 figures, Schahgaldian cited Suny, *Looking toward Ararat*, note 3 to Chapter 13; for 1985 figures, Armen *et al.*, *Historical atlas of Armenia*, p. 33; for latest figures, CIA, *The world factbook* (Washington: Central Intelligence Agency, 2007); http://www.joshuaproject.net/peopctry.php?rop3=100516&rog3=RS.

of Armenians live in the former USSR outside former Soviet Armenia, most of them in the adjacent Caucasian states. This was both because of historical settlement patterns and the relative freedom to migrate internally in the period of the USSR's existence. Armenians continue to live in Turkey and the Middle East, while significant and increasing diasporic communities have settled in France and the USA. The US Armenians are particularly successful in economic terms and are said to have a per capita standard of living higher than any other Armenian diasporic community and one that compares favourably with other well-placed ethnic groups in the USA.

I only have space to comment on the two biggest and most influential Armenian diasporic communities outside the former USSR – those in the USA and France. There are perhaps three striking features of the Armenian diaspora in the USA – the relative public silence of the community until the mid-1970s; the more public role played since that time; and the growth of a powerful set of internal social and cultural organizations. Some of the initial silence was clearly a reflection of psycho-social trauma, known in more general terms as 'survivor syndrome'. The survivors often felt guilty and undeserving of their chance good luck. They were burdened with unresolved anger and found it difficult to enjoy their freedom and material success – it was as if their enjoyment would court another disaster and more misfortune, or would have been an insult to the dead.[39] Acute psychological states – reactive depression, anhedonia, hyperaesthesia and nightmares – have been widely reported by survivors. Even if we ignore these more extreme reactions, it is noticeable that the first and much of the second generation of Armenian-Americans adopted a privatized, inward-looking world of apparent conformity to the assimilationist ethic, *together with* a strong sense of difference, which was rarely displayed in the public domain.

Some of these confused feelings of acceptance and wariness emerge in an apparently autobiographical account provided by the Californian-born writer of Armenian descent, William Saroyan. He recalls his school days in Fresno and a dialogue with his teacher, Miss Chamberlain. She had reprimanded him for speaking Armenian in class and making the other pupils laugh. Was he making fun of her?

'No, we just like to talk Armenian once in a while, that's all.'
'But why? This is America, now.'
'The Americans don't like us, so we don't like them.'
'So that's it. Which Americans don't like you?'
'All of them.'
'Me?'
'Yes, you' … ['Americans always stick together']
'Well maybe we do, but then this *is* America, after all.'
'But we're here, too, now, and if you can't stand the only way we can be Americans, too, we'll go right on being Armenians'.[40]

The shift to a more public airing of the community's distinctive history can also be marked by a literary event – namely the publication of Michael J. Arlen junior's well-known book *Passage to Ararat* (1976). Michael Arlen senior, born Dickran Kouyoumdjian, was the son of a Bulgarian Armenian merchant who changed his name to gain acceptance in the English literary set. A friend of D. H. Lawrence and author of a highly-successful novel called *The green hat*, he was seen as the epitome of a successful assimilationist who had turned his back on the past and had found recognition and acceptance in his new environment.[41] The publication of Arlen junior's book is often seen as a refutation of his father's attempt at assimilation and, with it, the public passivity but private torment of the Armenian community. It helped to galvanize the US Armenian community into making the difficult journey back to the past and to assume its political identity. Some of this new-found energy went into extremism and wild acts of terrorism triggered by the assassination of a Turkish diplomat in Santa Barbara in 1973 by a 77-year-old survivor of the 1915–16 massacres. Attacks on other diplomats, on the Turkish airline and on Turkish property followed. Though all rationalizations for terrorism are morally suspect, it is easy to see that the 60-year silence about the genocide and the obstinate denials of the Turkish government were at some point going to provoke open rage rather than resignation and repressed anger.

A more considered response by the emerging generation was to build on the very considerable community organizations that had survived into exile or been newly created. Of these the Armenian Apostolic Church and the Dashnak party (the 'federal', anti-Soviet revolutionary party that was in power in the brief period of independence in 1918–20) are pre-eminent. The Dashnaks threw a spanner in the works when they provoked a split in the Church in 1933, arguing that the newly-elected Catholicos was a communist puppet. Most of these rifts were healed by the need for a united, non-sectarian committee to organize the commemorative events of 1975 and 1985 – the sixtieth and seventieth anniversaries of the genocide. To these inherited institutions have been added organizations that grew up in the diaspora itself, such as the Armenian General Benevolent Union, the Armenian Assembly of America, the Armenian Historical Research Association, the Zoryan Institute, the Hairenik and Baikar Associations of Boston, the Armenian Relief Society, and a host of others too numerous to mention. Much of this activity, particularly in educational and charity work, is promoted by wealthy Armenian patrons, including substantial foundations like the Calouste Gulbenkian Foundation. There are five Armenian newspapers in the USA, eleven day schools and many clubs and recreational activities promoted by the Armenian churches.

Perhaps the most important recent change in this organizational activity, however, has been the growth of a powerful Armenian political lobby in Washington. Armenian organizers in the USA have sponsored a bill in Congress to declare 24 April (the beginning of the massacres) a national day of remembrance of 'man's inhumanity to man'. They have learnt from, and made common cause with, the Jewish–American lobby, sponsoring joint exhibitions, conferences and publications. They have, as I shall explain more fully below, taken full advantage of the changing geopolitics at the end of the Cold War and found in Senator Robert Dole (at that time the Republican leader in Congress and a credible presidential candidate) a powerful friend. (It is said that he was treated by an Armenian–American surgeon after suffering grievous war wounds.)

What of the Armenian diaspora in France? Boyajian and Grigorian suggest that one difference between the Jewish and Armenian diasporas is that 'with rare exceptions the entire Armenian Community of the world is composed of survivors or their progeny. All were touched by the massacres'.[42] This observation is less true of the Armenians in France, who have a long history of settlement. (For example, the last king of Armenia is buried in St Denis.) The pre-1915 migration history, together with the strong assimilating tendencies of the French revolutionary tradition, has led to a more complex identity formation among Armenians in France. A subtle reading of this is provided by Martine Hovanessian who contrasts the Jacobin assimilationist tendency in France with the opposing philosophical principle, the 'right to be different'. This tension between these two trajectories is acutely sensed in the third generation because of the economic success of their parents and grandparents, because of the secularization of the community – few are regular churchgoers – and because 80 per cent of the current generation no longer speak Armenian.[43]

The desire to reaffirm an Armenian identity, or more strictly to affirm a double Franco–Armenian identity, is primarily related to two exogenous circumstances. First, the French state and its social institutions began to yield a little under the impact of a substantial number of North Africans and other recent immigrants who simply refused to bow to the Jacobin tradition. This allowed earlier 'recalcitrant' groups like the Jews to gain some breathing space and also permitted at least a cultural and intellectual affirmation of Armenian identity. Second, in the world 'out there' fundamental crises and changes were facing Armenians. The civil war in Lebanon in the 1970s generated a number of refugees who chose to come to France (France had governed the country from 1920 to 1956 and its cultural influence, particularly among the Lebanese Christians, was always strong). In 1975 and 1985 worldwide commemorations of the genocide were held. Three years later, in 1988, a massive earthquake shook Soviet Armenia, and the French Armenians were mobilized to send aid and money. Shortly afterwards, communism in the Soviet Union collapsed and by 1990 an independent state had been declared.

Young Franco–Armenians did not react by immediately identifying with the new state, affirming a 'Greater Armenia', or promoting a return movement. Rather, an interesting new kind of ethnicity emerged – a kind of cultural recovery[44] based on narrative, a memory of collective suffering in earlier generations and on a sense of empathy with Armenians outside France. The essence of this ethnicity was that it was *deterritorialized*, still affirming of France, its citizenship, culture and language, but also proclaiming a new 'virtual' community that stretched beyond the French frontiers.

SOVIET ARMENIA AND AFTER

As noted earlier, all that had been left of historic Armenia by the end of 1920 was a small impoverished Soviet Socialist Republic (strictly the SSR constitution was not adopted until 1922). It was a slim basis on which to recreate a homeland, but for once the geopolitics of the area worked in the Armenians' favour. Between the wars the Soviet Union saw Transcaucasia as a strategic area protecting its southern flank, a role that if anything was increased after the Second World War, when Turkey became a key forward point for NATO and the Cold War. While acknowledging that Beria 'decimated the leading Party cadres in Armenia', as he did elsewhere, Lang was surprisingly enthusiastic about the Soviet Union's trusteeship of Armenia:

> The social and economic life of Soviet Armenia made rapid strides ... Following World War II new factories and research laboratories have been opened up almost every month ... No one visiting Erevan, Leninakan and other cities of Soviet Armenia can fail to be struck by the general air of bustle, and the active pace of industrial and domestic construction work continually in progress.[45]

Are these the observations of a naive observer? Are there some data that suggest a reasonable degree of commitment to the homeland even during the period of the communist leadership? I can adduce the following. Some 300,000 Armenians served in the Red Army in the Second World War, many with considerable distinction. After the war Armenians came 'home' in considerable numbers from Turkey, Persia and the Lebanon, some 100,000 from the Middle East alone. Even during the Cold War, groups of diasporic Armenians made up the largest number of tourists. However, perhaps the clearest indication of wellbeing is in the dramatically increasing population of Soviet Armenia. Some of this is accounted for by increasing longevity (officially measured at 73 years in 1985) and better health care, but most of the increase has to be attributed to voluntary return migration. If the USSR population censuses are to be believed, the population of Soviet Armenia increased by two-and-a-half times from 1,320,000 inhabitants in 1940 to 3,317,000 people in 1985.[46]

Despite this evidence of the rebuilding of Soviet Armenia, the diasporic Armenian communities remained strongly divided – impelled in one direction by a deep suspicion of an old enemy, Russia, and (particularly in France and the United States) by the anti-communist policies of their countries of settlement. A contrary pull evoked pride in the achievements of their homeland within the Soviet Empire, imperfect and incomplete as that undoubtedly was.

The ideological divides wrought by the Cold War were set aside, first in response to the human tragedy of the earthquake in Armenia in 1988, when millions of dollars of aid poured into the country from the diaspora, and second when, with the end of the Cold War, the prospect dawned for a more open and public identification between the Republic of Armenia (proclaimed in 1990) and the Armenian diaspora. Some returned to serve in the new government; many invested in the future of the new independent state.

There is one large blot on this landscape. Unlike the benign form of deterritorialized identification shown by young French Armenians, some groups in the diaspora with long memories and bitter hearts decided that now was the time to recommence the long march towards Greater Armenia. First in their sights was Nagorno-Karabakh, the Armenian-dominated enclave within Azerbaijan. The pressure to reintegrate the enclave started with a demonstration in the Spring of 1988 when 20,000 people walked around the streets of Erevan shouting 'Karabakh, Karabakh!' The Armenian-dominated Soviet of Deputies in Karabakh voted 110 to 17 in favour of being transferred to Armenia. The cry was soon taken up in the diaspora. Telethons and political fund-raising drives were organized, and individual donations poured in. In one Californian telethon in February 1994, the Dashnaks raised $1.5 million.[47] The donations financed food and clothing, but also arms and ammunition. The political lobby also cranked into action, successfully pressing the US government to impose sanctions on Azerbaijan and generating over US$1 billion in aid for Armenia since 1991. In his well-informed account of the conflict, Tölölyan shows how different elites within the diaspora and different national sections of the Armenian diaspora took different views. For some the Azerbaijani government's intemperate statements and policies evoked the memory of 1915–16. A 'never again' movement in the diaspora fuelled a movement for violent resistance. The result was massive internal population displacement. Others took a more measured view. By 2007 the Armenian Assembly (the key diasporic association) and the key makers of Armenian foreign policy started working together to achieve a multilateral mediation of the Nagorno-Karabakh issue.[48]

CONCLUSION

We have seen that both Africans and Armenians conform well to the special attributes of a victim diaspora and the more general features of all diasporas. There was a greater element of voluntary migration from Africa than is often adduced, and the process was rather lengthy and involved both the Indian and Atlantic Oceans. Armenian population history was also complicated and tortuous. But both experienced a decisive 'break event' in their histories – Atlantic slavery in the first case and the 1915–16 massacres in the second. Both diasporas were widely dispersed and both clung on to a collective memory and myth about the homeland, its location and its achievements. For Africans, 'homeland' centred mainly on Ethiopia, an entity with both real and fuzzy frontiers constructed as much from legend as from history. For Armenians, although the biblical reference to Noah's ark landing on Ararat carries some significance, a great effort has been made to anchor a 'great tradition' in archaeological and historical studies. Celebratory studies have lovingly recreated the art, artefacts, buildings, churches, language, script, religious traditions and literature of a great historical nation.[49] One more cynical account of Armenian history cites the adage that 'a nation is a group of persons united by a common error about their ancestry and a common dislike of their neighbours'.[50] A lucid summary of why, amid its internal diversity, it is nonetheless valid to talk of a single Armenian diasporic identity has been provided by Tölölyan:

> First, those elements of popular culture that are shared across the diaspora (religion, music, some grasp of the genocide). Second, those transnational forms of discourse that circulate widely between elites and institutions across the (now partially democratized) web. Together these discourses, cultural practices and organizations link and mobilize different proportions of ethnic and diasporic members in different communities.[51]

This stress on the need for elites to mobilize opinion is witnessed in both the African and Armenian diasporas where explicit appeals are made to the wider communities to maintain the safety and prosperity of their homelands and to show solidarity when they are in danger. Notable acts of camaraderie were displayed by Africans when the Italians invaded Ethiopia and by Armenians in response to the events in Soviet Armenia after 1988. A substantial return movement existed in both cases, though, except when there was involuntary migration from the Middle East to Soviet Armenia, the numbers involved were not great. Most of the remaining criteria also seem to be congruous. A strong ethnic group consciousness, a troubled relationship with host societies (less evident among non-Middle Eastern Armenians), a sense of empathy with other co-ethnic members, and the possibility of an enriching, creative life in the diaspora – all apply in large measure to the two victim diasporas considered here.

FURTHER READING

- A useful book on Palestinians is provided by Helena Lindholm Schultz, *The Palestinian diaspora* (London: Routledge, 2003), while Walid Khalidi has compiled a moving photographic history of Palestinian life before 1948 in *Before their diaspora: a photographic history of the Palestinians, 1876–1948* (Washington, DC: Institute for Palestine Studies, 1984).

- Joseph Harris's pioneering account of *The African presence in Asia: consequences of the East African slave trade* (Evanston, IL: Northwestern University Press, 1971) is still worth consulting. There are many accounts of the Atlantic slave trade, but one of the most readable is Ronald Segal's *The black diaspora* (London: Faber & Faber, 1995).
- A tightly-focused but very instructive article on the role of elites in the construction of an Armenian diasporic identity is Khachig Tölölyan's 'Elites and institutions in the Armenian diaspora's history', *Diaspora: a Journal of Transnational Studies*, 9(1),(2000), 107–36. The journal is a rich source of material on all aspects of diaspora studies.

QUESTIONS TO THINK ABOUT

- 'Guinea', 'Liberia', 'Freetown' and 'Ethiopia'. Examine the real and symbolic aspects of these versions of an African homeland and their significance to those of African descent in the New World.
- How do the experiences and nature of the Armenian diaspora compare with the prototypical case of the Jews?
- How do the experiences and nature of the African diaspora arising from the Atlantic slave trade compare with the prototypical case of the Jews?
- Is there a class of diasporas that can usefully be considered as 'victim diasporas'. Are there other cases not on the list provided in the first paragraph of this chapter that should be there, or vice versa?

Figure 4.1 Mahatma Gandhi cut his political teeth in South Africa where he earned a formidable reputation as a lawyer defending the interests of upwardly mobile Indians, who had come to South Africa as indentured workers. © iStockphoto.com/Robin Cohen

4

LABOUR AND IMPERIAL DIASPORAS

Indentured Indians and the British

In my opening chapter, I suggested that instead of arising from a traumatic dispersal, a diaspora could be generated by emigration in search of work, to further colonial ambitions or in pursuit of trade. These circumstances can give rise, respectively, to a labour diaspora, an imperial diaspora or a trade diaspora. In this chapter I am concerned with the first and second categories (trade diasporas are discussed in Chapter 5). I have taken as my central example of a labour diaspora the Indian indentured workers deployed in British, Dutch and French tropical plantations from the 1830s to about 1920. There are many other possible candidate groups. For example, the Italians who made the transatlantic crossing, mainly to the USA and Argentina, in the late nineteenth and early twentieth centuries are one prominent example. Labour diasporas, it has been argued, were also constituted by the Turks and North Africans who entered Europe in the period after the Second World War.[1]

Clearly, it would be stretching the term to suggest that all groups who migrate internationally in search of work evolve into a diaspora.[2] Where, essentially, we are talking of individual, family or small group migration for the purposes of settlement, a diasporic consciousness may not develop, particularly if the immigrants concerned both intend to assimilate and are readily accepted. If, however, among overseas workers there is evidence over time of (a) a strong retention of group ties sustained over an extended period (in respect of language, religion, endogamy and cultural norms); (b) a myth of and connection to a homeland; and (c) significant levels of social exclusion in the destination societies, a labour diaspora can be said to exist. Weiner is considerably more restrictive, confining the notion of a labour diaspora to those who 'move across international borders to work in one country while remaining citizens in another'. His bifurcation works particularly clearly in the five countries of the Gulf (Kuwait, Qatar, Bahrain, the United Arab Emirates and Oman) that use vast numbers of foreign workers but resolutely deny them or their children the right of citizenship even through long residence or birth.[3]

A more specialized use of the cognate expression 'proletarian diaspora' can be found in Armstrong's work. He uses the term in contrast to a 'mobilized diaspora' whose members deploy their linguistic, network and occupational advantages to modernize and mobilize – thereby offering to the nation-state valued services and skills. By contrast, a proletarian diaspora, he claims, is characterized by low communication skills and comprises 'a nearly undifferentiated mass of unskilled labor', with little prospect of social mobility. In a sense, Armstrong's proletarian diaspora is a negative category – a group that has proved itself incapable of becoming an entrepreneurial 'mobilized diaspora'.[4]

There are two important qualifications to note here, one of which Armstrong also recognizes. First, within all diasporas, including the most economically successful, there are (sometimes large) proletarian elements. The emigrants from the Jewish Pale of Settlement included a high percentage of unskilled workers, though they were generally successful in using the labour movement or a high level of self-exploitation, to climb out of abject poverty.[5] The Armenians of Istanbul are another example Armstrong noticed. Generally thought of as a wealthy section of the Armenian diaspora, they none the less included a large proportion of people working as porters and in other menial occupations.

The second qualification is that over time occupational mobility can radically alter a group's profile. Two of Armstrong's exemplars of a proletarian diaspora are the Poles and Italians of interwar France who were predominantly concentrated in low-paying jobs and spoke French poorly. Though there still may be some clustering at the bottom of the occupational pile, it would be difficult to sustain this view of these two groups in the postwar period. In a similar way Italians, who were previously largely circulatory migrants, began increasingly to join the mainstream of society in the Americas after 1918.[6]

In my own principal example of a labour diaspora – the indentured Indian workers employed on the tropical plantations of the European colonial possessions – there is a more mixed picture of the changes wrought by time and circumstance. In some countries, Indians showed dramatic gains in terms of their political and social mobility. In others, dispossession and poverty were unrelenting. I anticipate my story, however. The only conceptual point to reiterate here is that diasporas are neither uniform in class terms at the moment of their migration, nor do they remain so over time.

A NEW SYSTEM OF SLAVERY?

The history of intercontinental migration is as much a history of the transport of unfree labourers by others as it is about the propulsion of independent labourers, employees, entrepreneurs and professionals moving by their own volition. I use the expression 'as much' not in a statistical sense (because, as is shown in Table 4.1, in the modern world system legally free migrants have far outnumbered coerced workers) but in terms of the political, economic and social significance of such workers.[7]

Table 4.1 **Indentured Indians and Indian population, 1980 and latest estimates**

Colony/Country	Period	Indentured workers	Indian pop. 1980	Latest Estimates 2007
Mauritius	1834–1912	453,063	623,000	850,558
British Guiana/ Guyana	1838–1917	238,909	424,400	384,547
Natal (South Africa)	1860–1911	152,184	750,000 (South Africa in total)	923,994 (South Africa in total)
Trinidad	1845–1917	143,939	421,000	422,643 (excluding mixed pop.)
Réunion	1829–1924	118,000	125,000	156,800 (excluding mixed pop.)
Fiji	1879–1916	60,969	300,700	343,584
Guadeloupe	1854–85	42,326	23,165	40,000 (source poor)
Kenya & Uganda	1895–1901	39,771	79,000	12,000 (source poor)
Jamaica	1854–85	36,420	50,300	61,500 (source poor)
Dutch Guiana/ Suriname	1873–1916	34,000	124,900	174,190
Martinique	1854–89	25,509	16,450	14,000 (source poor)
Seychelles	1899–1916	6,319	n.a	5,000 (source poor)
St Lucia	1858–95	4,350	3,700	4,095
Grenada	1856–85	3,200	3,900	3,698
St Vincent	1861–80	2,472	5,000	7,088
TOTAL in countries of indenture		1,361,431	2,952,495	3,403,697
TOTAL Indians overseas (2001)				17,000,000

Source: Colin Clarke *et al.*, *South Asians overseas: migration and ethnicity* (Cambridge: Cambridge University Press, 1990, p. 9). For latest estimates see CIA, *The world factbook 2007* (Washington: Central Intelligence Agency); http://en.wikipedia.org/wiki/Overseas_Indian_population; http://www.littleindia.com/news/132/ARTICLE/1346/2006-0-12.html; and Brij V. Lal, Peter Reeves and Rajesh Rai (eds) (2006). *The encyclopedia of the Indian diaspora* (Singapore: Editions Didier Millet in association with National University of Singapore).

Unfree labour was of crucial importance to the evolution of the modern world system. The key European mercantile powers underwrote their trading empires by the production of tropical commodities and the extraction of precious metals. The means they chose was the introduction of mass slavery and coerced labour to the Americas. The 'triangular trade' between Europe, Africa and the Americas was the lusty infant that was to mature as modern world capitalism. Slave labour in the plantations of the Caribbean, the southern states of the USA and Brazil, and *repartimiento* labour in Spanish America, provided the mother's milk to the newborn baby. But after the collapse of slavery, the new milch cow was indentured labour. The switch in the form of labour also involved a switch in the sourcing of the labour supply, from Africa to Asia.

Most indentured labourers were recruited from India, their time of recruitment, distribution and destinations being recorded in Table 4.1. The data also include the numbers remaining in the countries of indenture in 1980 and the latest estimates. I must make at least two interpretative comments on the table. The figures for East Africa in 1980 show a sudden fall from the previous decade because of the expulsion of Asians by President Idi Amin of Uganda in 1972. (In 1970, there were 182,000 Indians in Kenya and 76,000 in Uganda. By 1980 there were only 430 Indians left in Uganda.) Second, where there are dramatic leaps in numbers in the last column compared with the previous column, as in South Africa, this is sometimes accounted for by the subsequent free immigration of merchants and professionals, as well as, of course, by natural increases.

The extensive movement of Indians to faraway tropical plantations provides an instructive reminder of how far the planters were prepared to go in keeping their two desiderata for profitable production – abundant land and cheap labour. The recruiters were ruthless, the journey was horrific and the arrangements made for the legal protection of the workers were inadequate. The indenture was for a fixed period, usually for five or seven years. Many of the indentured Indians were physically moved into the slave barracks of the former African slaves – a poignant reminder of why they were there. The basic conditions are summarized in these terms: The indentured worker 'lived on the plantation which he was forbidden to leave without a pass, worked unlimited hours, was barred from taking any other employment, and in case of misconduct subjected to financial penalty and physical punishment. In return he received a basic pay, free accommodation, food rations, and a fully or partially paid return passage to India'.[8]

In his influential account Tinker, quoting a parliamentary speech by Lord John Russell, characterizes indentured labour as 'a new system of slavery'.[9] Despite the evidence that the planters saw Indian indentured labour as directly substitutable for slave labour, the analogy with slavery can be taken too far. Legally, the indentured workers and their offspring could not be bought or sold. Moreover, for some poverty-stricken Indians, intercontinental migration provided a window of opportunity for social mobility that the rigid caste system inhibited, if not totally prevented. A common in-group joke among contemporary Indo-Trinidadians is that while there were no Brahmins when the ships set out from Calcutta, by the time they arrived in Port of Spain (Trinidad) several gentlemen had assumed a puffed-up, priestly mien. Indenture also offered a free or sponsored return passage at the end of the contract, an option only taken up by 25 per cent of the Indians taken to the Caribbean and up to a third in some other territories.[10] The majority either re-indentured with the promise of free land or saved their pennies to buy land at the end of their indentures.

The dual aspect of oppression and the hint of better things to come is well captured by the poet, David Dabydeen, in this extract from his *Coolie Odyssey*, which graphically conjures up the arrival of the indentured Indians in Georgetown, Guyuna:

> The first boat chugged to the muddy port
> Of King George's Town. Coolies came to rest
> In El Dorado.
> Their faces and best saris black with soot.
> The men smelled of saltwater mixed with rum.
> The odyssey was plank between river and land,
> Mere yards but months of plotting
> In the packed bowel of a white man's boat
> The years of promise, years of expanse.
> At first the gleam of green land and the white folk and the Negroes,
> The earth streaked with colour like a toucan's beak,
> Kiskidees flame across a fortunate sky
> Canefields ripening the sun
> Wait to be gathered in armfuls of gold.[11]

THE SONGS OF *RAMAYANA* AND POLITICAL OUTCOMES

Did the Indian labourers abroad constitute themselves as a diaspora? A veritable political minefield exists in trying to answer this question. Indian nationalists strongly object to any attempt to separate out the three main Indian ethnic/religious groups – Sikh, Hindu and Muslim – for they see this as feeding destructive communalist sentiments in India itself. Sikhs, by contrast, insist on their difference and, as we shall see in Chapter 6, can invoke a distinctive history of Sikh settlement abroad (mainly as soldiers in the colonial employ or as free farmers), an intimate bond with the Punjab and, for some, a commitment to an independent state of Khalistan free from Indian oppression. The Muslim–Hindu distinction was less acute in the early Indian diaspora, as both groups faced similar conditions and Muslims rarely constituted more than 15 per cent of the indentured workers.[12] Parekh argues that there were three features that were particular to *Hindu* indentured workers and that helped them to create a distinctive diasporic consciousness – the reconstitution of family life, their religious conviction in general and, more specifically, the adoption of the *Ramayana* as 'the essential text of the Hindu diaspora'.[13]

The first aspect of the Hindu diaspora, the re-establishment of the family, was made difficult by the official policy of limiting the numbers of women allowed to between one and four for every ten men. Parekh suggests that 'a significant proportion of indentured women consisted of beggars, divorcees from lower castes, girls who had run away from homes, widows with low social status and even prostitutes'.[14] The enormous gender imbalance led to many breakdowns of normal family life. Women were passed around among several men, while there were endless opportunities for sexual jealousy and abuse. Wife beatings, even wife murders, were common. In Trinidad, over a period of just four years (1859–63), 27 Indian women were murdered by their enraged husbands. The relative scarcity of women has led one researcher to claim that under indenture 'probably for the first time in their lives, [women] got an opportunity to exercise a degree of control over their sexual and social lives'. However, she continued, men reasserted their control 'through the reconstruction, albeit in a different setting, of the Indian patriarchal family system'.[15] Given the level of abuse from Indian men, colonial officials and employers alike, it is probably an error to see the scarcity of women as that strong a bargaining counter. Scholarly consensus can be reached, however, in the observation that the Indian family was gradually reconstituted, often in an oppressive patriarchal form, but none the less in such a way as to provide a source of social cohesion and a site for reasserting communal life.

As for Hinduism as the religion of the diaspora, the Brahmins were at the forefront of the movement to reimpose a conventional ritualistic set of beliefs.[16] In some colonial settings, like that of the French Caribbean, they faced an uphill struggle in trying to confront the French demands for assimilation. The Christian missionaries also gained considerable numbers of adherents by combining their theological stick with the carrots of free education and the provision of orphanages. However, these were deviations from the norm. In general, orthodox forms of Hinduism became predominant in the diaspora and were the principal means whereby the Indian labour diaspora was reconnected to the 'Great Tradition' of India. Even where the authority of the Brahmins was challenged, diasporic Hindus did not generate alternative *yogis*, ascetics, *acharyas* and pandits of their own.[17] Instead, they relied on missions from India to supply their religious needs – the Sai Baba and Hare Krishna movements, for example, gained a significant following in Fiji after that country's postcolonial intercommunal conflicts.[18] Whether in orthodox or deviant forms, however, the vital attachment between diaspora and homeland had been re-established. 'Mother India' had reached out to her children abroad.

The third constitutive aspect of the Hindu diaspora was the adoption of the *Ramayana* as the key religious text. This occurred for four reasons. First, the book's central theme was exile, suffering, struggle and eventual return – a clear parallel with the use of the Bible by religious and Zionist Jews. Second, the text is simple and didactic, with a clear distinction between good and evil, a useful simplification in the harsh world of the plantation. Third, the *Ramayana* hammered home what the Brahmins and many conservative men wanted to hear. The eldest son should be dutiful, wives should be demure and obedient and clear roles should be defined for family interactions. Finally, as Hindu traditions go, the *Ramayana* was relatively casteless, but it especially stressed the virtues of the lower castes, namely physical prowess and economic resourcefulness.[19]

While this emphasis on how the Hindu diaspora 'made its world' provides a helpful contrast with the predominant scholarly concern of how the world was made for them, there were none the less some powerful extraneous pressures on the Indian diaspora that collectively, if not equally, afflicted all – Hindu or Muslim, men or women, Brahmin or Sudra. The indentured workers were housed in mass barracks, subjected to a harsh regime and separated from the rest of the society in which they found themselves. At the national level, indentured labourers and their offspring developed a troubled and often hostile relationship with the indigenous people and other migrant groups. The inter-ethnic tensions in countries like Guyana, Fiji, Uganda and South Africa provide cases in point.

Often, the issue of access to land and property started inter-ethnic conflict, though there was a high degree of variation in the outcomes of the Indians' struggle for a 'stake'. In Mauritius, for example, the former African slaves were not very numerous, and at the end of slavery they scattered to small fishing villages and to the edges of towns, leaving the plantations in the hands of the Franco–Mauritian elite. Gradually, Indians were able to extend their land claims and to promote a sizeable educated, urbanized, professional class that was to inherit state power at independence. In Fiji, by contrast, when indenture came to an end in 1916, 83 per cent of the land was owned by indigenous Fijians, 10 per cent was Crown land and only 7 per cent was freehold. Indians were regarded as intruders for whom short-term leases were the most that could be conceded. In the post-independence period they suffered extensive discrimination at the hands of the Fijian political elite. In a consultation conference on the 1990 constitution, following intercommunal tensions, one of the Indo–Fijian delegates made an impassioned plea to be allowed to have a permanent relationship with Fijian soil:

> Land has been raised as an issue very close to the hearts of Fijians. We have been told of the very special, almost spiritual, ties of the Fijian with land. For the Indo-Fijian the tie is no less ... A symbiotic relationship of love and balance develops between the Indo-Fijian household and the land. For four generations of Indo-Fijians, that land has now acquired a very special, sentimental and religious significance ... The Indo-Fijians have a saying about one's roots: 'One's roots are where one's umbilical cord is buried.' Mine is buried in that block of land in Mateniwai. Half of it is now 'reserved', but we continue to use it ... The other half of the land is now on tenancy at will. If ever we were to lose that piece, something within me will have died. I will have lost my roots. That piece of land holds me here, provides me with a sense of identity.[20]

The preoccupation of Indo–Fijians can, with modifications, be observed in the other overseas Indian communities of the Indian Ocean area.[21] Those who found themselves in Natal were desperate to acquire urban property in Durban and Pietermaritzburg, an aspiration the white authorities vigorously resisted. This was the issue on which a young Indian lawyer, Mahatma Gandhi, first cut his political teeth. While the Indian South Africans slowly secured a more agreeable economic situation, they were excluded from white political power and their relationship with indigenous Africans deteriorated, resulting in an outbreak of intercommunal violence in 1949. Indians in South Africa were thus thrust unwillingly into a 'V', not of their own making. Turn right, towards the white regime, and they were rejecting their fellow victims of apartheid; turn left, in the direction of black solidarity, and they became frightened of losing what status, rights and property they had acquired. Perhaps, not surprisingly, many remained uneasily where they were, like rabbits trapped before the headlights of an oncoming car.

Difficult as it was, the Indian community's situation in South Africa was a picnic compared with their plight in President Idi Amin's regime in post-independent Uganda. There they were the main targets of African economic nationalism. An emerging African petty bourgeoisie wanted their shops and houses, while the poor African customer was easily persuaded that Indian traders hoarded goods and charged high prices. The Indian community was forced into four choices: (a) stay where they were and adopt local citizenship, an option taken only by a handful; (b) return to mother India; (c) move on to happier settings like North America (where new groups of South Asian professionals, academics and entrepreneurs were heading); or (d) throw themselves on the mercy of the imperial power, Britain. Those who chose the last option, unpropitious as it seemed at the time, have in fact made remarkable progress, such that by the 1990s their socio-economic profile was well in advance of that of the indigenous British population.[22]

IMPERIAL DIASPORAS

In my next chapter I discuss the role of the trade diasporas, a number of which flourished during the period of mercantile capital. In several instances, commercial contact was followed by the settlement and colonization of the areas the merchants penetrated. Some countries were strong enough to arrest full colonization – China, for example, confined European and Japanese traders to special zones within the 'treaty ports'. But much of Asia and Africa was relatively easily overcome by imperialist adventurers, usually from Europe, and often dragging their home governments behind them. A number of countries remained unsuitable for European settlement, either because of particular difficulties of subduing local rulers or because the climate was unsuitable. (At the independence-day celebrations in Ghana, a toast was proposed to the mosquito, which had discouraged white settlement.) By contrast, the temperate zones were attractive to European settlers and large numbers of migrants volunteered, or were commandeered, to people the colonies. Where settlement for colonial or military purposes by one power occurred, an 'imperial diaspora' can be said to have resulted.

Nearly all the powerful nation–states, especially in Europe, established their own diasporas abroad to further their imperial plans. The Spanish, Portuguese, Dutch, German, French and British colonists fanned out to most parts of the world and established imperial and quasi-imperial diasporas. 'Quasi', because in a number of instances, localization or creolization occurred, with the new settlers marrying into the local community or turning against their homelands. The nationalist movements of Latin America were replete with leaders of Iberian descent who fought for freedom from Spain and Portugal. 'The Liberator' Simón Bolivar, for example, led the independence movements of Venezuela, Colombia, Ecuador, Peru and Bolivia. An imperial diaspora, by contrast, is marked by a continuing connection with the homeland, a deference to and imitation of its social and political institutions and a sense of forming part of a grand imperial design – whereby the group concerned assumes the self-image of a 'chosen race' with a global mission.[23]

THE SETTLEMENT OF THE BRITISH EMPIRE

Emigration from Britain from the seventeenth century onwards was one of the highest in volume and one of the longest in duration in the world. Given how extensive and lengthy this process was, it is hardly surprising that emigration took many forms. Some moved as exiles for religious or political reasons. Many, like the Irish famine migrants and those dispossessed in the 'clearances' of the Scottish Highlands, were forced to leave by grinding poverty, rapacious landlords or unsympathetic officials and politicians. But the bulk of British emigrants left because new opportunities – land and work to be blunt – were available in greater measure than in the British Isles. Shepperson put it this way: the great emigration, he suggests, cannot be explained alone by 'urban confusion, rural destitution, political inequality, religious restrictions, social injustices or educational handicaps endured by a section of the populace'. The British people 'were sufficiently advanced to aspire to social and political recognition more commensurate with individual ability, and to demand reasonable opportunity for the fruition of their material and intellectual endeavours'.[24]

However complex and mixed the motives, there was an underlying thread of state involvement. An emigration plan was first hatched in a state paper delivered to James I by Bacon in 1606. He suggested that by emigration England would gain 'a double commodity, in the avoidance of people here, and in making use of them there'.[25] The poor rates and overpopulation would be relieved and idlers, vagrants and criminals would be put to good use abroad. Once established, the principle was extended to other parts of the British Isles. Scottish crofters, troublesome Irish peasants, dissident soldiers (like the Levellers) were all shipped out in pursuance of the idea that they were of greater use overseas than they were at home. Not even the reverses of British power in the United States were attributed to a design fault in its pro-emigration policies. Against the *laissez-faire* doctrine of the times, the state was ready to be involved in emigration matters.

In the century between Waterloo (1815) and Sarajevo (1914), 17 million people emigrated from Britain, 80 per cent to North America – one can gauge the extent of this migration by recalling that the UK population in 1821 was 21 million. The bulk of British migrants went to the USA and to what are sometimes described as 'the colonies of settlement'. These were New Zealand, Canada, Australia, Rhodesia and South Africa. What linked these countries together was that most of them became 'dominions' in a formal, legal sense between the two world wars, but the description can also be used more analytically, for it aptly captures the superordination the settlers and their metropolitan backers sought to assert over the indigenous populations.

The push for an imperial diaspora probably reached its intellectual apogee in the work of the Cambridge professor of history, Sir John Seeley, who identified emigration as the key means of effecting 'the peculiarly English movement of unparalleled expansion'.[26] He was nevertheless critical of the inefficient way in which the movement was organized. The second part of his much-quoted aphorism is rather less well known than the first. After Britain 'conquered half the world in a fit of absence of mind, it peopled it in a mood of lazy indifference', Seeley remarked. Other backers of the pro-emigration cause also urged vigorous action by the authorities. As early as 1832, the poet laureate Robert Southey argued that the Irish needed to be given emigration opportunities further afield than the mainland:

> It is vain to hope for any permanent and extensive advantage from any system of emigration which does not primarily apply to Ireland, whose population, unless some other outlet be opened to them, must fill up every vacuum created in England or Scotland, and reduce the labouring classes to a uniform state of degradation and misery.[27]

While such musings were common to a number of commentators, the Scotsman Thomas Carlyle, provided a more explicit blueprint for state-aided emigration in 1843:

> Why should there not be an Emigration Service? and Secretary with adjuncts, with funds, forces, idle Navy-ships, and ever-increasing apparatus: in fine an effective system of Emigration: so that ... every honest willing workman who found England too straight ... might find a bridge built to carry him into new Western Lands, there to

organize with more elbow room some labour for himself? There to be a real blessing, raising new corn for us, purchasing new webs and hatchets from us; instead of staying here to be a Physical-Force Chartist unblessed and no blessing! ... A free bridge for Emigrants ... every willing worker that proved superfluous, finding a bridge ready for him. This verily will have to be done; the Time is big with this.[28]

The time became even bigger with this in 1845 when the potato crop in Ireland failed, a tragic misfortune that could not easily be alleviated by importing staples from England – the wheat harvest collapsed in that year. With his repeal of the Corn Laws in 1846, the prime minister Robert Peel had taken the decisive step to open Britain to foreign food imports and in so doing started the policy of cheap imported food that has been at the heart of British politics ever since. John Marriott, MP for York and at one time a lecturer and tutor in modern history and political science, saw the negative consequences of this bold move. With the collapse of the rural economy came overpopulation, unemployment and widespread poverty and with it a massive propensity to emigration, voluntary or state-aided. But the die had been cast and more and more emigrants were needed to sustain the system:

> In the short span of 150 years England has become a land of mines, forges and factories ... We have become an urban and suburban people, depending for food and raw materials on imported commodities which the overseas Empire is supplying in increasing proportions, and which it could produce in much large quantity but for the lack of labour and capital.[29]

The extent of emigration was so great that even supporters of the idea of an imperial diaspora became alarmed. One writer in *Sharpes London Magazine* (1852) considered that emigration

> is a medicine that may do a great deal of good, and which, at the same time must be administered with as much caution as any drug which poisons by gradually debilitating. Our people are our life's blood, and yet we appear to be dangerously easy on the subject of losing them ... What is the almost universal cry of the sons and daughters of England? Emigration. What is the advice that England gives to her distressed children? Emigrate ... That one word rings on the platforms of public assemblies, echoes through the walls of literary institutions, stares one in the face in colossal placards, thrusts itself into one's hand in the form of tailors' outfitting advertisements. It is the consolation of the idle, the refuge of the unhappy and the industrious, the watchword alike of the agitator and the philanthropist ... It is our scapegoat for everything that vice, folly, or public mismanagement had brought upon us – an

Alsatian for rogues of our own creation – a Slough of Despond, into which England many cast a little too much.[30]

As this author indicated, the idea and promise of migration had filtered down to all sections of the British population. In terms of their order of magnitude, self-sponsored migration was the most important, followed by government-supported, charity-supported, destination country-supported and trade union-supported movements.[31] Recent research has laid more emphasis on how, even in the context of government-supported schemes, financial and moral support from friends, family and the wider working-class community were necessary to advance practical plans for emigration. Without this help, it would be impossible to explain how 'some of the poorest elements in the British Isles were able to reach the most distant of the nineteenth-century emigrant destinations'.[32]

Emigration studies 'from below' are certainly likely to have a greater explanatory power for migration flows than the preoccupation with official and charity schemes, but the latter none the less illustrate official and humanitarian concerns. For example, the settlement of Australia by the British was regarded as an absolute priority by strategic thinkers because of the virtual certainty that Asia would be seeking what the Germans were later to call *lebensraum*. The race between Britain and Asia was on. Lord Northcliffe on his visit to Australia apocalyptically proclaimed:

> The key to your White Australia ideal is population. You must increase your slender garrison by the multiplication of your people. Only numbers will save you. The world will not tolerate an empty Australia. This continent must carry its full quota of people ... You have no option. Tens of millions will come to you whether you like it or not.[33]

As to voluntary bodies, there were at least two dozen private agencies to assist settlement of adults (including, for example, the Catholic Emigration Committee, the Salvation Army, the Society for the Overseas Settlement of British Women, the British Dominions Emigration Society) and 14 societies targeting juvenile emigration (including the Child Emigration Society, Dr Barnardo's Homes, the Church Army and the Church of England's Waifs and Strays Society). Special schemes, often endorsed and subsidized by the British and dominion governments, proliferated. One that caught my eye because of George Orwell's subsequent satirical use of the phrase was the Big-Brother Scheme to Australia. Started in 1924, the idea was that well-established Australian citizens would agree to act as a Big Brother to a Little Brother from the homeland. Boys between the ages of 14 and 19 were eligible for this scheme, but they had to have a school certificate (up to Standard 6), a health certificate and a testimonial of good character. Despite its inventiveness, by 1927 only 600 Little Brothers had made the trip.[34]

Empire settlement also provided an outlet for 'distressed gentlewomen', often left penniless by the common pattern of inheritance to the eldest son. Over the period 1899–1911, 1,258,606 women emigrated from Britain, many of them single and a surprising number in middle-class occupations such as clerks, teachers or professionals.[35] The movement for encouraging emigration by respectable women had powerful supporters. Edward Gibbon Wakefield, in *A view of the art of colonization* (1849) deplored the plight of women of the 'uneasy' or 'anxious' classes whom he thought were the very stuff needed in the colonies. They would favourably affect the dubious manners and morals of the colonists, spread religion and avoid being condemned to a reluctant barren spinsterhood. The women emigrants themselves were rather divided in their reactions to their new opportunities. One successful woman emigrant to Australia, Mrs Charles Clacy, published a best-selling book in 1853 recommending emigration to her English sisters on the grounds that they would find themselves 'treated with twenty times the respect and consideration you might meet with in England'.[36] This view was in marked contrast to one Rosa Payne who wrote from Melbourne in 1869 to warn that

> no one with the tastes, habits, or feelings of a lady should ever come out to Australia, it may do for mediocre governesses who can put up with the roughness, or I should say vulgarity of mind and great want of intellect but I would never advise a lady to try it.[37]

In many ways the policy-makers were naive about the likely outcomes of fostering a successful imperial diaspora. They assumed, for example, that trade flows would always be bidirectional, between motherland and diaspora. Marriott earnestly made the calculation that while 'every inhabitant of Canada buys British goods to the value of £2.18s.11d., each citizen of the United States buys only 9s. worth. Thus every Canadian is worth to us as a customer more than six Americans'. The presumption of loyalty to Britain in times of need was also assumed. Morale-boosting claims that there were 'no fewer than 6000 old Barnardo boys' fighting in the Canadian forces during the First World War lent further legitimacy to the idea that homelands and dominions were one in spirit and in political allegiance.[38]

And lest the press for mass emigration from below be diverted into the wrong direction, pro-diaspora journals warned would-be emigrants against going to the USA, lest Britons should 'cut themselves off from the great and good olive tree'. In 1840, the *Colonial Magazine* put it like this.

> Our advice is to emigrate to one of the British Colonies. There you have the laws, language and customs of your youth; you preserve an identity of interest with the parent state, and, under a wise system of colonial government, must ere long be adopted, you are still a citizen

of the British empire, and a part of that great Christian kingdom to which it is a pride and an honour to belong.[39]

As for the wretched Americans, the same magazine rather implausibly asserted they bitterly regretted casting off the parent country. When the *Great Western* liner anchored in New York, the magazine claimed, the 'intelligent and noble-minded populace fell into great lamentations, crying "England! revered England!! Great England!!! – land of my fathers, how I love thy very name; thy age commands my respect, thy power my admiration; I claim to be thy scion, yet feel myself to be an alien: would that I could return again into thy bosom".'

THE END OF THE DOMINION DIASPORA

Unfortunately for the imperial planners, many in the dominions could see no good reason to return, or even to stay close to Britannia's bosom. Essentially, the dominion diaspora was to fall victim to the very success of the colonial settlements. In some places, like South Africa, the British imperial diaspora was but one of the claimants for political hegemony – alongside the Boers and the indigenous Africans. Elsewhere, as British hegemony was established, powerful and wealthy farmers, professionals and industrialists began to emerge among the new immigrants themselves. They were to challenge the homeland and assert their right to tax, to trade and to legislate as they chose.

The Boston Tea Party, beloved of school history books, and the consequential loss of the American colonies, were the most celebrated and ultimately the most momentous examples of this phenomenon, but the hints of a similar rift were apparent even in more quiescent dominions. For example, during a trade dispute in 1903, six English hatters were held up in Melbourne harbour and denied permission to land. The affair was soon settled, but anti-Pommie sentiments had been aroused and they led the *Sydney Bulletin* to editorialize as follows:

> The right of Australia in fact has been established, definitely to keep out of this continent English-born citizens, if in her own interest she so chooses … What is important is the fact that Australia has proved her power to keep Australia for the Australians, and for such immigrants as Australians choose to welcome and has shown that an Englishman is not necessarily welcome because he is an Englishman. The six hatters have made history.[40]

A number of dominion diasporas established their right to self-government, though in each case (like in the USA) with deleterious effects to the indigenous population. The British settlers in Australia killed many Aborigines and virtually destroyed their way of life; the colonists in New Zealand crippled Maori culture; the Canadians forced the Inuit people into reservations. To each of these three countries the British government accorded formal Dominion status – namely self-government and a franchise to the settlers – while showing only token regard for the native peoples.

In all the dominions, a 'British' identity became hegemonic. English and Welsh law, the English language, the Anglican Church, English sporting traditions,[41] and Westminster-style political institutions either became paramount or were accorded a high status. Settlers fared less well in the remaining colonies to which the British migrated. In Kenya, the Mau Mau put paid to a wild attempt by the tiny settler group to declare 'white independence'; instead, decolonization placed power in the hands of the black elite. In Rhodesia, Ian Smith managed to sustain a Unilateral Declaration of Independence for about a decade, but he too was finally laid low by the force of an armed African struggle.

In South Africa, that most difficult of countries to classify and typologize, the contrary pulls of Boer and British ambitions (demonstrated by the Anglo–Boer War of 1899–1902 and by the counter force of African arms) inhibited the construction of a pure dominion society. Whereas the Boers organized successful shooting parties against the helpless San and Khoi (known in politically incorrect days as the Bushmen and Hottentots), the Zulu *impis* proved rather more formidable opponents to the British army. The fate of settler society in South Africa now hangs in the balance. Whereas the European population's political monopoly is at an end, its social and economic dominance is nevertheless likely to remain important.[42]

The relationship between the British at home and their dominion–diaspora abroad had been cemented by ties of kinship, economic interdependence and preferential trade arrangements, by sport, by visits and tourism, and by the solidarity wrought by the sharing of arms in two world wars and other encounters like the Korean conflict. Until quite recently, many New Zealanders, Canadians, Australians and white South Africans and Rhodesians/Zimbabweans stubbornly clung onto British passports as a means of affirming their British identity and hedging their political bets. Young men and women from the British diaspora abroad still often spend a *rite de passage* year in England. (They concentrate with a remarkable lack of imagination in Earl's Court in London: the nearest area between Heathrow and central London with a large rental market.)

Education, legal training and certification also bonded the dominions (and the Commonwealth more generally) to 'the mother country'. One small example is the Rhodes scholarship programme, which overwhelmingly draws on young men from the white dominions and the United States to its base at Rhodes House in Oxford. The programme was endowed by the famous British imperialist to celebrate the achievements of the imperial diaspora and to secure a cohort of key administrators for the empire. (After protests in the 1980s from former scholars a small number of black and female Commonwealth scholars were accorded recognition.)

The attempt to cling to a unified British home and diasporic identity defined primarily by descent and racial phenotype was, however, to be severely challenged on a number of fronts. First, it proved difficult to be too racially specific – the wider Commonwealth included a brown and black empire as well as the zones of white settlement. Second, with the postwar movement of Commonwealth citizens from India, Pakistan and the Caribbean to Britain, it became increasingly difficult to uphold the idea that a British identity was exclusively a white identity.

Despite various attempts in British nationality and immigration legislation designed to buttress a racially-based British identity, which fused white Britons to their diaspora in the dominions, a third and final factor undercut any neat correspondence between Britishness and whiteness. I allude to seismic shifts in the postwar international political economy, which impacted both on the UK and on the white British diaspora. The UK's historic decision to enter the European Economic Community (now the European Union) swept away any realistic possibility, though not the pretence, that it could maintain an independent world role. Public rhetoric that Commonwealth interests would be safeguarded was recognized, even at the time, as empty and tokenistic.

Events of similar impact were affecting the old white dominions. For the Canadians, already heavily intermeshed with the USA, signing the North American Free Trade Agreement in 1991 was seen as a sad though inevitable result of their geopolitical situation. The minority British diasporic communities in South Africa are gradually being corralled into accepting black majority rule. Thousands, perhaps even tens of thousands, may take up their opportunity to live in the UK, but over the next generation many will lose their 'patrial' rights and will slowly adopt a single, local citizenship. Australia and New Zealand still have close cultural, familial, sporting and linguistic ties to 'the mother country', but the entry of the UK into the European Economic Community represented a brutal familial rupture. Wool, butter and lamb exports were immediately affected, but the abandonment of the Commonwealth as an economic unit also had a profound psychological effect, particularly in Australia. Prime Minister Keating's angry outburst in April 1992 that Britain had deserted Australia in the Second World War by its precipitate withdrawal from the Far East was yet another slash at the old umbilical cord. New Australians from southern Europe and Asia rarely share the British link, republican sentiment is growing and the country increasingly relates more to the Pacific Rim and its hegemonic power, Japan. At the Commonwealth conference in November 1995, the New Zealand government complained bitterly that Britain had kowtowed to the French in supporting their nuclear tests in the South Pacific against the interests of its Commonwealth partners.

As I have argued elsewhere, until these more recent events the British abroad provided a crucial expression of (and gave vital reinforcement to) the evolution of British identity. Like other diasporic communities, exaggerated mannerisms and demonstrations of patriotism often made the British abroad more British than the British at home. The exaggeration of metropolitan manners, particularly in the case of the English, but not forgetting instances like the 'kilt culture' of the overseas Scots, derived directly from the imperial heritage – the heritage of the quasi-aristocratic rule over 'the natives'.[43] Anderson provided a penetrating insight into the origins of this manifestation of overseas 'Britishness':

> The administration of an empire comprising a quarter of the planet required its own special skills. Imperialism automatically sets a premium on a patrician style ... Domestic domination can be realized with a popular and egalitarian appearance, colonial never: there can be no plebeian proconsuls. In an imperial system, the iconography of power is necessarily aristocratic.[44]

Those old enough to have observed the British colonial administration at work would be struck by the force of Anderson's observation. In remote regions of Africa, Asia and the Caribbean, middle-class English administrators affected the manners of lords. Even working-class Britons who fled postwar Britain for the easy lifestyle available in southern Africa and Australia in the 1950s and 1960s soon adopted the overbearing *hauteur* of a racial elite.

The automatic and unthinking affinity between the British diasporic communities and 'home' is now largely gone. It addressed a vital nerve centre in the British identity, one that crucially coupled patricianship abroad to upper-class pretensions and mannerisms at home. The Britain to which the British diaspora looked was dominated by English aspirations and signified by the monarchy, the gentlemen's clubs, the benign feudalism of P. G. Wodehouse's novels, the *Spectator* and the *Daily Telegraph* (for the 'intellectuals'), *Punch* and the *Daily Mail* (for the not-so-cerebral), cricket at Lords, Henley, Wimbledon, preparatory and boarding schools, and the many other small nuances of dress, vocabulary, accent, manner and recreation that bipolarized the class structure. By signalling their putative association with the English upper part of that class structure at home, the British abroad were thereby also engaging in the much-venerated, and sometimes deadly serious, pastime of upward social climbing. Now social and political elites are firmly anchored in the dominion societies themselves.

CONCLUSION

Although they endured for a long time, the two forms of diaspora considered here, a labour and an imperial diaspora, can best be seen as transitional types. Few people in working class occupations – whether they are Indian workers in the plantation colonies or British workers in Australia – have a desperate desire to be horny-handed sons and daughters of toil forever. The idea of the 'honest worker', content with his station in life and only seeking to do a 'fair day's work for a fair day's pay' is largely an ideological construction of the nineteenth-century English bourgeoisie. That is not, of course, to say that dissatisfaction with one's lot is generally replaced by revolutionary zeal (as the Marxists hoped and expected). Instead, escape from the conditions of one's oppression takes a number of forms. Sometimes people escape into the imagination, deadening their life at work while creating alternatives in their leisure, hobbies or creative activities.[45] Many find solace in religious expression, as was shown by the revival of orthodox Hinduism and the *Ramayana* in the Indian labour diaspora.

However, more fundamental changes at the level of politics, educational provision and the economy were needed before the Indian labour diaspora and the British imperial diaspora could slough off their oppressive heritages. For the Indians, the predominant aspirations were to own land and property, or to become traders. Time and again bitter struggles over land rights occurred. In Fiji, the Indians were described by an Indo-Fijian writer as 'marooned at home' because they remained as squatters, estate workers and lease-holders.[46] In South Africa, an offer of land in exchange for reindenturing was withdrawn, but Indians managed to cling onto small plots (sometimes held by dummy white owners) or to enter profitable market-gardening.

As to becoming small traders, the bulk of the Indian labour diaspora could look to the 10 per cent or so of their co-ethnics who had come as 'free' or 'passenger' immigrants. There was a light sprinkling of religious leaders among this minority, but most were small traders, setting up shops to service the needs of the Indian community in terms of food, clothing and their religious and traditional artefacts. The Indian traders soon saw wider opportunities. Fearing competition, white merchants in northern Natal managed to ban Indian traders between 1927 and 1986, while the Afrikaners of the Orange Free State (alarmed also at the thought of a 'heathen' invasion), managed to stop all Indian settlement between 1881 and 1985.[47] All over the Indian labour diaspora, the success of petty entrepreneurship was to provide a role model for those emerging from rural impoverishment.

The Indian labour diaspora also needed to get itself politically organized if it was to begin the long haul to collective social mobility. As religious freedom was guaranteed in their terms of indenture, power was initially exercised by the subtle transmutation of religious ceremony into a popular protest. One notable demonstration of this took place in the so-called 'Coolie Disturbances' of 1984 in Trinidad when troops fired on a procession, killing 12 and wounding 107 marchers. Muslim indentured and free workers had been celebrating Hosay by carrying torches and *tadjahs* (representations of the tombs of the Prophet) to the sea. While being inspired by religious conviction, the marchers were also showing bravado by carrying lighted torches in defiance of an ordinance of the colony. The official investigator, the British governor of Jamaica, was not slow to pick up the growing self-confidence of the Indian workers:

> After residence of some time in Trinidad the Coolie not only becomes a man of more independent spirit than he was in India, but according to some reliable evidence, he often becomes somewhat overbearing ... There can be no doubt that the Coolies feel their power, or rather, I should say, have an exaggerated idea of that power.[48]

Through religious, cultural and finally political organization the Indian labour diaspora was able to gain considerable leverage in some of the countries of settlement. The diasporic communities were also becoming much more socially differentiated through the drip-feed of education. The teachers, doctors, lawyers, students, clerical workers and petty entrepreneurs who emerged from this process in the Caribbean have been subjected to ruthless pillory by the great, but certainly not warm-hearted, Indo-Trinidadian novelist and social commentator, V. S. Naipaul. Seen as 'mimic men' who imitated the ways of the West, without knowing their context and meaning, the emergent Indian middle classes have attracted all the conventional opprobrium of those with a little more caste, class or education. This does not, however, diminish their considerable educational and material achievements. Of course, many Indians remain on impoverished plots or in menial occupations in all the countries to which they were taken, but there is now sufficient progress in their acquisitions of land, property, education and income no longer to see the diaspora as overwhelmingly characterized by its proletarian character.

As for the British imperial diaspora, the initial impoverishment of the emigrants was generally offset by the grant of land in the countries of settlement, the subsidization of their passages and by imperial preferences and subsidies for whatever products they were able to wrest from the land. South African fruit and gold, New Zealand lamb and butter, Australian wool, Canadian maple and furs – the very objects of British household consumption were prefaced by an adjectival association with the imperial diaspora in the dominions. The settlers were also generally fortunate in their destinations. Most of the dominions turned out to have not only abundant land, but also rich mineral deposits. Add a century or so to when the bulk of the impecunious settlers left Britain and we find that their descendants start to compete and sometimes outstrip their metropolitan counterparts on the cricket pitch and rugby field, in terms of their longevity and health, their income and their level of education.

The British imperial diaspora is rapidly fading without the sustenance wrought by the intimate connection linking the mother country on the one hand, and the empire and dominions on the other. This is as much a consequence of the distancing from the side of the home country as it is from the dominions. The Fleet Street defender of the imperial idea, the *Daily Mail*, was founded by Harmsworth, as its banner head stated, to proclaim 'The Power, the

Supremacy and the Greatness of the British Empire'. Its editorials now rarely rise above the narrow domestic crudities of anti-European and anti-Labour Party campaigns. *Punch*, the bland satirical voice of a greater British identity, published its last issue in 1992. The library of the Royal Commonwealth Society, an old watering hole of dominion academics, sold up in the next year.

The echoes of worldwide racial bonding are still occasionally evident – in the Falklands campaign, in the proud commemorative marches of war veterans and in the activation of the British diasporic vote for the Conservative Party in the 1992 general election. But the collapse of empire, macro changes in the world situation facing Britain and its former dominions and the evolution of the empire into a multiracial Commonwealth have fragmented the unquestioned loyalty, and dissolved the essence, of the British imperial diaspora.

FURTHER READING

- The classic account of Indian indentured labourers is Hugh Tinker's *A new system of slavery: the export of Indian labour overseas, 1830–1920* (London: Oxford University Press for the Institute of Race Relations, 1974). Members of the Indian diaspora have been active in recording the fate and fortunes of Indians abroad. An excellent encyclopaedia is Brij V. Lal, Peter Reeves and Rajesh Rai (eds) *The encyclopaedia of the Indian diaspora* (Singapore: Editions Didier Millet in association with National University of Singapore, 2006).
- I cover here the case of the British in their dominions abroad, but students often like to extend the argument (or question it) using the case of contemporary British emigration. An engaging study of retirement migration to the Costa del Sol, the Algarve, Tuscany and Malta is provided by Russell King, Allan M. Williams, Tony Warnes, *Sunset lives: British retirement migration to the Mediterranean* (Oxford: Berg Publishers, 2000).
- A special issue of a journal has been turned into a useful survey of the British diaspora. See Carl Bridge and Kent Fedorowich (eds) *The British world: diaspora, culture and identity* (London: Frank Cass, 2003).

QUESTIONS TO THINK ABOUT

- Examine the various notions of a 'proletarian' or 'labour diaspora' and develop your own understanding of the term, taking as examples workers of foreign origin *not* discussed here.
- Is there such an entity as an 'Indian diaspora', or does it have to be broken apart into its three principal component parts – Sikh, Hindu and Muslim?
- With the help of some independent reading, characterize the balance between the voluntary and compelled elements in the British diaspora.

Figure 5.1 Chinatown in Vancouver, Canada. Chinatowns have proved an innovative means of being in, if not of, host societies. Besides, selling ethnic quaintness is big business. © iStockphoto.com/Robin Cohen

5

TRADE AND BUSINESS DIASPORAS

Chinese and Lebanese

Trade diasporas in the classical world became familiar to modern western European scholars through Homer's writings. Surprisingly, both the *Iliad* and the *Odyssey* contain generally negative views about the role of commerce. The Greeks (rather like the Romans later) preferred the 'noble' ideals of military conquest, plunder and colonization to trade. They relied for commercial affairs on the Phoenicians, the legendary 'Bedouin of the sea', who exchanged products and knowledge as far afield as Spain, Britain, Greece, Babylon, Persepolis and Thebes. Used of the Phoenicians in early modern history, the expression diaspora was revived to allude to networks of proactive merchants set up to buy and sell their goods along established trade routes. This drew the meaning of the word closer to the Phoenician prototype.

The term 'trade diasporas' was first given a reasonably precise definition by Abner Cohen, who insisted that there had to be evidence of moral community if the notion was to carry conviction. A trade diaspora was 'a nation of socially interdependent, but spatially dispersed communities'. A degree of moral cohesion is necessary if risks are to be taken, or an often vulnerable minority is to survive or thrive. A close degree of kinship also permits trusting someone with large advances for what might be long-delayed and uncertain returns. Family and kin, the creation of a common commercial culture and religion, among other factors, provide the ties that bind.[1]

A similar note is struck by Curtin, who argues that trade diasporas can be considered the 'most common institutional form' after the coming of urban life. Merchants from one community would live as aliens in another town, learn the language, the customs and the commercial practices of their hosts then start the exchange of goods. He continues:

> At this stage a distinction appeared between the merchants who moved and settled and those who continued to move back and forth. What might have begun as a single settlement soon became more complex ... The result was an interrelated net of commercial communities forming a trade network, or trade diaspora – a term that comes from the Greek

word for scattering, as in the sowing of grain … Trade communities of merchants living among aliens in associated networks are to be found on every continent and back through time to the very beginning of urban life.[2]

In his comprehensive account, Curtin documents diasporic networks of traders in Africa, Anatolia, Mesopotamia, pre-Columbian America, Armenian and China.[3] Often vast wealth was accumulated, while in some cases a lucrative trading monopoly, combined with great diplomatic skill, allowed 'middlemen' to transform themselves into the notables of small but viable city states. The most significant example of this outcome is found in sixteenth-century Venice, which commanded the trade between Europe and Asia and supported an advanced artistic, cultural and civic life. (The influence of the Turks in the eastern Mediterranean and the growth of competitive nation-states in western Europe ultimately put paid to Venice's powerful commercial position.)

Allied to trade diasporas and imperial diasporas (discussed in my previous chapter) was an intermediate type, which might be described as an 'auxiliary diaspora', a term related to Tinker's 'imperial auxiliaries' or 'auxiliary minorities'.[4] Auxiliary diasporas profited from colonial expansion but were composed of ethnically different camp followers of military conquests or minorities permitted to provide retail shops by the colonial regimes. Often the small numbers representing the imperial power meant that local hostility was directed instead to the more visible and often more numerous auxiliaries, who were seen to be 'foreigners' allied to the colonial administration. Chinese traders in the European colonies of Southeast Asia, the Lebanese in the Caribbean and West Africa, and the Indians in East Africa, all had some features of an auxiliary diaspora, but the autonomous expansion of their own trading networks also impelled their arrival in the European colonies. Not all auxiliaries were traders. Take the case of the Sikhs, whom various British colonial administrations deployed in the military.[5] The presence of such auxiliary minorities was later to have important consequences as nationalist movements sought to homogenize their populations – forcing the auxiliaries to choose between local citizenship, repatriation, or rescue by the former metropolitan power. Although there are peculiarities that derive from the auxiliary aspects of some diasporas that deserve special attention, I only have an opportunity here to deal with the general features of trade diasporas, taking the Chinese and Lebanese as the exemplary cases.

THE MAKING OF THE CHINESE DIASPORA

Given the common stereotype in the West of the Chinese as innovative and successful traders, it is interesting to learn that historically merchants were almost totally subordinate to the mandarinate, at least up to the end of the Tang dynasty.

Rather like the ancient Greeks, they also had to struggle against a Confucian heritage that left them near the bottom of the social scale. It was only after the tenth century, when the maritime trade with the southeast provinces of China became substantial, that the status of the traders began to improve. Wang provides a compelling picture of the Hokkien traders, looking in particular at their settlements in Manila from the 1570s and in Nagasaki after 1600.[6] In response to competition with the Dutch and Portuguese, the Spanish officials in Manila welcomed the Chinese as a means of building up the colony. Within 30 years the Chinese population had reached 10,000 and a thriving trade in silks, tools, textiles, food, furniture and porcelain commenced. Those who did not convert to Catholicism retained their primary cultural links with south China and began to develop a pattern of circular migration, best described in English as 'sojourning' – of which more anon. As for the Hokkiens in Nagasaki, their own effectiveness was limited by the periodic disapproval of their activities by their own government. The Japanese also gave preference to the European mercantile companies backed, as they were, by their royal charters and their capacity to negotiate treaties on behalf of impressive sounding royal houses. Despite these handicaps, the Hokkiens showed their adaptability by adopting Buddhism and, by the middle of the seventeenth century, a substantial maritime empire had been developed, notably by the Zheng family. Because they were lowly provincial merchants, Wang contends, they 'had to live by their wits, cultivate the fine art of risk-taking, and, at the crunch, could count only on their family–village system and strong local Hokkien loyalties to help them through hard times'.[7] The connection with 'home' was thus both instrumental and necessary.

The story of these Hokkien trading communities can be used to make apparent one important distinction between trade and imperial diasporas. The former were not state-sponsored and state-backed, the latter were. In the case of the Chinese this led to an inner resilience and a high level of family and clan solidarity, which in turn gave birth to the famous Chinese capacity for 'adaptability'. One of the most propitious examples of 'adaptability' arose in Singapore which, when the British occupied it, was nothing but a sleepy fishing village. Sir Stamford Raffles invited Chinese traders to come to Singapore in the nineteenth century to develop the port. They arrived in considerable numbers, quickly learnt European laws and trading practices and soon began to speak English for commercial purposes. Raffles was delighted: Singapore's prosperity was 'the simple but almost magic result of that perfect freedom of Trade which it has been my good fortune to establish', he boasted.[8] Free trade plus the Chinese traders would have been a more accurate rendering of the magic formula.

As with the British, so it was with the other colonial powers. The French encouraged Chinese immigration to French Indochina, Mauritius and Réunion, while the Portuguese and Dutch followed suit in Macão and Batavia, respectively. The founder of the Dutch colony in Batavia, Jan Pieterson Coen, enthused: 'There are no people who can serve us better than the Chinese.' Coen was so excessive in his zeal to acquire Chinese immigrants that he sent expeditionary parties to kidnap some on the mainland while blockading Manila and Macão so that the junks would be diverted to Batavia. However, the Chinese traders had ambivalent attitudes both to the colonial powers and to their places of settlement.[9] They were not thus 'auxiliaries' in a strict sense. Rather, they were loyal to thriving entrepôts and profitable arrangements, not caring over much whether the British, French, Portuguese, Malays, Dutch or Indians were in charge of the political superstructure.

The lack of commitment to local political life in the places to which the Chinese migrated was linked to the practice of sojourning rather than settling. There are a number of ways of explaining the Chinese traders' retention of a strong connection with 'home'. I have already suggested that sojourning was intrinsic to the group's coherence and its commercial survival. Pan advances some additional thoughts. She suggests that a preoccupation with identity and genealogy is characteristic of a group that was intrinsically marginal, even in China – nearly all the 'overseas Chinese' were not from the Han centre of the country, but from the peripheral regions of Fukien and Kwangtung. Despite being Sinicized, they were also of somewhat different ethnic origins; more akin, it is said, to the inhabitants of Vietnam, Cambodia and Laos. Then too there was the almost mystical attachment to *hsiang* ('home') which was never an immense entity like 'China', but rather could mean a village, a home town, familiar countryside or simply the place of emotional attachment. Pan continues: 'For commitment to one's native place, one's ancestral home, few people could beat the Chinese.'[10] Attachment to *hsiang* was also closely associated with filial duty. How else could one perform ancestral rites, look after aged grandparents or undertake ceremonial visits to the family grave?

Although her view closely mirrors the sentiments of many overseas Chinese, it has the danger of assuming the status of a timeless and unvarying cultural norm. A more dynamic view would be to see how the practice of sojourning evolved and why so many Chinese abandoned it in favour of permanent settlement. Wang has been the key scholar in elaborating the origins and changing meaning of 'sojourning'.[11] The first essential change was to persuade the Chinese authorities to move beyond a position that regarded the traders abroad as more than merely 'outcasts' or 'waifs'. This recognition first dawned in the 1880s, when the Chinese equivalent term *hua-ch'iao* appeared in treaties with the French and Japanese. In these agreements, the government of China abandoned its traditional disdain of the merchants abroad and sought to protect their rights. This was partly an expression of gratitude to the 'temporarily resident Chinese people and irregulars in Vietnam' who had gained official Chinese approval by militarily opposing the French. For the Japanese it was more of a *quid pro quo*, with the Chinese government feeling constrained to ask for protection of its residents in Japan in response to a similar request on behalf of the Japanese in China.

Official recognition of the overseas Chinese helped to legitimate their comings and goings. Successful endeavour abroad also reflected the shortcomings and constraints of the home country. By the end of the nineteenth century, the Chinese nationalists, revolutionaries and republicans found a ready following among the *hua-ch'iao*. One popular manifestation of this was the Song of Revolution, which appealed to their patriotism, attacked materialism without political engagement and asked for contributions to the anti–Manchu cause. Extracts from this song make the message transparent:

> Let me call again to the *hua-ch'iao* overseas
> Compatriots to the distant ends of the earth!
> Only because of the need to feed yourself
> Did you leave home to wander the seas ...
> You are no mandarin back in your native home.
> Your descendants remain inferior to others
> Without protection none can get very far ...
> What use is the cumulation of silver cash?
> Why not use it to eject the Manchus?
> Ten thousand each from you isn't much
> To buy cannons and guns and ship them inland
> Buy a hundred thousand quick-loading rifles
> Aimed at Peking with easy success!
> The Manchu barbarians destroyed, peace will then surely follow,
> A republican polity immediately assured!
> The *hua-ch'iao* can then vent their feelings
> And the Westerners retreat to call you brothers
> Much better than building fortunes and pleasures
> Which can do nothing when death appears.
> It is hard to be happy all one's life,
> You need but little conscience to feel shame.
> What then is the most shameful matter?
> To forget one's ancestors involves the greatest hate!
> If not that, to register as a foreign national
> Forgetting that you come from Chinese stock.
> In life, you may gain an awesome fame
> After death how can you face your ancestors?[12]

This appeal is interesting for a number of reasons, not least of which is the claim to a common ethno–nationality and an attack on the Manchu as aliens. One of the most enthusiastic supporters of this song was Sun Yat-sen, the founder of the Chinese Nationalist Party, whose followers had distributed hundreds of thousands of copies of it. Although born in Guangdong, Sun Yat-sen was educated in Hawaii and Hong Kong, where he trained and practised as a doctor. Sun's key commitment was to the maintenance, restoration, safety and prosperity of the homeland (to allude to one of our own listed features of a diaspora), and a key means to realizing these ends was to mobilize the entire diaspora. He even wished to re-Sinicize those who had been assimilated in their countries of settlement and 'entered into the foreign registers', that is adopted local citizenship. They too could be redeemed and have their 'Chineseness' restored. The support of the diaspora was ultimately to prove vital to the success of the 1911 revolution, the key event that allowed Sun and his followers to make of China a modern nation-state.

THE CHINESE AS MINORITIES

The 1911 revolution can be regarded as marking the waning of the conventional 'sojourner option' for the Chinese diaspora. The strategy of working and trading abroad but maintaining a close political, social and cultural relationship with *hsiang* was to prove difficult to sustain for three reasons. First, it was irreconcilable with the emerging nationalisms of the former colonial world, particularly in Southeast Asia. Second, as with all overseas communities, second or third generations became culturally localized and began to drop away old habits associated with the past. Third, after the Chinese Revolution in 1949, the ideological rift between the People's Republic and the diaspora was often too great to be bridged and the practical arrangements for continuing an oscillating system of migration became increasingly troublesome.[13]

The story of Malaya's decolonization provides a good example of the impasse. With the end of the Second World War, the pace of decolonization rapidly increased, but the sponsored migration of trade and auxiliary diasporas by the former colonial powers created an *a priori* problem – who exactly was to constitute the nation? As Lian shows, in the attempt to articulate a Malayan identity, the non-Malays – Indians and Chinese – were scapegoated as alien minorities. They were different in appearance and religion, they appeared not to want to take part in the process of nation-building and, perhaps most tellingly, they occupied positions in the economy that the nationalist elites or their clients craved. The suspicion of the Chinese by the Malays was somewhat unjust in that the Chinese population of the Federated Malay States and the Straights Settlements (Singapore) was increasingly less footloose. The figures speak for themselves. In 1911, in conformity with the sojourner pattern, less than 24 per cent of the Chinese in the Straights were locally born, while only 8 per cent were locally born in the Federated Malay States. Twenty years later, the Chinese constituted 70 per cent of the population in the Straights, 38 per cent of whom were locally born; by 1957, 73 per cent were native born. The Chinese could not win. If they continued with their traditions of oscillating migration, they were not showing proper commitment to the anti-colonial struggle. If they indigenized – as increasingly after 1949 they felt constrained to do – they were a threat to the Malays.[14]

The Malays forced through a form of citizenship that insisted that a *bumiputra* ('prince of the soil') had to speak Malay, practise Islam and follow Malay custom.

The Chinese demanded impartiality and an acceptance of cultural and religious pluralism. For a while, the powerful political personalities of the time, Lee Kwan Yew and Tunku Abdul Rahman, patched together various political compromises and managed to form a federated Malaysia. The federation only lasted for two years (1963–65) until, under the impact of Sino–Malay riots, Singapore withdrew to become an independent state. For the first and only occasion a section of the Chinese diaspora constituted itself not as an ethnic minority, but as a majority in its own state. Singapore is best conceived of as a 'city-state', the basic business of which is anchored around the import–export trade and providing financial services to the global economy. In this sense, Singapore remains true to the trading origins of the Chinese merchants Raffles first invited there. It is to the global economy what Venice was to the early modern world, not perhaps in its overall dominance, but rather in its function as the political embodiment of a successful trade diaspora.

All other parts of the Chinese diaspora constituted themselves as minorities, with significant concentrations in all continents other than Africa.[15] Over the period 1848–88 alone, over two million Chinese found their way to such diverse destinations as the Malay Peninsula, Indochina, Sumatra, Java, the Philippines, Hawaii, the Caribbean, Mexico, Peru, California and Australia. The Chinese diaspora today comprises 33 million people (excluding Taiwan and Hong Kong), compared with 1,321 million at home. I have laid emphasis on the Chinese as a trade diaspora, but in fact historically the Chinese emigrants fell into three distinct classes – indentured workers (the so-called 'coolies'), free artisans and traders.[16] We are not centrally concerned with the first two groups here, but it may be helpful to say a little about the 'coolie trade', for it impacted on the other two parts of the diaspora.

Comparatively little has been written on this theme by Chinese authors because the experience was a source of some embarrassment to China, indicating its weakness in the face of imperialist labour recruiters. However, Ong breaks new ground by taking a much more positive view of the achievement of the indentured labourers. Their endurance, he submits, was a copybook demonstration of the virtues of deferred gratification. Endless backbreaking work laying the railways across the USA or working in tropical plantations and mines was better than starvation at home. Moreover, those who decided to stay after their indenture formed the nucleus of the Chinatowns that are so evident in many large cities. To the former indentured workers were added the artisans like tailors, blacksmiths, ships' chandlers, cobblers and carpenters. Those merchants who abandoned or modified their practice of sojourning thus had a ready-made ethnic enclave in which to trade.[17]

The growth of Chinatowns became the unique institutional vehicle for the Chinese to be in, but not necessarily to become of, the societies in which they settled. The beginnings of the biggest of the world's Chinatowns, in New York, can be traced to one shop; as late as the mid-1960s it only covered six blocks with 15,000 people. By 1988 there were 300,000 residents; 450 restaurants employed 15,000 people, while 500 garment factories hired about 20,000 Chinese women.[18] Pan describes the area in these terms:

> Chinatown has stuck to its own ways the longest, a classic, self-contained ghetto that was haunted by the Exclusion Acts and little freshened by new blood. The residents huddled together for comfort and let the rest of the world go by, a world which merely seemed a place apart in the eyes of some and loomed up to frightening heights in the eyes of others ... Those who gravitated towards Chinatown found an enclave clad in the whole paraphernalia of immigrant Chinese communities, from secret societies to clan associations, each group looking after its own, the whole presided over by the Chinese Consolidated Benevolent Association (CCBA), a staunch supporter of the Kuomintang ... The last thing [the CCBA leaders] wanted was to engage with the larger world, the world of city politics and administration – for so long as the Chinese community kept to itself, so long as the Chinese looked to the traditional associations for all their needs, these men rule the roost in Chinatown.[19]

Kwong, a social scientist who lived for many years in New York's Chinatown, is also sceptical about whether integration into the larger society will take place: 'Powerful interests in and out of Chinatowns are served by keeping the majority isolated from American society.'[20] The functions of Chinatowns are nonetheless changing radically. Overseas Chinese in precarious situations used New York's Chinatown to shift their money. Kwong further argues: 'While the rich moved part of their business operation to the United States, the less wealthy put their savings in the care of relatives, who made deposits in Chinatown banks to avoid complicated rules governing non-residents. Many banks were set up precisely to facilitate such transactions.'[21] Investments in property and their relatives' businesses, as well as speculative ventures, have created a hothouse economy in the Chinese enclaves.

As far as outsiders are concerned, Chinatowns are also transmuting as global tourism finds in them what the guidebooks call 'authentic', but what are often newly socially-constructed versions of supposedly traditional Chinese practices. Tourist buses, herbalists, acupuncturists, kitchenware shops, sages, masseurs and restaurants proliferate as the Chinese learn to offer yet another commodity to the global marketplace – their ethnic quaintness. However, beyond the tourist gazes and the bubble worlds of the Chinatowns, the new generations of the Chinese settlers, as well as those joining them from Hong Kong and Taiwan, are entering into professional and business life in significant numbers.

Because of the growing interdependence of the US economy with the Chinese Pacific economies of Taiwan, Hong Kong and China, many west coast Chinese in particular are becoming 'hypermobile' migrants, who establish a family in one society, start a business in the other and are constantly moving between the two. These *Tai Ku Fe En* ('spacemen') may have a professional practice or business in (say) Taiwan, yet locate their families in Los Angeles to maximize educational opportunities or as a safe haven in the event of political instability. Others are more explicitly traders, facilitating commerce across the Pacific Ocean and using their homeland and diasporic networks to do so. The increased mobility arising from the regionalization and globalization of the marketplace, together with the neo-liberal turn in the People's Republic, has greatly invigorated, rather than diminished, the Chinese trade diaspora.[22]

THE GREAT LEBANESE EMIGRATION

The Lebanese trade diaspora comprised two initially distinct groups, merchants and labourers, whose fates converged in the countries to which they emigrated. From the seventeenth to the nineteenth centuries, relatively prosperous independent merchants had set up networks spanning the burgeoning trade between the Middle East and Europe. Significant settlement took place in Egypt and in Livorno, Marseilles and Manchester. If we downplay the somewhat fanciful connection with the Phoenicians, the pioneer Lebanese emigrants were Greek Catholics (Melkites) who controlled the trade with Egypt. Mount Lebanon,[23] the area round Beirut, was highly integrated into the modern world economy and stood at an important axis of trade, transport, communications and finance. Beirut was the financial capital of Syria and foreign banks and insurance companies proliferated. Railway and port companies, silk-reeling industries, banks, hotels and educational institutions all constituted the basis for a bourgeoisie, the size of which had no parallel in other Middle Eastern countries.

As the massive flows of emigration were to confirm, this picture of a thriving community was, however, somewhat superficial. Christians had always shown a great propensity to migrate, partly because of the communal clashes of the 1840s and 1850s and the sense that the Ottoman government was unsympathetic to their religious beliefs. To this sense of insecurity was added an underlying economic cause for emigration. The population of Mount Lebanon had increased dramatically, without a corresponding increase in local jobs. Indeed, the economy was distorted by its excessive dependence on finance and trade at the expense of industry and agriculture. What little industry there was turned on the trade in silk, which was subject to periodic decline as world prices fluctuated. Hashimoto advances an interesting hypothesis that those who acquired foreign currency in exporting silk thread and cloth in the good times were in a better position to go abroad later when prices collapsed.[24]

By the turn of the century, 'emigration fever' had gripped Lebanon. Figures from 1900 suggest that 120,000 had left the Syrian province, the vast majority from Lebanon. In the same year the American consul put the number of Syrians in the USA at 'over 50,000'. At the turn of the century there was a new census ordered for Lebanon, which some, probably correctly, thought was intended as a source of information to start the recruitment of Lebanese Christians as conscripts in the service of the Ottoman Empire. When the Balkan wars flared up again the threat of conscription produced a strong impulse to emigrate. By 1914, emigration was estimated at 15,000–20,000 people a year. Some 350,000 Lebanese had left by that year, over a quarter overall and, in some districts, a half of the home population.[25]

In the literature on the various Lebanese communities abroad, there is considerable confusion over how many of their number left voluntarily and how many were impelled by 'push' factors originating in the Lebanon. This description of the Lebanese in the USA is typical in its ambiguity:

> The Syro–Lebanese were not driven to America on a mass scale from either economic desperation, religious persecution, or political oppression although something like these conditions were more likely in Syria than in Mount Lebanon. By their own testimony, the immigrants came to improve their economic condition and to return home in a year or two, wealthier and prouder than when they left. It was while they were pursuing their get-rich-quick goal that they discovered the ideals of freedom, democracy and opportunity and they embraced them fervently. Later others would join the 'gold-seekers', for a variety of reasons such as evading personal problems or joining relatives. Muslims, Druzes, and some Christians escaped military conscription after 1908 and many who have suffered through the famine of the First World War also emigrated.[26]

The divided motives of the emigrants can be seen in the very dramatic switches in their occupational background. Data from Argentina (Table 5.1) show that over a 40-year period the ratio of merchants to labourers virtually reversed.

Table 5.1 **Declared occupations at point of entry: Middle East arrivals in Argentina (% in brackets)**

	1876–9	1900	1909	1913
Merchants	8135 (81.9)	1146 (72.3)	5763 (49)	904 (4.6)
Labourers	437 (4.4)	111 (7)	1906 (16.2)	9506(48.6)

Source: Ignacio Klich, '*Criollos* and Arabic speakers in Argentina: an uneasy *pas de deux*, 1888–1914', in Albert Hourani and Nadim Shehadi (eds) *The Lebanese in the world: a century of emigration* (London: I.B.Tauris for the Centre for Lebanese Studies, 1992) p. 265.

Although these data include all Middle Easterners arriving in Argentina, the overwhelming majority were Lebanese. While the change from merchants was steep enough until 1909, it became precipitant thereafter, probably indicating the consequences of the 1908 conscription. The data are, if anything, more impressive if we bear in mind that the Ottomans were reluctant to give travel papers to any Lebanese other than those in 'good standing' who were engaged in commerce and business likely to benefit the empire. Several documents subsequently uncovered by scholars talked of the embarrassment that would be caused to the Ottoman government by the arrival of impoverished or destitute emigrants. It is likely therefore that a number of Lebanese from modest backgrounds declared themselves to be merchants.

Even if the motives for emigration varied, aspirations did not. The two broad strands of Lebanese migration coalesced in the diaspora with very few of the immigrants accepting unskilled industrial employment; instead, most preferred to establish themselves as itinerant traders – pedlars. A number of case studies in Hourani and Shehadi's massive collection of case studies can be cited to confirm this general pattern:

- *Bishmizzini villagers*: 'Most became merchants, generally starting as itinerant pedlars';
- *Lebanese in Brazil*: 'The stories of wealthy former pedlars now retired to São Paulo or Rio de Janeiro encouraged more Syrians and Lebanese to move to the Amazon basin';
- *A Lebanese in Jamaica*: 'To the end of his life old Elias Issa, who had arrived in Jamaica in 1894, could show the mark on his back made by the box he has carried as a pedlar. After some years he was able to buy a donkey and then set up shop in Princess Street, later moving to Orange street';
- *Lebanese in the USA*: 'The vast majority of the pioneers – men, women and children – were drawn by the magnet of pack peddling. Despite its hardships, they preferred it to the drudgery of the factory and the isolation of American farm life'. 'Before the First World War a pedlar could average $1000 a year while white American labourers earned $650';
- *Lebanese in Montreal*: 'Of all the occupations in which the early Lebanese immigrants were involved, peddling was to have the most profound effect not only on their economic wellbeing, but also on their geographical distribution. Later Lebanese wholesalers opened up to replenish the pedlar's merchandise'.[27]

The reference to 'wholesalers' is a useful reminder that very large distinctions exist within the category of 'traders'. At least in his early life, 'old Elias Issa' and his ilk were certainly dependent on importers and wholesalers who were operating on a totally different scale. While many of the Lebanese continued in trade-related activities, the second and subsequent generations abroad became increasingly occupationally differentiated.

In his richly researched study of the Lebanese in West Africa, van der Laan also warns against seeing his subjects in too simplistic a way. He prefers the word 'trader' to 'middleman', explaining that not all trade was conducted between Africans and Europeans, with the Lebanese in the middle. With respect to the rice and kola trade, in which the Lebanese were heavily implicated, the buyers and sellers were all Africans. Again, after the 1930s the structure of foreign trade in Sierra Leone changed. The produce trade was faltering, but the trade in general merchandise continued, partly in response to the increased prosperity brought about by the mining of diamonds on a significant scale. 'Shopkeeping became more important than produce buying and there was ample justification for describing the Lebanese primarily as shopkeepers'.[28]

Whether shopkeepers or middlemen, by the late twentieth century, as a distinguished Lebanese scholar, Albert Hourani, remarks, the descendants of the Lebanese migrants boasted a president of Colombia, a prime minister of Jamaica, a majority leader in the US Senate, a Nobel prize winner for medicine, a president of the Royal Society, a world-famous heart surgeon and a prize-winning Lebanese-Australian novelist.[29]

THE LEBANESE DIASPORA: BUTTERFLIES AND CATERPILLARS

Were the Lebanese abroad no longer part of the society they had left behind? Hashimoto vigorously contests the idea of a divorce between home and abroad and uses an expressive metaphor to capture the sense of continual goings and comings. 'A butterfly', he declares, 'becomes a caterpillar again'.[30] People leave Beirut and the villages, then return from abroad, only to depart again not too long later. One illustrative figure of this tendency is that the percentage of return migrants between 1926 and 1933 was 41 per cent of the total number of emigrants.[31] The volume of this 'continually reversible population flow' is virtually unprecedented in populations that are so widely dispersed. The extent of the dispersal of the diaspora is demonstrated in Table 5.2 below.

The movement back and forth from the diaspora to Lebanon makes the distinction between stocks and flows of migrants difficult to gauge. The data are therefore imprecise, but adequate to illustrate that over about one-quarter of self-declared Lebanese do not live in the Lebanon at any one time. Such a proportion abroad is unusual, if not unprecedented. Puerto Ricans, for example are split half-and-half between the island and the mainland, often with several crossovers during an individual migrant's lifetime. However, Puerto Rico is contiguous to the USA and, since 1917, despite its special status as a 'free associated state' of the USA, Puerto Ricans have been entitled to US citizenship. Circulatory migrants from the Dominican Republic to and from the USA and from the neighbouring states to and from South Africa are also very common, but again the feature of contiguity helps to explain these large transversal flows, a factor that does not apply in the Lebanese case.

What draws the Lebanese overseas back to the Lebanon from such far-flung destinations? One important explanation is the extraordinary hold the imagined homeland has over the diaspora, despite bitter inter-ethnic conflict, civil war, Syrian dominance and Israeli invasions, the latest in 2006. Some of the ancient

Table 5.2 **The Lebanese diaspora by country of residence, 1990 and latest estimates**

Country	Number	Latest available	Note
France	800,000	28, 160	Lower figure from the French census (1999) and includes only Lebanese born with single nationality. Higher figure includes those with dual nationality and of Lebanese descent
Brazil	200,000	7, 000, 000	Higher figure is a rough estimate of those of Lebanese descent (2 million in São Paulo alone)
West Africa	200,000	100, 000	Many dual nationals in Nigeria, Sierra Leone, Ghana, Ivory Coast, Zaire and other countries. Unverified estimate
Argentina	200,000	300, 000	Unverified estimate
Australia	100,000	71, 310	The lower figure is the official count in the 2001 Australian census
Canada	100,000	143, 000	The higher figure is the official count in the 2001 Canadian census
Gulf/Saudi Arabia	200,000	140, 000	Includes some Palestinians
USA	400,000	410, 000	The higher figure is the official count in the 2000 US census, but using descent, not birth
TOTAL	2,2000,000	8, 192, 470	Cf. 2,897,000 in Lebanon (1991)

Source: Aaron Segal, *An atlas of international migration* (London: Hans Zell, 1993) p. 102; Official census data (Canada, Australia, USA, France); others are estimates derived from various web sites and should be treated with scepticism. Figures are also likely to be out of date, with high levels of emigration from Lebanon since 2006.

cedars of Lebanon were felled to build King Solomon's fabulous temple. In the nostrils of the poor Lebanese pack–pedlars remained the scents of cedars and mint, while their palates recalled the taste of mulberries, *kippi*, and the fiery red and soft white wines. An almost physically palpable nostalgia is evident in the survival and spread of Lebanese cuisine and in the literature and art of the Lebanese diaspora. The *mahhar* movement, founded in New York around the turn of the century, formalized the cultural movement; it included such notables as Khalikew Jibran (author of *The Prophet*). The contemporary Australian novelist David Malouf recalled his grandfather in this evocative poem:

> I find him in the garden. Staked tomato plants are what
> he walks among, the apples of paradise. He is eighty
> and stoops, white-haired in baggy serge and braces. His moustache
> once warrior-fierce for quarrels in the small town of Zable,
> where honour divides houses, empties squares, droops and is thin
> from stroking, he has come too far from his century to care …
> This is his garden,
> a valley in Lebanon; you can smell the cedars on his breath

and the blood of the massacres, the crescent flashing from ravines
to slice through half a family. He rolls furred sage between
thumb and forefinger, sniffs the snowy hills; bees shifting
gold as they forage sunlight among stones, church bells wading
in through pools of silence. He has never quite migrated.[32]

To the cultural movement in the diaspora were added many magazines, newspapers and social and quasi-political homeland organizations. The Lebanese
League of Progress, for example, was founded in the Americas in 1911, though
it tended to promote a Maronite–Lebanese nationalist position. Kindling
the putative association with their ancient role models, Phoenician clubs all
over the diaspora helped to cement the ties with the homeland, bridged the
generation gap and supplied practical assistance with travel costs. The Lebanese
airline, MEA (Middle East Airlines), provided a modernized, cheap form of
transport that linked all parts of the Lebanese diaspora, often in very difficult
circumstances.[33]

Trading links and cultural nostalgia may in themselves have been insufficient
to prevent the gradual erosion of a Lebanese identity in the diaspora had not the
politics of the Middle East intervened to reactivate an interest in the homeland.
Three particular blows fell hard on the Lebanon and ramified throughout the
diaspora. The civil war, beginning in the 1970s, reactivated the horrors of the
1850s and 1860s, this time with the landmine and submachine-gun replacing
the sabre and muzzle-loader. The beautiful trees and buildings of the Mount
could be seen disintegrating on the diasporic communities' television screens.
Politicized and bitter refugees fuelled emigration once again and renewed a
diasporic consciousness. To the blow of the civil war was added the subsequent
invasions and bombings of the country by the Israeli army and air force.
For some Lebanese this provoked identification with the Palestinian cause and
with Pan-Arabism. Despite the danger of creating an internal Palestinian force
that rivalled the power of the Lebanese state, some Lebanese argued that the
very existence of Lebanon seemed bound up with the creation of a viable
Palestinian homeland and opposition to Israel.

Others saw mortal dangers from elsewhere. Particularly for some Christian
Lebanese the invasion of Syria raised echoes of the Ottoman past. At first, the
impress of the Syrian government was much lighter than many feared, and the
country visibly rose from the ashes and from the bomb craters of civil war.
Tourists and Lebanese living abroad returned in significant numbers and the
shopping boulevards and cafés were back in business. Alas, this was not to last.
By 2006, Lebanon was sucked into the vortex of the Israeli–Palestinian struggle
as Gaza erupted, and terrorism from the Hezbollah bases in Lebanon provoked
a massive intervention into Lebanon by Israeli forces. Civilian casualties were
high, much infrastructure was destroyed and the painful cycle of emigration to
escape conditions in Lebanon recommenced. This time those at the head of the
queue were Lebanese 'with human, social and financial capital' and the authors

of a European Commission-sponsored report concluded that if 'Lebanon's environment of insecurity is not dealt with soon – and it is increasingly difficult to be optimistic on this point – large-scale migration will be the hallmark of 2007 and numbers may even rise more dramatically in the years to come'.[34]

CONCLUSION: ETHNIC ENTREPRENEURS AND TRADE DIASPORAS

I chose not to introduce this chapter with an extended theoretical discussion because, before drowning the reader in a welter of contending theoretical positions, I wanted first to describe the contours of the Chinese and Lebanese trade diasporas. It is now necessary, however, to recognize that our understanding of the experiences of these groups comes from a wider theoretical and comparative literature that tries to explain the extraordinary commercial success of some immigrant groups relative to the native-born populations or to other immigrant groups.

One comparative starting point is Max Weber's discussion of 'pariah people' such as the Jews and gypsies. These two peoples, Weber noted, had lost their territories, were confined to particular occupations and were endogamous in respect of dietary prohibitions, religious practices and social intercourse.[35] The Jews developed a form of 'pariah capitalism' that started with money-lending, then built to speculative investment and thence to banking and high finance. The caste-like attributes of these groups provided the basis for complete trust inside the group and an acute need to create some security against the threatening outsider. Clearly, there are some analogies between the pariah peoples and auxiliary trade diasporas like the Chinese, Lebanese and Indian traders, who were permitted to engage in commerce by the colonial regime but had a similar fear of being absorbed by the native populations. The combination of blocked opportunities, hostility from others and ethnic cohesiveness seem to create an advantageous sociological and commercial ethos in the ethnic group concerned.[36]

While these factors may be important, they are also insufficient. Is there a set of norms and values that has developed and prevails to predispose the group concerned towards commerce and entrepreneurship? Once again, Weber's fertile mind kicked off this debate with his much discussed thesis that there was an 'elective affinity' between Protestantism (especially its Puritan and Calvinist variants) and capitalism. I have already touched on this discussion in Chapter 4 in examining the British imperial diaspora. Weber's discussion of non-European religions (Confucianism, Hinduism, Islam and prophetic Judaism) is less flexible and more schematic than his analysis of Protestantism, with a tendency to freeze past practices as if they were a contemporary anthropological present.[37]

Nonetheless, many scholars of non-European societies find support for a modified Weberian thesis, not through exact textual reference to the eminent

97

sociologist, but rather by finding Puritan-like counter currents within the non-European societies and religions he described in such monochromatic terms. For example, Kennedy shows how conversion *either* to Christianity or to Islam in a number of African societies encouraged private accumulation and economic experimentation at the expense of kin loyalties. It was the movement towards an outsider status – it did not matter much which – that was decisive.[38] In Japan, the Confucian, Shinto and Buddhist legacies were all overcome in the Tokugawa period, which 'saw the full flowering of an emerging class of commercially oriented outsiders who would create the mould for Japan's economic culture'.[39] In the case of the two trade diasporas discussed in this chapter, I have already made clear that the Hokkien merchants were ethnically distinct and successfully fought against the Confucian hierarchy that left them near the bottom of the social order. Finally, though I have made less of the connection between a particular religion and trading success, in the Lebanese case there is a broad congruence between those professing one or other of the Christian faiths (Maronite, Greek Orthodox, Greek Catholic and Armenian Orthodox) and the likelihood both of migrating and of succeeding economically.

Besides Weber, another great scholar of comparative social systems, Arnold Toynbee, sees diasporas essentially as service agents filling the cracks and crannies between the great civilizations with which he is preoccupied. Toynbee's world comprised a progression of civilizations dominant until their deaths, a fate often brought about by self-inflicted wounds. He saw diasporas as 'abortive civilizations' or 'fossil societies' that nonetheless clung tenaciously onto their communal identities without the convenience of a physical frontier like a mountain fastness. Jews, Scots and Lebanese are mentioned in passing as examples of diasporas, but Toynbee's most arresting comment captures the psychological need to succeed in an economic niche:

> In the life of a diaspora, its psychological self-isolation would prove impossible if those who practised it did not, at the same time, develop on the economic plane a special efficiency in the exploitation of such economic opportunities as had been left open to them. An almost uncanny aptitude for economic specialization and a meticulous observance of jots and tittles of a traditional law are a diaspora's two main devices for providing itself with artificial substitutes for impregnable frontiers or military prowess.[40]

The unfortunately sexist but otherwise well-conceived concept of a 'middleman minority' is a somewhat similar notion to that advanced by Toynbee. Like the notion of a diaspora (in general) or a trade diaspora (in particular), the expression 'middleman minority' has been used to describe Jews, Indians, Chinese, Lebanese and Greeks. Rather than seeing middlemen minorities as being uncomfortably sandwiched between such grand categories as 'civilizations',

Bonacich sees them as being lodged between, in principal, any two ethnic groups that stand in a class-like relation of superordination and subordination. The dominant elite of the dominant group uses the middleman minority to foster economic development, but turns it into a scapegoat when things go wrong. The subordinate group benefits from the services the middlemen provide, but sees them as competitors or 'sojourners' who owe no fealty to their society of settlement.[41]

Are the Chinese and Lebanese trade diasporas to be discussed in terms of their pariah status, their auxiliary character, their religious distinctiveness or their role as service agents or 'middlemen minorities'? All these aspects are salient to their situation in some respects. However, one cannot help sensing throughout this array of related theory the siren voice or the unstated assumption of the superior validity of the nation-state (or, in Toynbee's case, the great civilization). Trade diasporas are presented as anomalies with unfortunate or intractable qualities that are puzzling and inconvenient. I would instead submit that the trading diaspora can be seen as an enduring and perhaps innovatory model of social organization that may be advantageous to the diaspora itself, its homeland and its place of settlement.

FURTHER READING

- Virtually anything written on the overseas Chinese by the distinguished scholar Wang Gangwu is worth reading, but you might like to look at this co-edited and comprehensive collection, Wang L. Ling-chi and Wang Gungwu (eds) *The Chinese diaspora: selected essays* (Singapore: Times Academic Press, 1998) 2 vols.
- The best collection on the various Lebanese remains Albert Hourani and Nadim Shehadi (eds) *The Lebanese in the world: a century of emigration* (London: I.B.Tauris for the Centre for Lebanese Studies, 1992) though some of the essays are of poorer quality and we need an up-to-date study, following recent dispersals.
- The great strength of the following book is its rich array of descriptive material on trade and diaspora networks, providing 19 chapters and a cornucopia of historical information on many territories. See Ina Baghdiantz, McCabe, Gelina Harlaftis and Ioanna Pepelasis Minoglou (eds) *Diaspora entrepreneurial networks: four centuries of history* (Oxford: Berg, 2005).

QUESTIONS TO THINK ABOUT

- What is a trade diaspora? Link your discussion to the wider social scientific literature on the connections between ethnicity, religion and entrepreneurial conduct.

- Why are Chinatowns so successful a mechanism for retaining group identities among the Chinese abroad and providing a service to the surrounding communities and the Chinese in Mainland China?
- Why is the Lebanese diaspora six times the size of the Lebanese at home? Pay particular attention to the role of external interventions in the affairs of Lebanese and inter-ethnic violence there.

Figure 6.1 A Sikh boy with his uncut hair, covered with a turban. Other self-imposed symbols of difference include an iron bracelet, a ceremonial sword and rather unusual breeches, though here dad has switched to blue jeans.
© iStockphoto.com/Robin Cohen

6

DIASPORAS AND THEIR HOMELANDS

Zionists and Sikhs

As I shall show in Chapter 7, it is not invariably true that diasporas require homelands in a strict territorial sense, though they normally include a notion of 'homeland' or a looser idea of 'home' in their collective myths or aspirations. Indeed, a homeland is imbued with an expressive charge and a sentimental pathos that seem to be almost universal. Motherland, fatherland, native land, natal land, *Heimat*, the ancestral land, the search for 'roots' – all these similar notions invest homelands with 'an emotional, almost reverential dimension'.[1] Often, there is a complex interplay between the feminine and masculine versions of homeland. In the feminine rendition, the motherland is seen as a warm, cornucopian breast from which the people collectively suck their nourishment. One Kirgiz poet fancifully claimed that the relationship between homeland and human preceded birth itself: 'Remember, even before your mother's milk, you drank the milk of your homeland,' he wrote.[2] Suggesting the same metaphor, the biblical Promised Land was said to be 'flowing with milk and honey'.

In other interpretations, the nurturing white milk of the motherland is replaced by the blood of soldiers gallantly defending their fatherland. Their blood nourishes the soil, the soil defines their ethnogenesis. *Blut und Boden* (blood and soil) was Bismarck's stirring call to the German nation, an evocation that Hitler renewed two generations later. Even in the wake of the post-1945 liberal–democratic constitutional settlement, the Germans were unusual in stressing a definition of citizenship and belonging – *jus sanguinis*, the law of blood – that emphasizes descent rather than place of birth or long residence. Thus, third and fourth generation 'ethnic Germans' from the former Soviet Union, many of whom no longer spoke German, were accorded instant citizenship in preference to second-generation Turks who had been born and educated in Germany.

Sometimes the images of motherland and fatherland are conflated. The androgynous British conceptions of homeland evoke the virile John Bull character exemplified in modern times by the indomitable wartime hero, Winston Churchill. They are also derived from the received history of Boudicca, Britannia, Queen Victoria and, perhaps more fancifully,

103

Prime Minister Margaret Thatcher. The last was fond of denouncing her fellow citizens as being overdependent on the 'nanny' welfare state. However, she too (as she accepted in a rare moment of self-awareness) was a nanny in another sense, administering to all the purgatives and punishments previously supplied only to the British upper classes by pitiless governesses.

Given the powerful sexual, psychological and affective attributes of 'home-land', it is hardly surprising that 'foreigners', 'strangers', or 'newcomers' are often identified negatively as 'the other' and used to construct the collective identity of 'the self'.[3] This is not to justify racism or xenophobia, merely to suggest that the social construction of 'home' uses fears and passions that are deeply etched in human emotions and weaknesses. Of course, there are a number of immigrant societies (the USA, Canada, Australia and Brazil among them) where an official ideology has been advanced that a new national identity can be forged with people of diverse origins. However, even these societies rarely escape periodic outbursts of nativism and display imperfect social integration.

Just as the evocation of 'homeland' is used as a means of exclusion, so the excluded may see having a land of their own as a deliverance from their travails in foreign lands: a homeland acquires a soteriological and sacred quality. In the opening chapter of this book I suggested that key feature of many diasporas is the idealization of the real or putative ancestral home and a collective commitment to its maintenance, restoration, safety and prosperity, even to its creation. In this chapter, I want to focus on two cases – one where a homeland was reinvented and recovered and another where it was invented, but failed to materialize. In the first example I continue the story started in Chapter 2 regarding the origins and character of the Jewish diaspora by examining its relationship to the state of Israel, now 60 years' old. I also expose the arguments of the 'post-Zionists' in the diaspora who reject the territorialization of Jewish identity. In the second case, the one that failed to reconstitute an independent homeland, I show how some Sikhs' ambition to create 'Khalistan' emerged both as a solution to oppression within India and as a response to demands in the Sikh diaspora.

BIRTH TRAUMAS: CAN ISRAEL BE A 'NORMAL' STATE?

The defining characteristics of the Jewish diaspora and the Zionists' dreams of a state of their own have been discussed in Chapter 2. Here I want to look at the special peculiarities that marked the creation of Israel, before turning to the reactions to this momentous event in the diaspora. Israeli politicians and Zionists alike assume that the creation of the state of Israel in 1948 was the logical development of Jewish aspirations since the original dispersals. Zionists imagine a Golden Age when Kings Solomon and David ruled and the Jews were united and free from fear. The establishment of Israel was seen as a means of recovering a lost Eden, resolving the causes of anti-Semitism and re-territorializing Jewish identity – making of Jews a nation like other nations. However, despite the constant attempts on the part of its Zionist founders and successive Israeli governments to foster normality, the circumstances that surrounded the birth of the Israeli state were far from normal, as I can illustrate by making just four points:

1   The founders of the state of Israel were largely secular Jews from the Polish–Russian Pale who reflected simply one of four political trajectories commonly articulated there at the end of the last century: (a) to stay and fight for justice through social-democratic and revolutionary parties; (b) to migrate to other parts of Europe and the USA (by far the most popular option); (c) to abandon themselves to inward-looking religious reflection; and (d) to emigrate to Palestine. Although time has softened these profound and bitter divergences of opinion, ultra-Orthodox Jews, even in Israel, do not accept the state of Israel. They regard its secular character with loathing and refuse to serve in its army.

2   Perhaps the most controversial and difficult issue for Zionists to accept is that while the founding of the Israeli state provided a measure of justice to Jews, it occasioned serious injustices for Palestinians. The displacements of the Palestinians have caused endless recriminations and soul-searching among all Jews, but in terms of my present concern with 'normality', this was a less unusual feature of nation-state formation than is sometimes supposed. As we saw in Chapter 3, it happened thus in the First World War when the Turks displaced 1.75 million Armenians. It happened with the partition of India and Pakistan in 1947 and again in the 1980s in the former Yugoslavia and the former Soviet Union.[4]

3   Because the Israeli state was established in the harrowing aftermath of the Second World War as a homeland specifically for Jews (and no others), it adopted a descent-based definition of citizenship, *jus sanguinis*, which had embarrassing similarities with the notions proposed by the Nazis. All immigrant Jews were given immediate recognition under the 'Law of Return', while resident Palestinians were only grudgingly and slowly given civic rights. As Haim Cohen, a former Israeli Supreme Court judge, remarked: 'The bitter irony of fate has decreed that the same biological and racist arguments extended by the Nazis, and which inspired the inflammatory laws of Nuremberg, serve as the basis for the official definition of Jewishness in the bosom of the state of Israel.'[5]

4   Finally, although Israeli political leaders lay great emphasis on the sovereignty and independence of their state, it is unlikely that it could have thrived (perhaps it might have survived) without three external supports: (a) German war reparations paid in repentance of the holocaust; (b) huge sums of money from the Jewish diaspora for development projects; and (c) the diplomatic,

military and financial help of successive US governments, their attitudes influenced by an influential US Zionist lobby.

To make my normative position clear, I strongly assert that none of the four points together or separately constitute the basis for some naive, counterfactual speculation that the Israeli state should not exist. Without it, the remnants of the holocaust Jews and the refugees from intolerance and famine in Ethiopia, North Africa, Russia and many other places would have perished. Nonetheless, the particularities that marked the rebirth of the Jewish homeland go a long way towards providing an explanation of why, even after 60 years, its legitimacy continues to be questioned by the states and nations surrounding it. These birth traumas also clarify why the fervent yearning for 'normality', in effect a desire for full acceptance by other nation-states, is unlikely to be realized in the intermediate future. Rather, it seems likely that for other states in the Middle East and for many external observers, the Israeli state will be regarded as an anomalous and destabilizing force in the region for many years to come.

ISRAEL AND THE DIASPORA

Just as the re-creation of a Jewish homeland triggered a complex set of reactions within Israel and the Middle East, so the very fact of Israel's existence posed a challenge to Jews in the diaspora. 'It bestowed on them the freedom to choose between their countries of birth and their ancient homeland.'[6] Perhaps it would be better to say that the choice was between their countries of birth and a *reinvention* of their ancient homeland. To insist on this point is to flag up the whole range of existentialist, essentialist, theological, political, cultural and psychological questions that marked the responses in the diaspora to the foundation of the state of Israel.[7] To get some sense of the scale and distribution of the Jewish population worldwide, I include some indicative data in Table 6.1 below.

In all of these countries fierce debates occur around the key issues defining the relationship between Jewishess and Zionism, between the state of Israel and life in the diaspora. I will say something in turn about positions and groups I would characterize respectively as Zionists, patrons, zealots, the religious Reform group and assimilationists. The special situation of those who leave Israel will also be considered.

Zionists

Probably the most common response in the diaspora to the creation of Israel was a sense of pride and fulfilment, and perhaps a feeling of relief that the remnants of European Jewry had been saved. Prior to 1948, when all energies

Table 6.1 **The top twelve Jewish populations (latest estimates)**

Rank	Country	Number	Notes
1	USA	6,500,000	Exogamous marriage rates 52%. Ageing population, likely to decline markedly
2	Israel	4,950,000	Growing population through immigration and higher fertility than diasporic Jews
3	France	600,000	Alternative estimate, 750,000. French censuses do not use ethnic categories
4	Canada	364,000	
5	Britain	275,000	Exogamous marriage rates for men, 52%
6	Russia	275,000	Alternative estimate, 650,000. Emigration slowing as economy improves
7	Argentina	197,000	Alternative estimate, 250,000. Emigration slowing as economy improves
8	Ukraine	112,000	
9	Germany	98,000	Alternative estimate, 115,000. Significantly growing population
10	Brazil	97,500	
11	South Africa	88,000	Alternative estimate 65,000. Population declining due to emigration
12	Hungary	55,000	Alternative estimate, 100,000

Source: http://www.simpletoremember.com/vitals/world-jewish-population.htm#_ftn11, using a mixture of government statistics and figures generated by Jewish organizations (consulted 3 August 2007). Statistics generated by diasporic organizations tend toward greater inclusiveness and are probably exaggerated.

were focused on the consolidation of the Zionist project, there was no direct conflict of loyalty between the state of residence and the reinvented homeland. What, however, was the role of the Zionist movement in the period after 1948? Some leaders advocated a three-tiered structure – with the Israeli state at the top, Zionist organizations[8] in the middle and the Jewish masses at the bottom.

Israeli politicians, like Ben-Gurion, who sought to assert Israel's political primacy but not lose its sources of support in the diaspora, often endorsed this hierarchy of power. This proposed structure was not, however, without its problems. If Zionists in the diaspora were to defer to Israel, they were exposing themselves again to the charges of dual loyalty that marked the most corrosive forms of conflict between Jews and their host states. Again, Zionist organizations proclaimed a kind of Leninist conviction that they alone were fit enough and perceptive enough to lead the Jewish masses. Like those who were subjects of the dictatorship of the proletariat, most of the Jewish masses in the benign countries of settlement were not that convinced that they should be led by elite cadres.[9]

The most compelling demand made by the Zionists was that young people, or those with skills, should abandon their life in the diaspora, however easy or profitable, in favour of *aliya* ('going up' or voluntary migration) to the homeland. The youth movements were particularly audacious in their claims on youthful idealism. One movement (which I joined as an adolescent in South Africa in the 1950s) provided a curious blend of scouting *à la* Baden-Powell, Germanic rural heartiness, Marxism and strident Jewish nationalism. There was also a soupçon of Russian revolutionary 'free love', which proved a good stratagem for recruiting. The movement was wholly secular and barely tolerated religious Jews. Those who were accorded the highest status in the movement would be expected to join Kibbutz Tzorah, established by South African Zionists, to give unstintingly of their mental and manual labour.

Patrons and proto-Zionists

Unlike these youthful idealists, for many wealthy and powerful Jews in the diaspora, the politics of homeland was the politics of the cheque book, the Jewish National Fund and occasional tourism. Established dynasties, like the Rothschilds and Montefiores, were spectacularly generous in funding or endowing agricultural settlements, hospitals, urban developments, schools and universities. Education provided a particularly attractive target for donations, with a proliferation of buildings all scrupulously inscribed with the names of the benefactors. Sometimes the more attractive veil of philanthropy covered a rather seedy past in profiting from prohibition or trading in arms.

The 'big givers' were, however, also followed by hundreds of thousands of those who responded to particular campaigns, bought trees for Israel ('to make the desert bloom again') or plopped notes, coins and cheques into the collection boxes dutifully taken around by volunteers. No doubt some of this group were committed Zionists who, perhaps through age or circumstance, felt unable to migrate to Israel. But the bulk of the 'small givers' were probably responding to a more diffuse set of moral imperatives. As in the case of the Armenians who survived the massacres (see Chapter 3), those who survived the holocaust often felt guilty and blemished because of their chance good fortune. One way of expiating this guilt while enjoying their material success and upward social mobility was to give generously to Israel. Besides, in the often tightly-knit Jewish diasporic communities it would attract disapprobation if one were not seen to be open-handed. This group, in short, comprised proto-Zionists, rather than Zionists proper. Their eyes did not burn with messianic zeal.

Zealots

Just such a description can be applied to my next category, the religious zealots. I have already mentioned the group that lived in Israel yet refused to recognize its secular state. For them, only the messiah could reunite the diaspora with its homeland. The secular Zionists who jumped the gun were to be despised rather than commended. Locked in little urban ghettos in Jerusalem, bent over the Talmud, the zealots emerged from time to time to stone women they thought improperly dressed or to turn back buses that ran on the Sabbath. As some of this group began to participate in Israeli politics, some kind of *modus vivendi* with the nation-state began to emerge.

This was to be ruptured by the arrival of new recruits from the American diaspora, zealots who combined their American love for big power politics with a chiliastic determination. The object of this was none other than the reinvention of a Greater Israel said to be sanctioned by biblical boundaries and including the area known as the West Bank (west of the Jordan River). The result was intractable contests of authority between the state authorities, who had finally conceded the need to accommodate some of the Palestinians' demands, and the new zealots – trying to create a reality on the ground by establishing settlements of their own. The construction of a 'barrier' or 'wall' (the term used is contested) to separate the West Bank settlers from their Palestinian neighbours and potential terrorists demonstrated how powerful a force this group had become in Israeli politics by the turn of the twenty-first century.

Religious reform groups

It is worth making clear that religious hostility to the state of Israel existed beyond the ranks of the ultra-Orthodox Jews. A Reform (namely liberal or progressive) rabbi, Elmer Berger, delivered a crucial speech in 1942 in which he provided an 'ideological platform' for a position that asserted that Judaism was by its nature anti-nationalist and had only survived because of its universal principles. These 'could be transmitted from country to country and era to era', while other peoples and nations disappeared from the face of the globe. He had little time for the Golden Age of Israel, regarding the much-lionized periods of Kings David and Solomon as marked by moral turpitude rather than spiritual achievement. He bluntly maintained that the Zionists had sanctioned and perpetuated racist and fascist theories that wrongly claimed Jews had no place outside a homeland.[10]

The Reform groups, on the contrary, vigorously asserted that it was possible and necessary for a viable, creative and intellectually challenging life to exist outside the homeland. This involved the continued assertion of the universal principles of Judaism. In practice, the Reform groups developed a rather anodyne version of Judaism, with less emphasis on the prophetic parts of the Bible, less interest in following intricate religious observances and much more emphasis on 'fitting in' with neighbours and host societies. The general thrust of their position was to 'normalize' within the diaspora rather than return to the homeland and to become a model minority while still retaining the right to worship in their own way.

Assimilationists

Many Jews in the diaspora have, of course, gone much further than the Reform Jews – having abandoned Judaism, or indeed any religion. Even a loose connection with their ethnic background and history is slowly beginning to erode. This phenomenon has been particularly pronounced in France, the UK and the USA, which together contain more than half the world's Jews outside Israel. By the 1980s 40 per cent of UK Jews were marrying exogamously – a key indicator of assimilation. In the USA, the 1991 National Jewish Population Survey concluded that more than half the country's young Jews were marrying Gentiles, while only a small proportion of their spouses were converting to Judaism. Again, by the mid-1990s, 'most alarmingly from the standpoint of community cohesion, only a minority of Jewish children live[d] in households where all the members are Jews'.[11]

The assimilationist position is especially damaging to the Zionist view of the diaspora because people are simply voting with their feet – and these are pointed towards the affluent suburbs in affluent countries, rather than in the direction of Jerusalem. As I made clear earlier, there have always been Jews who have been keen to escape the confines of their ethnicity and their religion. However, many of them consciously identified with a political struggle in their countries of settlement, which they saw as more salient to their lives than the assertion of their Jewish identity. A conspicuous minority among those who worked for revolution in Russia, for labour unions in New York, for the anti-apartheid movement in South Africa, or for progressive social movements in France were of Jewish descent.

What is more threatening in the current context is that Jewish identity is threatened not by a sense of rebellion, but by one of indifference. This is the obverse side of succeeding in a pluralist and tolerant society. As Waldinger recorded, the USA has been kind to the Jews – in the mid-1990s, 40 sat in Congress, and Jews formed a disproportionate part of the professoriate in the elite universities, a number of which were governed by Jewish presidents. These same institutions excluded Jews only two generations earlier. Of the 400 richest Americans, 25 per cent were Jewish, while the group's income was twice that of the national average.[12] Political participation, professional prowess and personal property may not be everything, but they do attest that, in the more favoured parts of the diaspora, life for assimilated Jews is more fulfilling than the Zionists assumed was possible.

The post-Zionists

In a number of seminal publications, written separately and together, Daniel Boyarin and Jonathan Boyarin have mapped out the terrain of a post-Zionist Jewish identity.[13] They start with the telling, if somewhat Talmudic, point that a Jewish culture was initially constructed in the diaspora. Abraham, supposedly the first Jew, had to *leave* his native land to find the Promised Land. The land of Israel was *not* therefore the birthplace of the Jewish people. This observation provides the starting point for an alternative rendering of Jewish history and, in particular, the suggestion that one of its most enduring characteristics is 'the impossibility of a natural association between this people and a particular land – thus the impossibility of seeing Jewish culture as a self-enclosed, bounded phenomenon'.[14]

Despite all the dangers of antagonizing the host societies in which they find themselves, the Jewish diaspora tradition must, the Boyarins proclaim, continue to insist on the respect for difference within 'a world grown thoroughly and inextricably interdependent'.[15] Jewish identity can never anchor itself in a self-satisfied resting place, or manifest itself as a form of nativism; it has to find expression through a perpetual, creative diasporic tension. The Boyarins find in this deterritorialized notion of Jewish identity a new idea as powerful as the Jews' contribution to the notion of monotheism. This idea is simply that *peoples and homelands are not necessarily and organically linked.*

In rather evangelical terms they aver that if this message is understood it could help prevent the bloodshed produced by the ethno-nationalist struggles of recent years. They even proclaim that far from the Israeli state being hegemonic over the rest of Jewry (as the Zionists demanded), Israel should reimport a diasporic consciousness. This would mean that the Israelis would understand that the *bona fide* Jewish tradition requires sharing space with others, that there needs to be a complete separation of religion from state, that the Law of Return needs to be revoked and that they should seek to build a multinational and multicultural society. Thus the wheel comes full cycle.

Yordim, *sabras* and transnationals

Zionists assumed that the migratory flow would be unidirectional, from the diaspora to the homeland. It was therefore particularly galling that there were some who wished to leave Israel. Return migration has proved especially painful for those who have once gone on *aliya*, but have now returned to the *golah*. This group is pejoratively known as *yordim*.[16] The Zionists argue that while life in Israel is one of normality, health and independence, life in the diaspora is neurotic, deficient and schizophrenic. Shusterman provides an instructive account of the philosophical journeys paralleling his decision to return to the USA after 20 years in Israel. As with many other writers, he associates the creation of the nation-state with modernity and suggests that the Zionists have grafted onto this coupling the idea of normality:

> We find in all these premises a modernist faith and privileging of the normal, the autonomous the essential and the authentic. Not surprisingly, the radical Zionism these premises support – that only life in Israel can be fully and authentically Jewish, can definitively and

decisively resolve our problems of Jewish identity and unity – is a very modernist view. It is one guided by a goal of stable unity and definitive closure with the final return of all Jews to Israel.[17]

In the only book-length study of the Israeli diaspora Gold argues that we need a threefold understanding of Israeli migration. Many of his subjects do indeed accept that life outside Israel is ultimately intolerable and see themselves as sojourners who have been unfortunately, but temporarily, displaced. A second group, who conform to more general patterns of migration, have simply left Israel for personal, professional or economic reasons and do not particularly engage in speculation about their status as *yordim*. In particular, those who were born in Israel, the *sabras*,[18] often study, work and live abroad without the self consciousness often found in Jews born in a diasporic context. A third and final group are transnationalists, whose migration is to be understood as conforming to the increasing globalization of information, economic, cultural and migration flows. This group optimizes 'freedom and opportunity by retaining links to multiple national settings' including, of course, Israel.[19]

THE ORIGINS OF THE SIKH DIASPORA

I turn now to my second case. Like the Jews, the Sikhs are ambiguously a nation, a people, an ethnic group and a religious community. The religion was founded by Guru Nanak (1469–1539) in the Punjab area of north India. Under his leadership, and that of the following nine gurus, a distinctive religious community emerged. Its theology was syncretic, drawing freely from its parent religions, Islam and Hinduism, but in the process many elements were jettisoned. Caste, for example, was effectively abolished. The extent of egalitarian relations between all Sikhs, men and women, is also notable, but so too is the masculine, militaristic ideology of Sikhism. This last feature seems to have arisen from the forcible conversion to Sikhism of another Punjabi-speaking people, the Jats, over the period 1563–1606.

Apparently, the guru at the time, Arjun Dev, thought that proselytizing was best done in the form of a holy war. From this experience emerged the central Sikh ideal of a soldier-saint, a concept not unlike that of a Christian crusader. Collectively, the soldier-saints were enjoined to form a brotherhood (no sisters here) to advance the cause of Sikhdom. The brotherhood was called the *Khalsa*. (The imagined homeland of the Sikhs was later to be named Khalistan.) As with the *Khalsa* itself, Sikhs are rather fond of naming their icons with an initial 'K'. Uncut hair, curled under a turban, is called *kes*. Other symbols of difference include an iron bracelet, worn on the right wrist (*karha*), a ceremonial sword (*kirpan*), a comb in the hair (*kangha*) and rather unusual breeches (*kachha*). Other groups lived in the Punjab and also spoke Punjabi,[20] so the adoption of the five Ks, as they are known, is best understood as a form of 'social marker', forcing recognition of difference from non-Sikhs as well as affirming a sense of community among Sikhs themselves.

At the political level a complex set of localized loyalties were welded together under the leadership of Maharajah Ranjit Singh, who died in 1839 after 40 years on the throne. In his well-known history of the Sikhs, Khushwant Singh described the Punjab at that time as 'one of the most powerful states in Asia'.[21] The Punjabis controlled the fate of the Afghan throne, contained the Chinese in Tibet and stopped British expansion from the southwest. The crucial strategic importance of the Punjab was well understood by all the principal players. Cut off by the Himalayas to the northeast, the Punjab valleys were the crucial axial point between central Asia and Hindustan. Later the Russians also sought to penetrate the area. Kipling's famous novel *Kim* tells the story of how an abandoned Anglo-Indian boy was trained to become a secret agent to spy on Britain's enemies in the Punjab.

I divert. The narrative needs to recommence with the decline of the Punjab state in the period after 1839. The struggles over Ranjit Singh's succession were chaotic – with misfortune, miscalculation, venality and brutality (one maharajah was manually disembowelled by his rival) seriously weakening the political and military capacities of the Punjabis. The British spotted their opportunity. They invaded in 1845, and four years later the Punjab was theirs. The very suddenness of the collapse – from kingpins to underdogs in a decade – led to a fabulation and reconstruction of the Ranjit Singh period as a golden age. The lustre assigned to his rule has been further burnished by time and distance. Then, so the legends state, all Sikhs were united and powerful. Then, their ideal of the soldier-saint was consummated.

On this occasion the British had the sense not to throw sand into Punjabi faces. They demilitarized the Punjab, restored law and order, stimulated agriculture and favoured the Sikhs for employment, particularly in the army.[22] In the Sepoy Mutiny of 1857,[23] when the rest of northern India turned on the government, the Sikhs sided with the British. As one British governor-general remarked, the future of the Sikhs 'was merged with that of the British Empire in India'.[24] Though the British administrators made a positive economic contribution, the distinctive cultural and religious identity of the Sikhs began to erode. That gentle but omnivorous religion, Hinduism, began to reassert itself, while the disbanded Khalsa soldiery became dacoits engaged in 'thuggeeism' (from which the English word 'thug' was derived). One of Ranjit Singh's sons, the five-year-old Duleep Singh, who had been officially proclaimed Maharaja in 1843, was dispatched to a sad exile in Britain. He was educated in Scotland, became a Christian and was given a sufficient allowance to set up as a Norfolk country squire. However, his past never quite left him. In a long letter to *The Times* in 1882 he denounced British rule in the Punjab and rediscovered his Sikh faith. Denied the right to return to the Punjab, he was arrested in Aden and exiled to Paris, where he died in 1893.[25]

As to the soldiers recruited, the British colonial army provided a window of opportunity to serve and sometimes to stay in various parts of the empire. Malaya was one of the first ports of call for Sikh soldiers; then they found their way to Fiji, New Zealand, Australia and Canada. In the Canadian case, a detachment of Sikh soldiers returning indirectly to the Punjab from Queen Victoria's jubilee in 1897 landed in British Columbia. These soldiers spread the word to the rural districts of the Punjab that there were opportunities for agricultural workers on the railways and in the lumber mills. In response, 5,000 Sikhs arrived in Canada between 1904 and 1907.[26] Although Sikhs, as equal subjects of the king, were technically free to migrate anywhere in the empire, racists in Australasia and Canada soon made their lives hell. They succeeded in halting immigration from Asia by deploying popular prejudices and mobilizing white opinion against the newcomers. One popular song in British Columbia ended with this chorus:

> Then let us stand united all
> And show our fathers' might,
> That won the home we call our own,
> For white man's land we fight.
> To oriental grasp and greed
> We'll surrender, no never.
> Our watchword be 'God save the king'
> White Canada for ever.[27]

Despite this campaign of hatred, Sikhs excluded from Canada found their way to the USA and to other parts of the British Empire, including the metropolis itself. Although the bulk of the movement to Britain was after 1960, even in the 1920s and 1930s Sikhs were evident in the Midlands, Glasgow, Peterborough and London in the role of door-to-door sellers of hosiery, knitwear and woollens.[28] The number and global distribution of the Sikh diaspora in 2005 is listed in Table 6.2.

SIKHS: THE LURE OF HOMELAND

The loyalty of the Sikhs to the British Empire was poorly rewarded. Not only did they have to suffer immigration restrictions, the 100,000 troops in the First World War were paid less than British servicemen and were restricted in their duties. British privates sometimes did not salute their superior Sikh officers, which caused great offence. These insults did not prevent the Sikhs winning a hugely disproportionate number of awards for gallantry in the field. The Sikh veneration for honour required no less.

To the racism of the white dominions and the battlefields was added another grievance – repression in the Punjab. Returning soldiers are nearly always

Table 6.2 **The Sikh diaspora, by country of residence, 2005**

Place	Date of arrival	Population
Europe		
United Kingdom	1960–	336,179
Denmark	1981–	2,000
Germany	1981	25,000
France	1982–	2500–3000
Belgium	1984–	3500–5000
Netherlands	1984–	1500–2000
Americas		
Canada	1905–13	7500–10,000
	1960–90s	100,000–125,000
USA	1905–13	7500–10,000
	1960–80s	100,000–125,000
Mexico	1930–	1000–1500
Argentina	1950s	500–2000
The Far East		
Malaysia	1865–1940	30,000–45,000
Singapore	1865–1940	25,000–30,000
Australia	1890–1910	5000–7500
New Zealand	1890–1910	2000–3000
Fiji	1890–1910	1200–2500
Philippines	1910–30	2000–5000
Thailand	1920–40	2500–5000
The Near East		
Afghanistan	1900–30	2000–2500
United Arab Emirates	1970–80	10,000–25,000
Iraq	1970–80	7000–10,000

Source: Gurharpal Singh and Darshan Singh Tatla, *Sikhs in Britain: the making of a community* (London: Zed Books, 2006) p. 32; Darshan Singh Tatla, *The Sikh diaspora: the search for statehood* (London: UCL Press, 1999) pp. 42–3 citing a wide variety of data collected over the period 1969–88.

a force for radicalism. Coming home after arduous and dangerous service, they are confronted with the contrast between the high ideals used to build fighting morale and the realities back home. Thus it was with the Sikh heroes of 1914–18. They found the revolutionary Ghadrite movement (acting partly in sympathy with the Bolsheviks) had been ruthlessly suppressed; the summer monsoon had failed; new taxes had been imposed; while a virulent strain of influenza had wiped out 100,000 people.

On 13 April 1919, at Amritsar, six people were killed and 30 wounded after peaceful protests. The mob turned on the British banks and the Christian clergymen who had been trying to proselytize in the area. The killing of five Englishmen and an assault on a missionary provoked the British to a frenzied response. They surrounded a large crowd near the Golden Temple and opened fire without provocation, killing 379 and wounding over 2,000 people.

The Amritsar massacre is probably the most notorious act of colonial oppression in any part of the British Empire. The rage of the Sikhs was augmented by the horror felt all over India at this attack on unarmed civilians. An all-India nationalist, rather than sectarian, consciousness was the primary reaction to Amritsar, but the event also marked the reawakening of Sikh political activism and religious enthusiasm. The old litany *rāj karey gā Khalsa* (the Khalsa shall rule) was loudly proclaimed again. As it became evident that the British would have to go, Sikhs reasserted their historic 'right' to rule the Punjab, even though they constituted a minority within the area. The demand for a Sikh state paralleled Muslim calls for a separate Pakistan. The entreaties of the Sikhs were successfully resisted by the powerful and popular Indian nationalist party, known in short as 'Congress', which feared that irredentism, secession and separatism would fragment the unity of the anti-colonial struggle.

In the Sikh diaspora, the post-1948 disposition was, however, rarely accepted without demur. Many Sikh community associations were absorbed in the politics of their host societies, forming self-help groups and seeking forms of political representation, often in alliance with other Indian groups. Nevertheless, the politics of the Punjab were never far away. In addition to the Congress Party, the Akali Dal and various communist bodies all had close allies in the diaspora. In particular, the Akali Dal took on the role of articulating the idea of a separate Sikh identity, though, unlike the Khalsa and temple management organizations, Akali supporters were often turbanless and clean-shaven secular leaders. The Akali Dal developed effective and well-supported organizations in Britain, Canada and the USA, which kept in touch with one another as well as with the Punjab. The International Golden Temple Organization was set up to collect money for the central shrine of Sikh belief, while a World Sikh Festival was held in 1982. These connections provide further evidence of one of the features of all diasporas, namely the social construction of a sense of empathy and solidarity with co-ethnic members in other countries of settlement.

The expressed need for a separate Sikh homeland was notably articulated in the 1950s and 1960s by a former finance minister of the Punjab government, Jagjit Singh Chohan, who raised the issue of a Sikh homeland in Britain, Canada and the USA.[29] He also placed a half-page advertisement in the *New York Times* (12 October 1971) claiming that the Sikhs had been misled at the time of independence:

> At the time of the partition of the Indian subcontinent in 1947 it was agreed that the Sikhs shall have an area in which they will have complete freedom to shape their lives according to their beliefs. On the basis of the assurances received, the Sikhs agreed to throw their lot with

India, hoping for the fulfilment of their dream of an independent, sovereign Sikh homeland, the Punjab.

In fact a few of the supporters of a Sikh homeland had already begun using the expression 'Khalistan' rather than 'Punjab' as their rallying cry. A consul-general's office for the non-existent republic of Khalistan was set up in Canada, while a monthly magazine, *Babbar Khalsa*, was issued alongside a Khalistani passport and Khalsa currency. The lure of a homeland was that it appeared to offer an escape from what was represented as Hindu domination. In one supporting magazine in Britain the author implored Sikhs to

> realize that there is no future for them in an India dominated by Hindus. The honour and prestige of the community cannot be maintained without state power. The sooner we realize this challenge the better it will be to set up our objective of establishing a sovereign Sikh state in the Punjab. We cannot keep ourselves in bondage for ever. Our leaders are like beggars in New Delhi asking for this or that.[30]

The movement for Sikh autonomy or for a separate homeland might have slowly dissipated but for the storming of the Golden Temple in July 1984 by Indian security forces. The temple is not only the highest seat of religious and temporal authority for the Sikhs (analogous to the significance of St Peter's for Catholics) it also was the symbolic centre of a world without boundaries. Unlike the overseas Chinese or caste Hindus, who attracted a high level of disapprobation for leaving their homeland, Sikhs 'suffered no loss of rank or merit from travel overseas'.[31] Sikhs could constitute themselves as a viable congregation wherever there were five worthy members, but the Golden Temple none the less retained its importance as a site for pilgrimage and a home for the *Akal Takhat* (the 'throne' of the Sikhs), an artefact that was destroyed by the Indian army in 1984.

What precipitated this extraordinary event? By early 1984 Sikh separatist unrest had led to a severe clampdown by the Indian government and the declaration of emergency rule. After the separatists were said to have stockpiled arms in the complex of the Golden Temple, Delhi sent in troops. They killed the leading Sikh militant and about 700 of his followers. The horrors did not stop there. Three months later Prime Minister Indira Gandhi was assassinated by two of her hitherto utterly loyal Sikh bodyguards. The bond of trust between Hindus and Sikhs had snapped.[32] Some 2,000 Sikhs were killed in communal riots and Sikhs responded by terrorism and violence, adding several thousand more to the casualties.

Sikhs in the diaspora were not slow to pour gasoline on the flames. The most notorious episode, which was blamed on Canadian Sikh extremists, was the crash of an Air India plane off the Irish coast on 23 June 1985, killing its entire complement of 329 passengers and crew. Members of the Babbar Khalsa in Canada were immediately arrested, but suspicion soon fell on one Inderjit Singh Reyat, who was extradited from Coventry to Vancouver where he was convicted of placing bombs at the Narita airport in Japan and on the fateful Air India plane.

The more constitutional Sikh parties and associations desperately tried to distance themselves from terrorism and managed to win some political support in Canada, the USA and Britain. The World Sikh Organization and the International Sikh Youth Federation, in particular, mobilized tens of thousands of Sikhs in peaceful demonstrations for an independent Sikh state. New organizations, like the Khalistan Council, sprang into being and there was a general shift to the youth and the militants in the *gurdwara* (temple) management committees and political associations. In the wake of the storming of the Golden Temple, the editor of a New York publication *Sikh News* made a suggestive comparison between the Sikh, Jewish and Palestinian diasporas. All three, he argued, were subject to oppression and injustice (in my terms they were 'victim diasporas'), but

> the Jews have transformed their dreams into a reality. The Palestinians' cause, though equally just, has been poorly served ... Now the question arises, 'How do the Sikhs appear to the world?' The Indian government would like nothing better that the international community should brand us 'terrorists'. The Sikh nation's cause has to be fought simultaneously on three fronts: (a) the hearts and minds of our people; (b) the international community; and (c) the Indian government. Are we like the Jews struggling to right a momentous wrong or like the Palestinians with little sense of their past, a chaotic present and little hope for the future? If the shoe fits, wear it.[33]

Though this is a cruel outline of the Palestinian struggle, the author captures the sense of incoherence in Sikh responses to the events of 1984. The reactions in the diaspora were ones of shock, fury and outrage, but they lacked a clear focus or any inspired leadership from the Punjab. The Sikhs in India began to disintegrate into rival factions. In particular, the urban-based Delhi intellectuals distanced themselves from the 'dung-heap' politicians in the Punjab. In one notable *volte face*, the historian Khushwant Singh denounced the continuing militancy in the Punjab as 'thuggery' and condemned the assassination of Indira Gandhi.[34] In the first (1977) edition of his *History of the Sikhs* he had insisted that 'the only chance of survival of the Sikhs as a separate community is to create a state in which they form a compact group, where the teaching of Gurmukhi and the Sikh religion is compulsory, and where there is an atmosphere of respect for the tradition of their Khalsa forefathers'. In marked contrast, the 1991 edition denounced the 'lumpen sections of Sikh society mindlessly propelled by the Khalsa death wish'. His other statements on self-determination had also been toned down and sanitized.[35]

'Amritsar' has come to haunt the Sikhs, first because of the events in 1919, then in 1984. The dream of an independent homeland is structured around those two dates, which have provoked determined resilience as well as a sense of despair. For the foreseeable future, advancing the Sikh claim for a nation-state looks unlikely to bear fruit. But memories are long and the desire for this expression of modernity and territoriality is great. It is possible, as is suggested below, that with the general deterritorialization of all social identities, Sikhs may find they are able to develop functional diaspora-wide alternatives to a state. Though probably supported by the majority of the Sikh diaspora, this solution is unlikely to have much appeal to the die-hards who continue to nurse their grievances and bitterly resent the failure of their cause.

CONCLUSION

I have suggested in this chapter that the relationship of the diaspora to the homeland is both complicated and fraught. That relationship is represented by nationalists (in our case studies of the Zionist and Khalistani movements) as basically unproblematic. Nobody of course imagines it is easy to create or reinvent a homeland – international support, armed intervention, a propaganda war and community mobilization – are accepted as necessary parts of a successful attempt to do so. But nationalists implausibly believe that once their goal has been attained all will be well.

Of course this is far from the truth. The manner and consequences of achieving statehood may be complex and controversial. For example, if terror accompanies the struggle for statehood (as it did with the Stern gang in Palestine and the Babber Khalsa in Canada) this cannot but mark the character of the state. If Khalistan were ever established, it would face an identical dilemma, with respect to the people already living there, as the one that faced the neophyte state of Israel. What would happen to the 65 per cent of the population of the Punjab who are *not* Sikhs? Given that there are no 'empty lands' left in the world, can statehood for one people ever be achieved without perpetrating injustice to other ethnicities, thus bringing into being new victim diasporas with new grievances.

One unacknowledged problem for the nationalists is that contemporary demands for statehood are essentially anachronistic. To demonstrate this we need for a moment to return to the crucial historical conjuncture when the nation-state emerged. Jacobson puts forward a compelling argument that the idea of a deterritorialized universal (Catholic) Church was 'flattened' by the rise of Protestantism.[36] This placed a premium on the linking of specific nations, affiliated with distinct churches, to demarcated lands – thus the emergence of designations like the Church of Wales, Church of Ireland, Church of Scotland, Church of England or Dutch Reformed Church. This nationalization of the church was reinforced by economic and ideological imperatives.

One often-cited writer, Nairn, has traced the origins of the nation-state to the development of a successful bourgeoisie and active intelligentsia seeking to reconcile their relative political weaknesses with their relative economic power.[37]

This potent vinculum between territory, polity, economy, ideology and religion was historically far more delimited than most nationalists concede. This is not to say that there are not other historical conjunctures that give rise to nationalism, such as an anti-colonial struggle or the implosion of an empire, though these circumstances are rarely as propitious. It is true, for example, that there is a proliferation of internationally recognized nation-states: nearly four times the number that comprised the United Nations membership in 1945. Yet many of these are flag-and-postage-stamp states with no prospect of wielding international influence or, in some cases, effectively governing their populations. Irredentism and ethnic conflict are common.

Brutal as it is to say this of the Khalistanis, they may have boarded the historical train too late. In the Israeli case, the quest for national sovereignty was driven through *against* the tide of history, and the ideological and practical penalties for establishing a nation-state without the favourable nexus mentioned earlier are still onerous burdens. Sixty years after its establishment, the Israeli state continues to struggle for legitimacy. Equally, the Jewish diaspora is hopelessly fragmented in its attitudes to the homeland. While the Zionists occupy many public platforms, the extent of indifference, challenge or hostility to their position is often underestimated. Though, at the moment, the post-Zionist position is barely known, its protagonists are probably articulating the wave of the future. In short, the endless quest and bitterly-fought campaigns for statehood may be like trying to imprison the butterfly of ethnic identity in too small a net with too dense a mesh. Perhaps the butterfly should be permitted to fly in its own direction at its own whim?

FURTHER READING

- A book focusing partly on the mobilization of Sikhs to create a state is Darshan Singh Tatla's *The Sikh diaspora: the search for statehood* (London: UCL Press, 1999), while an excellent study of one community is provided by Gurharpal Singh and Darshan Singh Tatla in *Sikhs in Britain: the making of a community* (London: Zed Books, 2006).
- Two recent accounts of Israeli–diaspora relations can be found in David J. Goldberg, *The divided self: Israel and the Jewish psyche today* (London: I.B.Tauris, 2006) and Edward Alexander and Paul Bogdanor (eds) *The Jewish divide over Israel: accusers and defenders* (New Jersey: Transaction Publishers, 2006). The latter is focused on the left intelligentsia in the diaspora.

- André Levy and Alex Weingrod (eds) *Homelands and diasporas: holy lands and other spaces* (Stanford: Stanford University Press, 2004) provide an informative set of case studies that usefully supplement and extend the two cases discussed in this chapter.

QUESTIONS TO THINK ABOUT

- Is the idea of homeland intrinsic to the idea of diaspora? Taking cases of other diasporas not discussed in this chapter suggest why the lure of homeland attracts so many diasporic organizations?
- What are the main problems affecting the relationship between Jews in the diaspora and the Israeli state?
- Why did the attempt to create Khalistan fail? Compare the Sikh case with other examples of a failed or imperfectly-achieved homeland project.

Figure 7.1 A Caribbean man looks out on the 'Black Atlantic'. As ideas, people and popular culture criss-crossed between Africa, the Americas and Europe a fluid, deterritorialized diaspora has emerged. © iStockphoto.com/Robin Cohen

7

DETERRITORIALIZED
DIASPORAS

The black Atlantic and the lure of Bombay

Throughout my account I have suggested that ethnicities and homelands have to be considered as multifaceted, historically contingent and socially constructed entities. In the case of Jews, Parsis, Sindhis and Sikhs, for example, it is unclear to what extent their religions, historical experiences or assumed common ancestries jointly or separately are mobilized to determine their collective identities over time. There also may be wide differences between self-descriptions (the emic dimension) and characterizations by outside observers (the etic dimension). This is true too of homelands or the looser idea of home. As we saw in Chapter 3, for Africans of the 'first diaspora', home was Guinea, Freetown, Liberia or the emblematic idea of Ethiopia. Now 'new' African diasporas are more likely to identify with their post-colonial independent states – like Nigeria, Ghana or Zimbabwe.

Despite acknowledging the many ambiguities surrounding the notions of ethnicity and home, in some cases we need to slacken these vital moorings of the concept of diaspora even further – seeing collective identities and homelands/homes as a fluid, vibrant and frequently changing set of cultural interactions. The need to do this arises for three reasons:

1. Patterns of international migration that once would be assumed to be merely unidirectional – 'migration to' – are being replaced by asynchronous, transversal, oscillating flows that involve visiting, studying, seasonal work, temporary contracts, tourism and sojourning, rather than whole-family migration, permanent settlement and the adoption of exclusive citizenships.[1]
2. Diasporas are often formed not only by one traumatic event (the marker of a victim diaspora), but by many and different causes, several only becoming salient over an extended historical period. This can lead to double or multiple displacements and in atypical cases to a 'travelling culture'.[2]
3. Events in the homeland can take such an adverse turn that new centres of belonging can emerge – in effect one or more sites in the diaspora can materialize as functional equivalents of the original homeland.

How then do we loosen the historical meanings of the notion of 'diaspora' to encompass new forms of mobility and displacement and the construction of new identities and subjectivities? I propose we adopt the expression 'deterritorialized diaspora' to encompass the lineaments of a number of unusual diasporic experiences.[3] In these instances ethnic groups can be thought of as having lost their conventional territorial reference points, to have become in effect mobile and multi-located cultures.

It is easy enough to think of some population groups that might qualify as travelling cultures on the grounds that they have always had a wandering character – the Tuaregs, Bedouins, San, Qashqa'i, Maasai and Berbers come readily to mind. However, if home has always been on the move, it is doubtful that the word 'diaspora' can add anything useful to the expression 'nomad', other than providing a novel label. A much more intriguing example is the case of the Roma (popularly known as Gypsies), who have a narrative of ethnogenesis in India, but have lost any sustained connection with the Indian sub-continent. Treating the Roma/Gypsies as a diaspora provides a stimulating challenge.[4] However, in this chapter I have selected migrants of African descent from the Caribbean as a paradigmatic case of a deterritorialized diaspora. I examine the fact and fortune of Caribbean emigrants in various destination countries and interrogate the shared experiences, intellectual and political visions, and religious movements that cement African–Caribbean cultural and migratory experiences. At much shorter length, I consider also the examples of Sindhis and Parsis, who perfectly demonstrate the argument that new centres of economic, cultural, social and religious identification can develop as the links to a homeland become more and more tenuous.

THE CARIBBEAN: MIGRATION AND DIASPORA

I turn now to my principal case study of a deterritorialized diaspora, the people of the Caribbean, at home and abroad. The main population of the area has been both multiply displaced and continues its migratory traditions – from Africa, within the Caribbean archipelago and to far beyond the region. The earliest settlers of the Caribbean, the Caribs and Arawaks, generally failed to survive the glories of Western civilization – nearly all died from conquest, overwork and disease.[5] Virtually everybody in the Caribbean came from somewhere else – the African slaves from West Africa, the white settlers, planters and administrators from Europe, the indentured workers from India and the traders from the Middle East. This does not, however, in and of itself disqualify any consideration given to the idea of a Caribbean diaspora, though settler and immigrant societies are normally conceived of as points of arrival, not departure, and sites of a renewed collectivity, not of dissolution, emigration and dispersion.

A stronger objection to the idea that the Caribbean peoples can form a diaspora (deterritorialized or not) is that they may be thought of as parts of other diasporas — notably the African victim diaspora, the Indian labour diaspora, various European imperial diasporas and the Lebanese trade diaspora. Again, surely it would conventionally be expected that, if they are free to remigrate, a significant proportion of any diasporic community should wish to return to their real or putative homeland. Yet, with the partial exception of the Europeans, Caribbean people of Indian and African origin have in recent years been notably disinterested in returning either to India or Africa.

Despite these considerable conceptual obstacles, Stuart Hall none the less is convinced that a distinctive Caribbean diasporic identity can be discerned. Caribbean identity, he argues, cannot be rendered simply as a transposition of an African identity to the New World because the rupture of slavery and the admixture of other migrants built into a Caribbean identity a sense of hybridity, diversity and difference.[6] Hall poses the question, 'What makes African–Caribbean people already people of a diaspora?' and answers as follows:

> Diaspora does not refer us to those scattered tribes whose identity can only be secured in relation to some sacred homeland to which they must at all costs return, even if it means pushing other people into the sea. This is the old, the imperializing, the hegemonizing form of 'ethnicity'. We have seen the fate of the people of Palestine at the hands of this backward conception of diaspora (and the complicity of the West with it). The diaspora experience as I intend it here is defined not by essence or purity, but by the recognition of a necessary heterogeneity and diversity; by a conception of identity which lives with and through, not despite, difference; by hybridity. Diaspora identities are those which are constantly producing and reproducing themselves anew, through transformation and difference.[7]

In this excerpt Hall is essentially concerned with the diasporic identity that Caribbean peoples created within the geographical bounds of the Caribbean. Another challenging question is the degree to which they affirm, reproduce and create a diasporic identity in the places to which they subsequently have moved. Before discussing this question, it is necessary to provide a quick brush-stroke picture of their migration history over the last century or so.

I have just mentioned that Indo-Caribbeans did not go back to India, while African–Caribbeans did not return to Africa. Strictly speaking, this was not always true. At the end of their periods of indenture about a quarter of the Indo-Caribbeans returned to India. In the African case, the British colonialists recruited a few dozen African–Caribbean train drivers for Nigeria, the French appointed an Antillean governor, Felix Eboué, in the Cameroons and a remarkable young psychiatrist, Frantz Fanon, who was later to become one of the most prominent of all third-world intellectuals, was assigned to the colonial medical service in Algeria. Some voluntary migration, including Garveyite and Rastafarian (see below) settlements, also occurred.

However, these were mere drops in the ocean of Caribbean people who decided to migrate to Panama, the USA and Europe. When Ferdinand de Lesseps, the famous Suez Canal maker, floated a new Panama Canal Company to link the Pacific Ocean to the Caribbean Sea, the Bourse went crazy with the prospects of great profits. In fact, the venture proved a long-drawn-out financial failure. The canal and railway works were dogged by mismanagement and the workers suffered greatly from malaria, snakebite, swamp fever, industrial accidents and bad treatment. The labour for this operation was drawn from many countries, but predominantly from Jamaica.

The African–Caribbean minority located in the strip of slums surrounding the Panama Canal Company area is descended from these workers. They have remained largely poor and underprivileged in the Panamanian context, with the key positions of authority and influence being occupied by Hispanics. Other small enclaves in Central America are drawn from Caribbean migrants brought there to establish banana plantations, or to undertake public works. Honduras and some small enclaves in Nicaragua and Guatemala (such as the charming Bay Islands) are inhabited by descendants of archipelago African–Caribbeans, often still fiercely resisting the abandonment of the English language, which they value as part of their diasporic identity. The main destinations of Caribbean emigrants are listed in Table 7.1.

AFRICAN–CARIBBEANS IN THE USA

As is shown in Table 7.1, the bulk of Caribbean emigrants went to the USA. They went in so many capacities that it would be impossible in this chapter to describe fully the Caribbean social structure in the USA.[8] Temporary contract

Table 7.1 **Caribbean peoples abroad, latest estimates in selected destinations**

Country	Number	Notes and source
USA		
Cubans	1,242,685	US Census 2000
Dominicans	764,945	Namely from the Dominican Republic. US Census 2000
Haitians	548,199	US Census 2000
Jamaicans	435,021	US Census 1990
UK	566,000	Approximate no. of 'black Caribbeans'. UK Census 2001
Netherlands	458,000	Approximate no. of Caribbean origin and descent. Estimate July 2006
Canada	415,334	Canadian census 2001
Panama	351,045	Estimated no. July 2006
France	337,006	French citizens from the Antilles. 1990

Source: CIA Yearbooks 2006, 2007; various official population censuses; Stephanie A. Condon and Philip E. Ogden, 'Questions of emigration, circulation and return: mobility between the French Caribbean and France', *International Journal of Population Geography*, vol. 2, 1996, p. 38.

workers cut cane in Florida; Cuban exiles went to Miami, Haitians often arrived as illegals or boat people; while many middle-class professional people from the Anglophone Caribbean occupied important roles in medicine, in teaching and in retail services. One of the oft-remarked on, but imperfectly researched, characteristics of the English-speaking Caribbean migrants in the USA is their extraordinary success and prominence, not only in the wider black community, but in American society more generally. Within some parts of the black community, Caribbean people are sometimes referred to, in a not entirely friendly way, as 'Jewmaicans'. The Caribbean community monopolizes the laundries, travel agents and hairdressing shops in several New York districts. Moreover, Caribbean people have played a prominent role in political activity – the Garveyite movement, the civil rights struggles and the Black Power Movement being the most notable.

AFRICAN–CARIBBEANS IN THE UK

In contrast to the USA, the fortunes of Caribbean migrants in Europe have been less happy. The possible explanations for this relative lack of success are complex: different groups may have gone to Europe, only largely unskilled positions were on offer there, and some migration (notably to the UK and the Netherlands) was 'panic migration' in response to impending immigration restrictions and without the networks of friends, relations and openings in business and education prefigured or prepared. A number of scholars, as well as Caribbean migrants, insist that the high levels of racial discrimination and disadvantage they experienced seriously jeopardized their chances of success.[9]

The bulk of Caribbean migration to the UK occurred in the 1950s, and came to a rapid halt in the early 1960s with the implementation of the Commonwealth Immigrants Act forbidding further unregulated migration. With the exception of 'the rush to beat the ban', the movement of migrants to the UK closely shadowed the ebbs and flows of the job vacancies.[10] Despite finding unskilled jobs, the early experiences of Caribbean people in the UK were often negative ones. They felt that their wartime loyalty had been unacknowledged and that they were treated as an unwelcome problem rather than as valued citizens of the empire coming to help the motherland. Besides this psychic shock of rejection, at a more practical level occupational mobility was limited, educational successes were meagre and the second generation showed high rates of crime and unemployment.

It is important, however, not be too mired in the negative images that both racists and anti-racists need for their respective political causes. British girls of African–Caribbean origin outperform both black and white British boys in school examinations. As in the USA, there is a disproportionately high representation of black athletes and sportspersons in the boxing ring, in track and field events, and in cricket and football.[11] African–Caribbeans are also well represented in broadcasting and in literary and artistic pursuits, especially the performing arts. Even though this is a somewhat backhanded compliment, the 1996 *British Crime Survey*, based on a sample of 10,000 people, showed that in the age group 16–29, whereas 43 per cent of whites claimed to have taken drugs, the figure for their African–Caribbean peer group was substantially lower, at 34 per cent.[12]

Perhaps more significant is that census data demonstrate that the level of ghettoization is low and has been falling since 1961. Using a sophisticated index of segregation, Peach illustrates that the levels of Caribbean segregation in London are about half those of African–Americans in New York. Moreover, only 3 per cent of the African–Caribbean population lived in 'enumeration districts' (the smallest census unit covering 700 people) in which they formed 30 per cent of the population or more. Taken together, these positive indicators may signify a first stage in a wider and deeper thrust to social mobility – in the third, if not the second, generation.[13]

CARIBBEAN PEOPLES IN THE NETHERLANDS AND FRANCE

The Netherlands received somewhat fewer Caribbean immigrants than the UK (Table 7.1). However, the numbers are much more significant when they are considered as a proportion of both the Dutch population and of the Caribbean source populations. Caribbean migrants arrived from all over the Dutch Antilles, but predominantly from the former Dutch colony of Suriname. So large was the departure that about half the population of Suriname was depleted. In that many people were persuaded to leave because of the prospect of independence with diminished Dutch support, the Surinamese in the Netherlands can be seen to fit into the category of 'panic migrants' mentioned earlier.

The Surinamese in the Netherlands divide, roughly equally, into two ethnic sections – Afro-Surinamese and Indo-Surinamese. The housing situation for many Surinamese is surprisingly favourable – their arrival in Amsterdam conveniently coincided with the abandonment of a 'white elephant' set of luxury apartments the local Dutch did not wish to inhabit. A comparative study of Caribbean migrants in Britain and the Netherlands yielded many similarities.[14] In another study, Cross maintains that exclusion on the grounds of culture, way of life or newness of incorporation is less salient than the class exclusion that arises from the collapse of blue-collar industries. In this respect, the cutting of welfare benefits in the UK in response to the ideology of neo-liberalism contrasts with the greater endurance of welfare provisions in the Netherlands. The circumstances of Caribbean migrants in the Netherlands may improve relatively given their more benign public provision.[15]

Caribbean migration to France arises in a different form from the cases just considered. The major source areas are the DOM (*départements d'outre-mer*) of Martinique and Guadeloupe. Because of the juridical status of the DOM as organic parts of France, migration to the continent is officially considered to be internal migration – simply as if one French citizen were to move from one mainland *département* to another. Of course it is important not to confuse formal rights with substance. Again, we notice a high predominance of unskilled, manual and public-sector jobs being held by people from the French Antilles, particularly in the 1970s. However, a significant white-collar salariat (for example in the banks and post office) has been recruited by the quasi-official labour agency in the islands. Because certification and formal qualifications are much more important in France than in either the UK or the Netherlands, French Antilleans with the requisite pieces of paper have been able to benefit from the strong meritocratic tradition.

Unlike the British Caribbean population, which has fallen, mainly due to retirement migration back to source countries, the French Caribbean population in the French mainland has moved from 165,945 in 1975, to 265,988 in 1982, to 337,006 in 1990.[16] Although it is difficult to track movements to and from the Caribbean, given that there are no immigration restrictions, Condon and Ogden find that return, circulatory and retirement migration are common, as are family visits and casual tourism. The younger generation of Antilleans living in France often talks of returning 'for their children's sake'. They place a high value on what they perceive to be their own culture, shared values and 'roots'.[17]

At a deeper level, French Antilleans have always shared a Faustian pact with the French state. Should they choose to abandon their Africanness and embrace mother France, they become French people, citizens, members of a world culture and civilization. Two possible consequences arise from this pact. The more positive is that the French live up to the revolutionary ideals of liberty, equality and fraternity. The most coherent defence of this position appears in Hintjens's iconoclastic book, in which she claims that decolonization is possible without formal statehood. She argues that in many cases decolonization can be seen as a form of denial, a shedding of the political and moral responsibilities of the colonial powers, an act of dismissal and disdain. For her, postcolonialism is also a political struggle for equality and recognition. It is even more potent if it can be deterritorialized and taken to the heart of the racist empires. The anti-colonial struggle, in short, is for equality within France.[18]

The more negative outcome, of course, would be if the path of assimilation were to turn out to be an illusion, a trap, ultimately a hoax. This would be the cruellest consequence of all – for the French Antilleans in continental France would become a liminal people, no longer able to express their distinctive ethnic identity or recover a sense of 'home'. Lodged in a state of limbo or liminality, they would experience a crisis of meaning, where institutions, values and norms dissolve and collapse. Their *communitas* would be reduced to a parody of the old ways and would be incapable of reconstituting itself in the new setting.[19]

THE BLACK ATLANTIC THESIS

Despite the different destinations and experiences of Caribbean migrants abroad, they remain an exemplary case of a deterritorialized diaspora. This arises first from their common history of forcible dispersion through the slave trade – still shared by virtually all people of African descent, despite their subsequent liberation, settlement and citizenship in the various countries of the New World and beyond. Partly, this is a matter of visibility. Unlike (say) in the cases of Jews or Armenians, where superficial disappearance is possible in Europe and North America if exogamy occurs, in the case of those of African descent skin colour normally remains a marker for two, three or more generations – despite exogamy. The deployment of skin colour in many societies as a signifier of status, power and opportunity, make it impossible for any people of African descent to avoid racial stigmatization. As one black British writer graphically puts it, 'our imaginations are conditioned by an enduring proximity to regimes of racial terror'.[20]

The most intellectually ambitious attempt to define a Caribbean deterritorialized diaspora is made by Paul Gilroy in *The black Atlantic*.[21] He strongly resists any attempt to hijack the experience of New World Africans to those particular to African–Americans, a tendency he found in some of the 'Afrocentric' positions of American black intellectuals. Rather, he sees the consciousness of the African diaspora as being formed in a complex cultural and social intermingling between Africa, Europe and the Americas. However, this does not lead to cultural uniformity, but rather to recognition of 'transnational and intercultural multiplicity'. Of course, some degree of unity must exist in the Atlantic Africans' diasporic culture for it to be deemed a shared impulse and form of consciousness. This emergent culture is characterized as 'the black Atlantic'. His major work (which needs much more exegesis than I have space to give it here) is also a comment on the nature of modernity, on the idea of a nationalism without a nation-state (or a territory), and on the idea of a 'double consciousness', prefigured in Hegelian phenomenology and expressed in the New World by the double heritage of Africa and Europe.[22]

How would we judge whether African–Caribbeans form a 'deterritorialized diaspora' and the key component of the black Atlantic? I would suggest that at least four elements should be present. First, there should be evidence of some cultural retention or affirmations of a primary origin in Africa. Second, there should be at least a symbolic interest in retaining links to Africa or the Caribbean. Third, there should be cultural artefacts, products and expressions that show shared concerns and cross influences between Africa, the Caribbean and the destination countries of Caribbean migrants. Fourth, and often forgotten in some intensely cerebral versions of diaspora, there should be indications that ordinary Caribbean peoples abroad – in their attitudes, migration patterns and social conduct – behave in ways consistent with the idea of a deterritorialized diaspora.

Retention and affirmations of an origin in Africa

With respect to the issue of cultural retentions, there are clear examples of an affirmation of Africa in the Maroon (runaway slave) communities of Jamaica, the Gullah islands (off Georgia) and the so-called 'Bush Negroes' of Suriname. Other, less dramatic, examples abound. Scores of anthropologists have minutely recorded everything from Santaria in Cuba, Shango in Trinidad and Candomblé in Brazil, Caribbean savings clubs, folklore, musical rhythm forms, popular art, cuisine and health practices.[23] This evidence of retention however, must not be narrowly understood as freezing African cultures in aspic. As with other migratory groups, New World Africans took the opportunity to throw off the shackles of their prior social constraints. Thus, the famous founding president of a free Haiti, Toussaint L'Ouverture, was as much Jacobin as African; while, arguably, during the Second World War the French Antilles were more loyal to the idea of the French nation than the metropolis itself. Equally, many Anglophone Caribbeans displayed a remarkable loyalty to Britain in both world wars and showed a fierce adherence to British educational, social and political institutions.[24] Using a reinterpretation of the work of W. E. B. Du Bois, Paul Gilroy supplies an insightful analysis of how African Americans and African–Caribbeans live within a 'double consciousness', stemming both from Africa and Europe.[25]

The links between Africa and New World Africans also took the form of literary, ideological and political movements. The African, African–American and African–Caribbean intelligentsia has long sought to define some cultural and historical continuity between Africans on the continent and in the diaspora. This movement has flowed in several directions. Kwame Nkrumah, the Ghanaian president, studied in a black university in the USA and articulated the ideas of an African personality and African unity. Léopold Senghor, the president of Senegal, advanced the idea of Négritude. The Trinidadian revolutionary intellectuals George Padmore and C. L. R. James were partly responsible for convening the watershed Manchester Conference of 1945, when the basic lines of struggle for African self-determination were articulated. In the case of the Francophone Caribbean, Aimé Césaire made his spiritual journey to Africa in *Return to my native land* (1956). He and other Caribbean leaders were also an important influence on Négritude and had a continuing dialogue with Africans and those of African descent in journals such as *Présence Africaine*.

Harney has ably analysed a number of literary figures from Trinidad whose works are imbricated in the evolution of a Caribbean diasporic consciousness. He shows how the creation of a postcolonial identity was the project of novelists Earl Lovelace and Michael Anthony. Valerie Belgrave and Willi Chen addressed the task of creating a new nationalism from Indo-, Sino- and Afro-Caribbean elements, while the writings of Samuel Selvon, Neil Bissoondath and V. S. Naipaul depicted the dilemmas of Caribbean migrants moving to Canada, Britain and the USA.[26]

Symbolic and vicarious links

Despite the small number of African–Caribbeans who actually returned to Africa, Caribbean visionaries were at the forefront of the Back-to-Africa movements and in the articulation of the idea of a common fate of African people at home and abroad. I have discussed the Garveyite and Ethiopian/Rastafarian movements in Chapter 3. Here I will simply add some details of how these movements served to link the different points of the Caribbean deterritorialized diaspora.

The most flamboyant, and immensely popular, of New World return movements was the Universal Negro Improvement Association (UNIA), founded by the Jamaican, Marcus Garvey. Garveyites were particularly strong in the USA, and representatives of small but ill-fated colonies were sent to Liberia and elsewhere on the continent. Garvey was born in Jamaica in 1887 and had travelled widely in the West Indies and Central America before starting the UNIA. He drew his inspiration from two main strands – the Maroon revolts, which showed even in the New World, and even after the experience of the Middle Passage and slavery, that blacks could still recover some of their African traditions. (He was also very influenced by the strength of the British imperial idea that people could bluff their way to political dominance by style, appearance and a belief in their own superiority.)

He was particularly unimpressed by what he found in the USA. He saw poor blacks beating their heads against brick wall situations in which they would never be accepted. This experience provided Garvey with the idea of setting up the Black Star Line, a shipping company owned by blacks with the intention literally of reversing the transatlantic slave trade. Though the line was never a great success, when Kwame Nkrumah came to power in Ghana, he adopted it as the name of Ghana's merchant marine.

Although Garvey had returned to Jamaica, with the exception of one large UNIA rally and a convention in Kingston in 1928, he was largely unsuccessful as a politician. He died in obscurity in London in 1940, but he had succeeded in further promoting the consciousness of Africa that had been well developed in Jamaica since the days of the Maroons. The deep spirituality that converted Christian Jamaicans, also enhanced the cultural link with Africa. They found in the Bible identification with the ancient Jews. Like the Jews who were dragged off to Egypt and Babylon to slavery, the Africans had been dragged off to the West Indies as slaves.

This biblical and African consciousness became fused together in November 1930, when a new prince, Ras Tafari, was crowned Emperor of Ethiopia and adopted the name Haile Selassie. Some poor, particularly rural, Jamaicans began to describe themselves as 'Ethiopians', or followers of the crowned prince Ras Tafari, namely Rastafarians. The emperor claimed descent from Solomon and Sheba, which made the Ethiopians a denomination of Christianity that dated back to the very foundations of the religion; and the fact that they had seen off an Italian army in 1898 became their symbol of resistance. An article published in the *National Geographic* magazine in January 1931, in which there was a discussion about modern Ethiopia that covered the coronation, was passed from hand to hand. This was no fiction. Here were pictures and an article in a white man's magazine! That the British had taken the coronation seriously enough to send the Duke of Gloucester, the son of King George V, to the event was regarded as further proof. The Jamaican national daily carried this letter.

> The whole Ethiopian race throughout the world, or at least the leaders of thought, should regard with the greatest degree of satisfaction the well considered decision of His Majesty's Government to send a deputation headed by a member of the British Royal Family to represent the great Anglo-Saxon people at the coronation of the only independent state among the millions of Ham's offspring.[27]

The movement rapidly spread from its origins in Jamaica, not least because Bob Marley, the celebrated reggae singer, spread the message through the popularity of his music. Yawney suggests that there may now be more Rastafarians living outside Jamaica than on the island, with many activists in the USA, Canada and Britain, as well as Africa itself.[28] Though the movement has often been dismissed as impractical and chiliastic, as Hall argues: 'It was not the literal Africa that people wanted to return to, it was the language, the symbolic language for describing what suffering was like, it was a metaphor for where they were … a language with a double register, a literal and a symbolic register.'[29]

Shared cultural expressions

The idea that there might be complex connections between Africa, Africans in the New World and African-Caribbean peoples abroad has been suggested by black writers and intellectuals for over a century. One poignant exploration of 250 years of the African diaspora is provided by the Caribbean-born writer Caryl Phillips, who chronicles the sense of disconnectedness and homelessness of those of African descent abroad and how they sought to reconstitute themselves as acting, thinking, and emotionally intact individuals. The title of his novel, *Crossing the river*, evokes the transatlantic slave trade and Gilroy's idea of a black Atlantic. The author hears the drum beating on the far bank of the natal land and sees the 'many-tongued chorus of the common memory' in West Indian pubs in England, an addicted mother in Brooklyn, a barefoot boy in São Paulo, the reggae rhythms in the hills and valleys of the Caribbean and the carnivals in Trinidad and Rio. Despite the trauma of the middle passage and the human wreckage that resulted, Phillips concludes his novel on an optimistic note. Beloved children arrived on the far bank of the river. They loved and were loved.[30]

Another novelist shows how Caribbean migrants to the UK carried language and popular expressions. In this passage the protagonist in Samuel Selvon's most famous novel, *The lonely Londoner*, significantly and ironically called Moses, tries with his friends to recapture life in Trinidad and adjust to their new life, after ten years, in London:

> [They] coming together for oldtalk, to find out the latest gen, what happening, when is the next fête, Bart asking if anybody seen his girl anywhere, Cap recounting an incident he had with a women by the tube station the night before, Big City want to know why the arse he can't win a pool, Galahad recounting a clash with the colour problem in a restaurant in Piccadilly.[31]

While vernacular language crosses the Atlantic in the way Samuel Selvon demonstrated, a more pervasive art form is music. Here, in a persuasive essay, Gilroy argues that: 'The contemporary musical forms of the diaspora work within an aesthetic and political framework which demands that they ceaselessly reconstruct their own histories, folding back on themselves time and again to celebrate and validate the simple, unassailable fact of their survival.'[32] The politics of black music are barely beneath the surface in the calypsos of Trinidad, reggae and ska from Jamaica, samba from Brazil, township jazz from South Africa, Highlife from Nigeria and jazz, hip-hop, soul and rap from the USA. In the expressive title of Gilroy's essay, Africans at home and abroad are 'one nation under a groove'.

Social conduct and popular attitudes

Much of the material on the Caribbean diaspora by the writers quoted is both challenging and theoretically sophisticated. But to what extent is a transnational identity a lived experience, demonstrated by migrants' social conduct as well as invented in the minds and emotions of writers, musicians and academics? To this question I do not propose a full reply – for only an extensive research project would yield empirically verifiable answers. However, I thought it might be educative to do what might be called a simple 'reality check' on the broad idea of a black Atlantic.

I did this by examining sample issues of the *Weekly Gleaner*, the self-declared 'top Caribbean newspaper' published in south London and comprising a digest of Jamaica's *Daily Gleaner*, together with local editorial matter and letters. That a newspaper of this type appears and sells is, in a sense, indication enough of the strength of a transnational Caribbean identity. What I thought particularly illustrative of the continuing relationship between the Caribbean communities in the UK and the Caribbean was a letter to the editor from a Mr R. Francis of south London. He complained about the discourtesy he had experienced on his last trip to Jamaica in banks, the customs service and government departments. I add the emphasis on the remaining part of his letter:

> I would like to express my view on the way in which *returnees* to Jamaica are treated *back home* ... Like other people, I am definitely homesick, I am scared of going back to Jamaica because of the treatment often meted out to returnees and people on holiday. Although *we are away* it should be understood that we have and will always contribute to the finance and development of Jamaica. *It is our country as much as it is those who have never left.*[33]

When one examines the advertisements, the link with 'our country' becomes much more concrete. The pages are stuffed with advertisements for shipping lines, airlines, freight handlers, money transfer services ('Send your cash in a flash', says one), plots for sale in Jamaica, architects, removal companies, vacation accommodation and export houses selling tropicalized refrigerators 'good with the correct voltage and specification *for your country*'. Readers are offered shares on the Jamaican stock exchange and access via a cable company to 'Black Variety Television'.

SINDHIS AND PARSIS IN BOMBAY

Are there other examples of deterritorialized diasporas? I would like to draw attention to two intriguing examples, both centred on Bombay. The first concerns the Sindhis, historically settled in the area currently defined as the southernmost province of Pakistan. Sind had a prior independent existence, but the British governed it for a little over 100 years, from 1843–1947. The navigable Indus River, which debouches into what was once called 'the Sindhi Sea' (now the Arabian Sea), bisects the area; ancient Greek, Persian, Arab and Sindhis mariners were tied into far-reaching trade networks long before the arrival of the Europeans.[34] The province is strategically salient, with a long frontier with India and a key port connecting Sind to Central Asia and the wider Gulf and Indian Ocean business and trade networks.

Concentrating particularly on the case of Hindu Sindhis (most of whom accept the teaching of Guru Nanak, the first guru of Sikhism, but remain within the Hindu camp), Falzon takes up their story.[35] The first diasporic wave was generated at the beginning of the British occupation and constituted a classic trade diaspora (see Chapter 5) but the second, and far more numerous, accompanied the grisly end of British rule and partition. The Hindu Sindhis found themselves in Muslim Pakistan and moved *en masse* to India, notably to Bombay and its satellite town, Ulhasnagar (redubbed Sindhunagar, because of the many Sindhis there). There were already strong administrative, educational and trade links with Bombay and exit to Bombay by sea was the safest course of action for the refugees.

India has been kind to the Sindhis, with the Bombay-based community at large being regarded as politically integrated and economically successful. The emblematic evidence of this success was the election of L. K. Advani to the deputy prime ministership of India and the prominence (sometimes notoriety) of the fabulously-wealthy Hinduja brothers. Like the Hinduja brothers who have spread their wings, many Indian Sindhis have moved on, settling in perhaps 100 further countries, sometime linked to the pioneer Sindhi traders. Do they constitute a deterritorialized diaspora? Falzon argues that 'the notion of a (distant) homeland is still central to the Hindu Sindhi's diasporic imaginary', but that the idea of recovering a homeland in historic Sind is generally and increasingly seen as a political impossibility. By contrast, the benefits of forming an economically successful transnational network centred on Bombay are apparent to all, except a few 'cultural entrepreneurs' who wistfully look to their lost homeland.[36] Some are even prepared to argue that partition in 1947 was a 'blessing in disguise', while one poet enthused:

> Oh Sindhi! May God be with you
> May you spread happiness
> Wherever you find your people, call it home.
> Wherever you find Sindhis, call it your Sind.[37]

While the Sindhi population of Bombay remains substantial, the diasporic Sindhis often own second homes there and return to sample the remembered pleasures of the city, to see friends and relatives, to participate in the thriving marriage market for their sons and daughters and to handshake with new and old business partners. As Falzon explains, Bombay has become the 'cultural heart' of a deterritorialized diaspora:

> Business reputation, personal narratives, indicators of wealth, virtue and a host of other aspects of the person and, more importantly, the family, are periodically transported to Bombay from every corner of the world, and through interaction in the city, re-exported to the various localities of the diaspora. The city's five-star hotels, expensive restaurants and sari emporia provide an excellent opportunity for the type of conspicuous consumption for which Sindhis are stereotypically but hardly erroneously famous wherever they are located.[38]

Bombay (renamed Mumbai by nationalists) is, of course, a famously cosmopolitan city with famous diasporic intellectuals like Salman Rushdie who celebrate its diversity. The central characters in his novel *The Moor's last sigh* are drawn from the city's Cochin Jews and Portuguese Christians and the city has been home, or a point of transit, for many diasporic peoples.

There is an Armenian church in Meadows Street established in 1776. In 1864, Ewald notices, 'more than half of the (probably under-reported) two thousand Africans in Bombay earned their living as sailors or in related maritime work'.[39] Given this diversity, it is perhaps not therefore surprising to find a substantial Zoroastrian community in Bombay – where they are known as Parsis. The Parsis became an established part of the landscape of the city as early as 1640, while the British East India Company conceded that their funeral practices (where vultures eat the dead) could be carried out at the Tower of Silence at Malabar Hill in 1673.

As Hinnells explains in his monumental study of the Zoroastrian diaspora, the Parsis in Bombay became the major cultural and religious centre for the worldwide community from the eighteenth century onwards.[40] He considers the cases of some 11 other diasporic communities (in Hong Kong, East Africa, Britain, continental Europe, the USA, Canada and Australia) showing how endogamous norms, social mobility and late marriage have steadily reduced this ancient community to about 100,000 members. However, the main threat to the Zoroastrians has been manifested in their natal homeland, Iran (formerly Persia) where, since the revolution of 1979, emigration or conversion has reduced the community to about 22,000. Founded centuries ago, Zoroastrians had once succeeded to the throne of Persia, before being driven out by Muslim rule in AD 652. While some holy relics remain as Chakchak in Iran, which is still a site for pilgrimage, the diaspora has become nearly entirely deterritorialized, with its main religious and cultural reference points anchored in Bombay.

CONCLUSION

Theodor Adorno once remarked that 'it is part of morality not to be at home in one's home'.[41] Certainly this seems to be a recurrent theme in the story of Caribbean peoples abroad and in the cases of other multiply-displaced diasporas. In this chapter I have sought to show how the Caribbean migrants constitute a deterritorialized diaspora by addressing three preliminary questions. What was the history of settlement in the Caribbean and migration from the area? What were the fates and fortunes of Caribbean peoples in the different destination areas? Were there systematic differences between those who went to North America, the UK, the Netherlands or France?

In fact all sorts of cultural and political compromises with a diasporic identity arose, particularly, I would suggest, among the French Antilleans in metropolitan France. For example, if we take the four criteria I suggested for assessing whether a Caribbean deterritorialized diaspora existed, the level of cultural retention and interest in an original natal homeland was lowest among those from the Francophone Caribbean. Not of course that it was absent. For Césaire, as for many in the Anglophone Caribbean, the idea of return was subliminal, figurative and symbolic. But there remains a significant difference between the two language groups. In the English-speaking Caribbean and in the USA, the idea of a link with Africa spread beyond the intelligentsia to the masses – through the Garveyite and Rastafarian movements.

In popular culture – particularly in music, literature, carnival, the visual and performing arts and language – there was considerable cross-pollination of ideas, images and concepts over the waves and the air waves, exactly in conformity with the black Atlantic thesis. The frontiers of the region are beyond the Caribbean – in the consciousness of Caribbean people to be sure, but also in their social conduct, migration patterns and achievements in their places of settlement and sojourn. However, I would like to share something of a preliminary corrective to the idea of a black Atlantic. Susan Craig has noted that it is not without coincidence that 'the enterprise of the Indies' as it was called in Columbus's time, joined the major continents of the globe (Europe, Africa *and* Asia) to the Americas and that with the help of Caribbean labour, the Panama Canal added the Pacific. Thus, whatever the sophistication and complexity of the black Atlantic thesis, at root it is a historical simplification, which cannot fully explain the process of indigenization and creolization in the Caribbean. Nor can it account for the complexities arising from the large Asian presence in the Caribbean and *its* subsequent diasporization.[42]

The idea of a deterritorialized Caribbean diaspora needs therefore to be somewhat separated from the more limited notion of a black Atlantic, but the core concept of deterritorialization seems to work well in explaining how multiply-displaced groups, like the Sindhis and Parsis, reaffirm their worldwide interconnectedness even though the connection to their natal homeland has effectively been lost or seriously compromised by events outside their control. It is perhaps important to stress that Africa does not disappear from the Caribbean imaginary, just as Hindu Sindhis and Parsis still remember Sind and Persia, however distantly. Rather than a complete process of erasure, the conditions in the natal homeland have become so hostile (and the relatively benign conditions in parts of the diaspora so attractive) that the recovery of homeland has been deferred indefinitely and displaced by newer centres of religious, cultural and economic achievement.

FURTHER READING

- The theme of deterritorialization of identities is notably addressed by James Clifford, 'Traveling cultures', in Lawrence Grossberg *et al.* (eds) *Cultural studies* (New York: Routledge, 1992) pp. 96–116.
- Paul Gilroy's *The black Atlantic: modernity and double consciousness* (London: Verso, 1993) is highly influential and merits careful reading, though several

of my very good students have struggled with it and it would be fair to students to note that lucidity is not the prime virtue of the book.

- A lifetime of scholarship can be found in John R. Hinnells's *The Zoroastrian diaspora: religion and migration* (Oxford: Oxford University Press, 2005). Though long (875 pp.) the bits you are interested in can easily be extracted from the whole.

QUESTIONS TO THINK ABOUT

- Does a deterritorialized diaspora require at least some vestigial recognition of an original homeland to build its sense of social cohesion?
- Using published sources and the web, investigate the spread of carnival from Brazil and Trinidad to parts of the Caribbean and to Europe and North America. What does this tell you about how a deterritorialized diaspora is socially constructed?
- In this chapter I have covered only the cases of the Caribbean peoples, the Sindhis and the Parsis and hinted that the Roma/Gypsies are a possible candidate for a deterritorialized diaspora. Taking the Roma as one example and selecting one or two other cases not mentioned here, explore other aspects of deterritorialized diasporas.

Figure 8.1 A pilgrim in Japan. Cheaper travel has accelerated such 'homecomings' in all diaspora religions. Shinto priests hold at least 15 festivals each year to welcome pilgrims to Taisha, Japan © iStockphoto.com/Robin Cohen

8

MOBILIZING DIASPORAS IN A GLOBAL AGE

As has been demonstrated throughout this work, diasporas are in a continuous state of formation and reformation. Their situation can change, often dramatically, in response to tumultuous events and more subtle changes in religious epicentres, homelands and hostlands. Migrants can be dispersed to one, some or many destinations. They can settle in some places, move on, or regroup. New waves of migration from an original homeland can transform the predominant character of the diaspora concerned. More fundamentally, as Van Hear puts it, 'diasporas can be made and unmade'.[1] These contingent features of diasporas are given added force in the contemporary period, which can loosely be described as 'the global age'.[2] Within the rich array of possible understandings of the global age, I would like to emphasize four aspects that have particular bearing on the mobilization of diasporas:

1. *A globalized economy* that permits greater connectivity, the expansion of enterprises and the growth of new professional and managerial cadres, thereby changing but creating new opportunities for diasporas;
2. *New forms of international migration* that encourage limited contractual relationships, family visits, intermittent stays abroad and sojourning, as opposed to permanent settlement and the exclusive adoption of the citizenship of a destination country;
3. *The development of cosmopolitan sensibilities* in many 'global cities' in response to the multiplication and intensification of transactions and interactions between the different peoples of the world; and
4. *The revival of religion as a focus for social cohesion* through dispersal, renewed pilgrimage and translocation resulting in the development of multi-faced world religions connected in various and complex ways to the diasporic phenomenon.

Each of these four aspects of globalization has, in different ways, opened up new opportunities for diasporas to emerge, re-emerge, survive and thrive. Let me consider them in more detail in turn.

DIASPORAS IN A GLOBALIZED ECONOMY

It is a commonly expressed belief that enhanced flows of technology, information, capital, trade and migration are remaking the world by sweeping all forms of localism aside. Yet, there is a curious fatalism and determinism in such accounts that elides any elaborated consideration of the pertinent institutions and agencies that animate this process. This sense of predestination is derived from the almost total hegemony of neo-liberal economic thinking in official circles and in the media, which naively assumes that 'the market' is all that is needed to dynamize the global economy. Usually forgotten are the institutional and social mechanisms that manage and structure the market place and the agents who engage in market transactions.

Take, for example, the case of the emigration of Japanese professionals and managers who have moved abroad with their expanding transnational corporations. In his readable and innovative account, Kotkin calls this movement a 'diaspora by design'. He argues that because the Japanese had historically been frustrated in their plans for conventional colonization, they enlarged their influence in the world economy through other means:

> Among the principal agents for this expansion were the *sogo shosha*, or trading companies ... Initially the move abroad was on a small scale and rather poorly coordinated. Lacking any foreign markets, the first foreign operations, those of Mitsui, were conducted out of the Japanese embassy in London ... By the 1930s nearly a half million Japanese were living temporarily abroad as 'birds of passage', including agents for the *zaibatsu* [subsidiaries], independent traders and students. At the top of this worldwide network stood the new breed of college-educated managers ... who created a large network of related companies, often quite independent, whose products and services they could in turn finance then distribute through their global network.[3]

The most important Japanese colony in Europe is in the UK where, by 1990, Japanese factories, banks, corporate offices and insurance houses had investments totalling US$16 billion. These enterprises employed 45,000 Japanese nationals in 1996, but this figure included only those Japanese who had registered with the embassy in London. The total is likely to be over 150,000. Despite its size, the group has remained largely invisible through the development of its own social institutions. A number of golf clubs, hotels, spas, Japanese schools (there are more than 230 worldwide), temples, cinemas, booksellers, restaurants, night-clubs, bars and markets are patronized almost exclusively by overseas Japanese.

A globalized economy has also mobilized and expanded the functions of the older trade and business diasporas discussed in Chapter 5. Traders place orders with cousins, siblings and kin 'back home'; nieces and nephews from 'the old country' stay with uncles and aunts while acquiring their education or vocational training; loans are advanced and credit is extended to trusted intimates; and jobs and economically-advantageous marriages are found for family members. By being attached to a strong and tightly-integrated diaspora, family- and kin-based economic transactions are made easier and safer. Social sanctions provide a cheaper, more effective and more discreet means of collecting bad debts than repossession orders and legal action. And success in business brings not just material rewards, but social approval and prestige, accorded by the valued reference group. Diasporas allow small and family businesses to adjust to a global scale and to assume a more rational, functional, productive and progressive character. A network of mutual trust of global proportions builds up as capital and credit flow freely between family members, wider kin, fellow villagers and even more loosely associated co-ethnic members.

In essence, these flows are similar to the lines of credit that were established by the trade diasporas in, say, early modern Europe or by the Chinese in Southeast Asia (see Chapter 5). However, electronic banking and communications have vastly speeded up transactions and their sheer volume and diversity make them difficult to track and police – for example, by the tax authorities of various countries. Many sectors of capital benefited from the deregulation of foreign exchange markets, but diasporic traders and businesspersons were particularly advantaged. On the one hand, they could no longer be accused of 'unpatriotic' conduct if they dealt with suppliers abroad or 'out-sourced' manufacturing contracts to their 'home' countries. On the other hand, they were often best placed to reactivate links with countries that, through war or political ideology, had not previously or fully been sucked into international markets. With the collapse of official communism after 1989, diasporic segments like the Canadian Ukrainians or American Poles were able to revitalize business links with their countries of origin.

The Vietnamese, Cubans and Chinese abroad are also actively engaged in economic relations with their respective home countries. All three countries have gradually been forced to abandon any attempt at autarky and have joined the global rat race, usually with the mediation of their diasporas. For example, since 1979 China has received $60 billion in foreign investments and about the same in loans; and the Chinese in the diaspora were responsible for a staggering 80 per cent of the total sums involved. In fact, 1979 marked the turn of the Chinese towards capitalism, disguised by Deng's claim that all he was doing was decentralizing economic control. Overseas Chinese took the opportunity to reconnect with their villages and ancestral homes through the influential *guanxi* – elaborated networks of relatives, friends and associates. Legitimate enterprises, the drugs trade and special economic zones – where capitalist relations prevailed – were established on a massive scale. At the disposal of the 55 million overseas Chinese (Hong Kong and Taiwan included) was $450 billion; in 1995 this sum was 25 per cent larger than mainland

China's own GNP.[4] No doubt the proportions have changed as China's pace of economic growth has rocketed, but much of the energy to fuel the takeoff has come from the Chinese diaspora. In 2006, a local survey revealed that Shenzhen alone had an investment volume of US$20 billion from overseas Chinese who also owned 20,000 companies.[5]

NEW FORMS OF INTERNATIONAL MIGRATION

We can recall that the warning to the biblical Jews was that they would be 'scattered to all lands' if they disobeyed the Mosaic Law. A number of diasporas covered in this book – the Jewish, Indian, Lebanese and Chinese to name a few – were indeed widely scattered to many destinations. However, international migration also followed much narrower and more predictable channels – from a colony to a metropolis, between contiguous territories, along language lines or where bilateral migration contracts were signed. Now changes in the cost, ubiquity and awareness of mass transport have uncovered fresh destinations for migrants, so that in addition to the well-trodden routes to North America, western Europe and Australia, the oil-rich states of the Middle East and the economic hothouses of East Asia have increasingly been brought into the global migration arena. In the age of globalization, unexpected people turn up in the most unexpected places. Their more diverse geographical spread creates a more truly global basis for the evolution of diasporic networks.

Momentous political changes affecting migration at the points of supply have paralleled these shifting destination patterns. Between 1945 and 1989, the political and military duopoly of the USSR and the USA seemed firmly to cement the bipolar world. The cement was unexpectedly friable. Indeed, many people gasped as they saw on their television screens emblematic chunks of the east hammered off the Berlin Wall. The break-up of the postwar international balance of power has radically altered the character of international migration. As the communist regimes imploded and Western investment and goods poured in, it became impossible to maintain the old restrictions on travel or emigration for work and settlement. An additional axis of migration from relatively poor to rich countries has thus been opened up (East–West as well as South–North migration), giving renewed life to the diasporas of Russians and of east and central Europeans that had earlier evolved over the period between 1870 and 1914.

Regional conflicts have also assumed a new character. Without the Soviet Union to prop up its clients or face down the USA, the social consequences of regional conflicts, including migration, burst more readily through the weaker international constraints of the post-Cold War world. Sudden migration flows have been one of the most prominent manifestations of the conflicts of the post-1989 era. The first Gulf crisis, for example, led to the involuntary repatriation of two million Arab and Asian workers and residents; among them were hundreds of thousands of the Palestine diaspora, who were uprooted from the lives they had rebuilt in the Gulf States and forced to seek refuge again in Jordan and elsewhere. The Caribbean showed a similar dynamic. Now that the Soviet Union no longer subsidizes Cuban sugar, Cuba's economy has collapsed and the pressures for emigration to the USA have increased. On the nearby island of Haiti, the anti-communist rhetoric of the ruling class was no longer deemed necessary or convincing, so the USA withdrew its support. The consequent flows of migrants and refugees have considerably changed the size and character of the Cuban and Haitian diasporas.

Despite the increased mobility of people in the global age no countries welcome mass migration. Members of diasporic communities have benefited from the wooing of business migrants and the relative laxity in respect of family migration, especially to the USA.[6] Again, despite the rigorous official control of immigration, there has been an extensive and rapid development of a 'migration industry' comprising private lawyers, travel agents, recruiters, organizers, fixers and brokers who sustain links with origin and destination countries. Such intermediaries are driven by the cash nexus and make no distinctions, except in terms of price, between refugee and migrant, professional or unskilled, illegal or legal migration. Points of departure and arrival are also linked by friendship, kin and the ethnic networks that migrants organize.

Restrictions on entry for settlement have also given new life to an old diasporic practice – that of 'sojourning' (the cyclical pattern of emigration and return) characteristic of the Chinese, but also evident in many cases including the Mexicans, Dominicans, Puerto Ricans and Italians.[7] As Wang points out, many of today's 'global' migrants are people of considerable wealth and portable skills – a different group from the unskilled labour migrants of the nineteenth century and the refugees and tightly-controlled contract workers of more recent decades:

> new classes of people educated in a whole range of modern skills are now prepared to migrate or remigrate and respond to the pull of centres of power and wealth and the new opportunities in trade and industry. Even more than the traditional sojourners of Southeast Asia, these people are articulate, politically sensitive and choose their new homes carefully. They study the migrant states, especially their laws on the rights of immigrants and the economic conditions for newcomers ... Furthermore, many are masters not only in the handling of official and bureaucratic connection but also in the art of informal linkages.[8]

Networks established in colonial times have now been superseded by the emergence of selective migration opportunities in Canada, Europe, the USA and Australia. Sojourners to the new destinations are helped by the global communications and transport revolutions, by the need for states to attract foreign investment through the multinationals, by the stronger legal protection accorded to minorities in the receiving countries and by the adaptable tradition of sojourning itself. A diasporic consciousness, with a foot in two or more locations, is highly attuned to contract-driven moves, and to family and clan networking and sojourning as opposed to permanent settlement in a destination country.

COSMOPOLITANISM, GLOBAL CITIES AND THE BRIDGING ROLE OF DIASPORAS

That power is concentrated is a commonplace, but this is not the same thing as knowing *where* power is concentrated. The global shifts in the location of financial services, industrial plant and other constituents of the world economy impose a defining spatial grid on the patterns of global power. The most important nodes in this spatial lattice are what have come to be called 'world cities' or 'global cities'.[9] The location decisions of transnational corporations are by no means the only factors involved, yet they are important agents in this process. The placing of their corporate headquarters is of particular salience. Here, high-level investment and disinvestment decisions are reached. Advertising and purchasing financial, legal and political services further concentrate power in particular cities.[10]

The reconfigurations of global space and the new connections between global cities serve to advantage diasporas. Members of diasporas are almost by definition more mobile than people who are rooted solely in national spaces. They are certainly more prone to international mobility and change their places of work and residence more frequently. In previous eras and still in some places, when periods of febrile nation-building take place, their internationalism was a distinct disadvantage and a source of suspicion. In the age of globalization, their language skills, familiarity with other cultures and contacts in other countries make many members of diasporas highly competitive in the international labour, service and capital markets. In the context of global cities, this applies irrespective of whether they are competing for professional advantage or in the unskilled labour market – after all, waiters, porters or prostitutes who can address international customers in their own languages are also likely to have a distinct edge over their competitors.

Cosmopolitanism and localism

In global cities, two counter-tendencies, cosmopolitanism and localism, potentially challenge a diasporic orientation. As Vertovec and Cohen have argued:

> For the majority of the population, living their lives within the cultural space of their own nation or ethnicity, cosmopolitanism has

[hitherto] not been an option. However, in the contemporary world, cultural and linguistic diversity is omnipresent, and the capacity to communicate with others and to understand their cultures is available, at least potentially, to many ... Travel and immigration have led to the necessity of cheek-by-jowl relationships between diverse peoples at work or at street corners, and in markets, neighbourhoods, schools and recreational areas ... Such everyday cosmopolitanism might be regarded as a newly recognized form of behaviour.[11]

Through these everyday interactions, a wider outlook might supersede diasporic identities anchored on a single ethnicity or religion. It is at least a plausible hypothesis that increasing intercultural opportunities might, in some cases, act as a catalyst to move local cultures first into a diasporic space then, via multiculturalism or pluralism, to a more cosmopolitan outlook. There is, however, a much more visible counter-tendency to cosmopolitanism, namely nationalism, ethnic particularism, religious fundamentalism, racism, sexism and other forms of social exclusion, all of which seem to be on the increase, despite globalization. To simplify a more complicated picture, let us call this narrowing tendency 'localism'.

Thus, one perverse feature of globalization at the cultural level is that it has also solidified and even enhanced localism through the fragmentation and multiplication of identities. How do we understand this apparent paradox of particularism in the midst of globalization? In effect, we are witnessing counter-global movements, which operate locally and globally while drawing their inspiration (normally unconsciously) from a felt need to confront and oppose the anonymous, rational, bewildering, progressive and universal elements of globalization. This requires a return to the local and the familiar. Stuart Hall is perhaps the most insightful observer of this condition:

> The face-to-face communities that are knowable, that are locatable, one can give them a place. One knows what the voices are. One knows what the faces are. The re-creation, the reconstruction of imaginary, knowable places in the face of the global postmodern which has, as it were, destroyed the identities of specific places, absorbed them into this postmodern flux of diversity. So one understands the moment when people reach for those groundings.[12]

A 'reach for groundings' can mean a retreat from global realities, an incapacity to respond to the challenges of the ever-widening marketplace and to the new ethical and cultural demands stemming from globalization. To meet both needs, for a meaningful identity and a flexible response to burgeoning opportunities, for a resolution of the contradictory pulls of cosmopolitanism and localism, a double-facing type of social organization is highly advantageous. Just such an organization exists in the form of a diaspora.

147

The bridging function of diasporas

Pointing in two directions is not just a contemporary function of diasporas. They have always been in a better position to act as a bridge between the particular and the universal. Among other arenas, this has allowed them to act as interlocutors in commerce and administration. A few examples must suffice to make this point historically. According to Armstrong, the Spanish Jews were 'indispensable for international commerce in the Middle Ages'.[13] The Armenians controlled the overland route between the Orient and Europe as late as the nineteenth century. Lebanese Christians developed trade between the various parts of the Ottoman Empire. Diasporic groups introduced innovative economic techniques – the Chinese introduced tin mines in Malaya and Borneo, while the Huguenots introduced lace-making to Britain and viniculture to South Africa.

Many members of diasporic communities are bi- or multilingual. They can spot 'what is missing' in the societies they visit or in which they settle. Often they are better able to discern what their own group shares with other groups and when *its* cultural norms and social practices threaten majority groups. Such awareness constitutes the major component of what the Jews call *sechal*,[14] without which survival itself might be threatened. It is perhaps because of this need to be sensitive to the currents around them, that, in addition to their achievements in trade and finance, diaspora groups are typically over-represented in the arts, in the cinema and in the media and entertainment industries. Knowledge and awareness have increased to the point of cosmopolitanism or humanism, but at the same time traditional cultural values, which sustain solidarity and have always supported the search for education and enlightenment, have not been threatened. (Awareness of their own precarious situation may also propel members of diasporas to advance legal and civic causes and to be active in human rights and social justice causes.)

The combination of cosmopolitanism and ethnic collectivism is an important constituent in successful business ventures. Probably the most upbeat analysis along these lines is provided by Kotkin in a comparative study of why some peoples seem more successful as entrepreneurs than others. In his quest, he provides case studies of five 'global tribes' – the Jews, the British, the Japanese, the Chinese and the Indians.[15] Gone, for Kotkin, are the traumas of exile, the troubled relationship with the host culture and other negative aspects of the classical diasporic tradition. Instead, strong diasporas are the key to determine success in the global economy. He writes:

> Rather than being a relic of a regressive past, the success of global tribes – from the Jews and British over many centuries to the Chinese, Armenians and Palestinians of today – suggests the critical importance of values, emphasis on the acquisition of knowledge and cosmopolitan perspectives in the emerging world economy. In an

ever more transnational and highly competitive world economy, highly dependent on the flow and acquisition of knowledge, societies that nurture the presence of such groups seem most likely to flourish ... Commercial opportunism overwhelms the narrower economic nationalism of the past as the cosmopolitan global city-state takes precedence and even supplants the nation.[16]

Naturally, not all diasporas have equal success in entrepreneurship. Kotkin argues that economically successful diasporas are likely to possess three desiderata, namely: (a) a *strong identity*; (b) an *advantageous occupational profile*; and (c) a *passion for knowledge*.[17] Each of these needs some elaboration.

Whether a *strong identity* is derived from internal clannishness, external rejection or a combination of the two, a definite ethnic or religious identity engenders a distance from the larger society, which can be used for creative and productive purposes. Characteristically, early immigrants came from the same village or region, they may have shared the rigours of a journey,[18] and when they arrive they share accommodation and rely on each other for friendship and mutual protection against a threatening world. As an example of the latter, Kwong avers that as late as the 1980s many apartments in New York's Chinatown had wall-to-wall beds occupied by the tenants in successive shifts. As more people arrived ancillary accommodation would be found, but the core accommodation would become a *fong* (literally a room) where 'through games of mah-jong or poker the immigrants made contacts to obtain jobs, found partners for joint ventures, and discussed the pooling or borrowing of funds for new businesses'.[19] Above the level of the *fong* would be the village association, often formed by those who shared a similar family name. Migrants from contiguous village associations who spoke a similar dialect might be joined to form a *huiguan*, a district association. And when the going got tough, armed gangs of tongs or triads would be formed to protect property, monopolies or monopsonies.

Rather like a stack of Russian dolls, starting with the smallest and ending up on a considerable scale, members of a diaspora (in this case the Chinese) became locked into one another, reaching down to reaffirm their unshakeable loyalties and reaching up to the marketplace with the confidence born of their strong sense of identity. Such diasporas are thus both inside and outside a particular national society. They are outsiders as well as participants and, as spectators, are able to compare and learn from 'how things are done' in other societies as well as in the one in which they find themselves.

Compared with the members of the host society, those who belong to a diaspora characteristically have an *advantageous occupational profile*. They are often more strongly represented in the professions and in self-employment and less vulnerable to adverse shifts in the labour market. The more prosperous members of a diaspora may possess two passports and savings, investments and bank accounts in more than one county. Diasporas thus foster self-help, a family or collective project and a risk-minimalization strategy that transcends national borders.

A *passion for knowledge* is usually reflected in a desire for education or, to be more specific, a passion for certification. Characteristically, the choice of qualification coincides with the possibility of migration, forced or self-chosen. Degree certificates, vocational or professional qualifications are the passports of the successful members of a diaspora. Members of a diaspora may choose to work abroad or calculate that they may have no other choice. But a passion for knowledge is also adequately or even spectacularly served by intense curiosity. Those with *sechal* or gumption often do not need formal education because they quickly intuit business niches (for example in textiles, communications, or the retail sector) left by other more established groups. Again Kwong provides some useful observations of the Chinese:

> Younger generations of Chinese are achieving upward social mobility through education. They have earned respect for their intellectual achievements, particularly in the difficult subjects of science and technology. There is truth to the belief that Chinese families stress education ... Good grades in school and entering a first-rate college are praised not only by the family but by relatives and family friends. There is constant pressure and supervision of the young to develop discipline and, most importantly, to internalize their parents' values as their own. As a result, many youths grow up with a high regard for hard work and accomplishment. The Chinese immigrants are not unique in this way. Earlier immigrants, such as the Jews, and more recent groups, such as the Koreans, also value education highly.[20]

What such accounts of ethnic entrepreneurship signify is that economic and cultural analyses are complementary. The crudities of neo-liberal economic-speak need to be abolished in favour of a more sophisticated sociological account, the implausibly invisible hand of the market replaced by the intimate handshake of ethnic collectivism: as it is with business ventures, so too is it with the marketplace of ideas, with the plastic and performing arts, with literary endeavours and with other forms of cultural production. Diasporas score by being able to interrogate the universal with the particular and by being able to use their cosmopolitanism to press the limits of the local.

RELIGION AND DIASPORAS

The connection between religion and diaspora was there virtually from the beginning. Not only did diaspora enter its conventional use in Jewish history via the Greek translation of the Bible (see Chapter 2), Baumann points out that in the first century AD Christians adopted the term, altering its 'soteriological meaning according to Christian eschatology'. He continues:

> The New Testament uses the noun *diaspora* and the verb *diaspeírein* three times each. Without going into detail on the complicated usages, the individual writers of the different Biblical stories and letters interpreted the early Church 'as a pilgrim, sojourning and dispersed community, in the understanding that it is the eschatological people of God'. On earth Christians living in dispersion would function as a 'seed' to disseminate the message of Jesus. The Christians' real home, however, was the 'heavenly city Jerusalem', the goal of Christian pilgrimage.[21]

There are, indeed, a number of Christian communities who behaved precisely in conformity with the tradition Baumann describes. The Mennonites (sixteenth-century Christian Anabaptists) are a case in point. Dispersal took place as a result of internal schisms (often over seemingly minor theological differences), in reaction to overt persecution, or as a response to attempts by states to bring religious communities into their tax regimes and place them under state authority. For those who believed only in the Kingdom of God, spreading the seed of Christianity to other parts of the world seemed the obvious thing to do. The Mennonites ended up largely in small rural communities, dispersing to 51 countries all over Africa, Europe and the Americas. A Mennonite theologian, Alain Epp Weaver, argues that there is (or perhaps should be) a close parallel between Christians and Jews. Both, he maintains, took erroneous turns in subordinating themselves to state power – for the Christians it was the Roman Emperor Constantine (AD 280–337) who established Christianity as a state religion, while for the Jews it was the creation of the state of Israel. By getting themselves entangled with temporal institutions Jews and Christians foolishly abandoned their spiritual missions. Both, Weaver argues, 'are called to an exilic, diasporic faith which embodies an alternative politics amidst the Babylons of the world'.[22]

Reconnecting the faith through pilgrimage

Ninian Smart described, though rather briefly, the fate of religious diasporas in global times.[23] The background to his argument is that, with the increased pace of connectivity, especially in respect of cheap long-distance travel, even rather poor religious communities can maintain contact with the principal epicentres of their religions: the Jews with Jerusalem and the Wailing Wall, the Catholics with Rome and Lourdes, the Hindus with Varanasi and the Ganges, the Sikhs with Amritsar and the Golden Temple, the Muslims with Mecca and the Kaaba, and so on. Contact often takes the form of pilgrimage to sites of religious significance – the fires of religious passion often being nurtured by long separation followed by ritualized forms of connectivity, such as the Hajj. The Hajj, the fifth pillar of Islam, is a source of inspiration and bonding for the Islamic world community, the *umma*. Those who are medically fit and can afford the journey are obliged to travel to Mecca at least once in their lives: about two million do so each year. Occasionally, the facilities are overwhelmed by the enthusiastic crowd. In 2006, 345 pilgrims on the Hajj lost their lives in a stampede near the three pillars where the devil appeared to Abraham and where they are enjoined to throw stones.

Christian pilgrimages have also experienced a massive revival with the reduced cost of international transport and greater accessibility.[24] Perhaps the most famous example of this is the case of Lourdes, a small town in the French Pyrenees. Each year, millions of people travel to Lourdes.[25] The town only has a permanent population of 15,000 but it has 270 hotels and is second nationally only to Paris in terms of the number of tourist beds available. As is often the case with places of pilgrimage, the religious aura surrounding Lourdes arose from the mysterious appearance of a religious figure. In this case a 14-year old girl is said to have seen the Virgin Mary 18 times in 1854. The water of Lourdes is thought to be blessed and many who are sick (some in wheelchairs or on hospital trolleys) come to the town in the hope of emulating the 66 officially-recognized miracle cures. Pilgrimages have also acquired new importance in other religions. Increasing numbers of Buddhists and Taoists are returning to Mount Tai in northeast China, where the shrines were vandalized by Maoist Red Guards but restored after 1976. Shinto priests hold at least 15 festivals each year to welcome pilgrims to Taisha, Japan.

Religions in diaspora or diaspora religion

Through the enhanced opportunities for pilgrimage, through other forms of renewal, and through proselytizing, certain religions then take on the character of 'world' or 'global' religions. Smart and his colleagues, who allude to a newspaper started in the mid-1980s that styled itself 'an international bimonthly newspaper fostering Hindu solidarity among 650 million members of a global religion', provide an illustrative case.[26] Despite some counter-tendencies towards pluralism and multi-faith protestations, world religions often seem to develop a proclivity towards ecumenism, orthodoxy or fundamentalism. This is evident (and much feared) in Islam, but also arises in religions that have hitherto been understood to be without a single, narrowly-defined set of beliefs and practices. Even Hinduism and Buddhism, for example, are moving in more fundamentalist and even aggressive directions, the former with the support of the Vishwa Hindu Parishad and Bharatiya Janata Party in India, the latter under the auspices of the World Federation of Buddhists.

It is difficult to know how to theorize the connection between religion and diaspora. Part of the problem is that there are relatively few prior attempts to do so. As Baumann notes, historians of religion 'quite aware of earlier experiences of ambiguity in transferring culturally and religiously bound terms, shied away from applying the notion [of diaspora] to non-Jewish traditions and peoples'.[27] Smart's initial formulation laid emphasis on the ways in which, with dispersal, religious beliefs adapted to new cultural settings and how, in return, the development of diasporic religious communities and their exposure to foreign influences, transformed the organization, practices and beliefs of the religion as a whole.[28] The Zoroastrians (also discussed in Chapter 7), followers of one of the oldest religions in the world, provide an extreme example. As Hinnells explains:

> As Zoroastrians continue to migrate around the world not only in greater numbers but also and perhaps more significantly, in a greater proportion compared with the population in the 'old country', so the threat of dispersal seems to make ever closer the apocalyptic scene of the extinction of the world's oldest prophetic religion.

Yet, as Hinnells explains, some Zoroastrians are more positive about the future; for, just as they accept that the move from Persia to India in response to Muslim persecution was a necessary survival strategy, so they think of the dispersal from India as another stage of 'moving on'. They are not so much a travelling culture, as a travelling religion, though Bombay has effectively become a displaced homeland because of the many religious sites located there.[29]

A second reason why theorizing the connection between religion and diaspora is fraught with uncertainty is that in several notable cases religion is closely imbricated with ethnicity and is sometimes inseparable from it. Armenians are often followers of the Catholic Armenian Church or the Armenian Orthodox Church; many Irish and most Italians are Catholics; Judaism and Sikhdom unite many diasporic Jews and Sikhs. Such an overlap between faith and ethnicity is likely to enhance overlapping forms of social cohesion and to create situations where it is difficult to decide whether one is describing a faith or an ethnicity. However, that is only one of three possible scenarios. What about the many situations where a diaspora includes many secular members or members of different faiths? How, for example, do the very substantial minorities of non-Hindus fit into the broad category of 'the Indian diaspora'? Again, think of the expression 'Muslim diaspora' (which generated 1,700,000 hits on a Google search in August 2007) where many ethnicities and nationalities are buried within a supposedly single 'diaspora religion'. Even in a small neighbourhood in London it is possible to find Muslims from Turkey, Bangladesh, Kosovo, India, Pakistan, Nigeria, Somalia and Iran, professing an adherence to the *umma* and their Islamic faith, but often not even sharing a common language.

In an ambitious synthesis, Vertovec draws the threads of the argument together.[30] He suggests that we might understand the connections between religion and diaspora in the global era in terms of 'the patterns of change' that follow migration and minority status, those that arise because of their dispersed condition, and those that accompany transnationalism and global religious change. His full account needs to be read in the original, as I only have space here to pick out some edited highlights. As minorities, Vertovec argues, religious groups will mobilize around the creation of devotional congregations (for example, raising funds for erecting a temple) and the recognition of their cultural practices (for example, their preferred form of dress). As dispersed members of a religious faith, the newly formed congregation will be engaged in a process of respatialization as new identities and networks have to be re-engineered a long way from home. Sacred and secular space will constantly be under renegotiation with the surrounding communities and with other coreligionists. Finally, changes that arise as a result of transnationalism and the globalization of religions include greater connectivity of dispersed religious communities, more horizontal linkages, which often displace traditional authority, and a greater politicization of religious demands. Vertovec instances the use of a Cuban religious shrine in Miami for mobilizing anti-Castro campaigns and the rise of transnational religious terrorism.[31]

CONCLUSION

It is quite difficult to establish the exact causal connection between globalization and 'diasporization' (to coin an ugly word). The relationship recalls Weber's powerful theory linking the emergence of Protestantism and capitalism. He thought there might be an 'elective affinity' between the two. A similar thought is found in a popular song that suggests that 'love and marriage go together like a horse and carriage'. I would hesitate to pronounce on the wisdom of this view, but I like the simile. Globalization and diasporization are separate phenomena with no necessary causal connections, but they 'go together' extraordinarily well.

That there is no direct causal link is evident from the fact that the earliest diasporas precede the age of globalization by 2,500 years. Again, even if we argue that contemporary diasporas are different sorts of social organization from those of the ancient Jews or early Christian communities, it would be an enormous exaggeration (or indeed completely wrong-headed) to suggest that the many changes in technology, economic organization, modes of travel, production, communication, the movement of ideas or the syncretization of cultures that underpin the process of globalization are *caused* by the existence of diasporas.

However, these changes disproportionately advantage diasporas and leaders of diasporic communities are able to exploit them to mobilize the group concerned. Many social and economic actors, including states, international organizations and transnational corporations, propel a world economy. These may be the sinews binding the ends of the earth together, but the flesh and blood are the family, kin, clan and ethnic networks that organize trade and allow the unencumbered flow of economic transactions and family migrants. Again, whereas the location of global economic, political and communication power is now debouching to particular cities, diasporas are often concentrated in such cities and profit from their cosmopolitan character. Deterritorialized, multilingual and capable of bridging the gap between global and local tendencies, diasporas are able to take advantage of the economic and cultural opportunities on offer.

Globalization has enhanced the practical, economic and affective roles of diasporas, showing them to be particularly adaptive forms of social organization. As diasporas become more integrated into global cities, their power and importance are enhanced. Their relative solidarity and integration are particularly evident in relation to the local populations among which they live. Of course many powerful and wealthy actors profit from globalization. However, there is often a striking discrepancy between the fate of diasporic communities and the condition of the local working class, where the predominance of unemployment and the temporary and precarious nature of jobs have virtually destroyed any sense of solidarity. This has led to feelings of uncertainly, isolation and often destructive individualism. By contrast, the more mixed profile of diasporas, with many being educated and professionally qualified and others able to engage in *collective* capitalism, has allowed them to avoid the worst impact of global restructuring. By working and living successfully in the most sensitive nodes of the world economy, the global cities, diasporas reinforce, even if they do not exclusively propel, a further stage of globalization.

In a complex world, full of uncertainty and even fear, it is comforting to express a known and familiar identity – with the warmth of an extended family and the intimacy of a shared religion, language and way of life. Perhaps the crucial aspect of organized religion that has ensured its survival is its adaptation to ethnicity, nationalism and now globalization. As Robertson puts it: 'The long-term adaptation of religion to society ... is one of the most significant general features of the history of religion(s) and certainly of the analysis of religion.'[32] However, the construction of a religion or an ethnicity that is tunnel-like is as dangerous as having none at all. Horizons and opportunities narrow and the group can become a target for envy, stereotyping and discrimination, even violence. The form of adaptive behaviour that meets the needs of a complex world is for a group *simultaneously* to hold to its ethnicity and/or religion and also establish transnational and intercultural ties, first with groups sharing similar origins and characteristics, and then more widely. This strategy, this game of life, can be deployed to mobilize diasporic ties and sentiments and bend them to more cosmopolitan outcomes and purposes.

FURTHER READING

- A very readable account of how diasporas connect to the global economy is provided in Joel Kotkin, *Tribes: how race, religion and identity determine success in the new global economy* (New York: Random House, 1992).
- The standard account on the emergence of global cities is Saskia Sassen, *The global city* (Princeton, NJ: Princeton University Press, 2001). First published in 1991, the new edition contains some important updates.
- Theorizing the connections between religion and diaspora is a fraught task. For a suggestive start try Steven Vertovec's 'Religion and diaspora', Working paper, Transnational Communities Programme (University of Oxford, WPTC-01-01, 2001) http://www.transcomm.ox.ac.uk/working %20papers/Vertovec01.PDF.

QUESTIONS TO THINK ABOUT

- What are 'diasporas by design'? Has an increasingly globalized economy undermined diasporas or created new opportunities for them?
- Can diaporas bridge the countervailing tendencies toward cosmopolitanism and localism that seem to be characteristic of our global age?
- Elucidate the advantages and the difficulties of making the connections between religion and diaspora.

Figure 9.1 Wittgenstein's rope analogy provides one way of understanding how different strands go into the making of a diaspora. © iStockphoto.com/Robin Cohen

9

STUDYING DIASPORAS

Old methods and new topics

In studying a complex theme like the history, rebirth, development and proliferation of diasporas, one has to start somewhere. For over 2,500 years, one notion of the word 'diaspora' had been overriding – it was one that highlighted the catastrophic origin, the forcible dispersal and the estrangement of diasporas in their places of settlement. As I have shown in Chapter 2, this interpretation of diaspora may have strong biblical support but it is, in any case, too narrow an interpretation even of the experience of the paradigmatic case, the Jewish people.

In trying to interrogate, supplement and transcend the dominant tradition, I considered various theoretical, methodological and taxonomic alternatives to give adequate recognition to the more diverse experiences of other transnational ethnic or religious communities that designated themselves, or were designated by others, as diasporas. For example, I noticed that one might have 'masculine' or 'feminine' versions of a diaspora. As Helmrich had stated, the patriarchal connection to the word is quite strong, the scattering or dissemination of seeds being closely related in Judeo-Christian and Islamic cosmology to male sperm.[1] A more gender neutral, or perhaps feminine, inflection was given by Malkki who argued that arboreal metaphors – like 'roots', 'soils' and 'family trees' – are more intimately related to ideas of kinship and national identity.[2] Though interesting, I found this gender split to be too limiting and, in any case, was not persuaded that discourse analysis on this or other diasporic themes could provide anything but the most superficial insight into the diasporic condition.

Instead, I turned to more fundamental methodological strategies. For the purposes of comparison I wanted a means to classify the units of comparison by bundling like with like, and contrasting like with less like and unlike. For this I adopted a typology. Such an exercise has an old provenance; for example, medical historians date the key intervention in their field to Thomas Browne's *Pseudodoxia epidemica*, published in 1646.[3] As I explain in the next section, taxonomies and typologies can work rather well, but you must be aware of how they abstract from reality by purposive exaggeration. Max Weber's 'ideal types', developed early in the twentieth century, were particularly helpful in constructing my typology.

When it came to understanding how the main features of diasporas knitted together I turned to other powerful methods eminent thinkers had adumbrated. First, I benefited from an observation made in 1874 by the natural scientist, Jevons, who proclaimed: 'A perfect intelligence would not confine itself to one order of thought, but would simultaneously regard a group of objects as classified in all the ways of which they are capable.' Second, I was influenced by Vygotsky's idea of a 'chain complex', a definitive attribute that keeps changing from one link to the next. The variable meaning is carried over from one item to a class of items with no 'central significance' or 'nucleus'. Finally, I was struck by Wittenstein's image of a rope 'which does not attain its strength from any fibre that runs through it from one end to another, but from the fact that there is a vast number of fibres overlapping'.[4] The analogy of a rope (Figure 9.1) was particularly suggestive in that it provided me with a legitimating mechanism with which to compare systematically how different diasporas conformed to the normal, but not invariable, features of most diasporas. Put another way, all the relevant fibres are part of a similar phenomenon, but they are not the same part of that phenomenon. While the diaspora rope may be visible and strong, discarded fibres of meaning shrivel and innovative strands of meaning are added.

After I look at typologies and compare diasporic features, I turn to emerging themes in diasporic studies – the increasing use as agents of development in home areas and the changing role of diasporas in international politics. Negative views of diasporas are recorded before I conclude the book with some final remarks.

HOW AND WHY DO TYPOLOGIES WORK?

In trying to supersede the exclusively catastrophic rendition of a victim diaspora, I developed at least four other types, which I have characterized earlier in this book as trade, labour, imperial and deterritorialized diasporas (Table 1.2, p.18). However suggestive such descriptions are, they should not be understood too obviously. Constructing a taxonomy of diasporas is a highly inexact science, partly because the taxa concerned are overlapping or change over time. For instance, as circumstances altered, the prototypical case, the Jews, can be regarded as a victim, labour, trade *and* deterritorialized diaspora. Despite the weight of previous interpretations, even an imperial phase is evident in the Zionist colonization of Palestine. Again, although the early phase of the Indian diaspora (1834–1914) made it a strong example of a labour diaspora, the current period of India's emergence as an incipient super power also coincides with its export of very large numbers of professionals and entrepreneurs, fundamentally altering the nature of the Indian diaspora.

In natural science the purpose of taxonomy is to develop relatively stable measures of consistency, pattern recognition and dimensionality with a view to evolving an agreed and impartial vocabulary that will sustain for some time.

Of course, natural scientists also recognize that revisions are necessary as paradigms shift and new discoveries and observations arise. A whale becomes a mammal and ceases to be a very large fish. But these changes are gradual compared with the agitated patterns arising from human sociality and conduct. Weber explicitly recognized that 'social reality presents a ceaseless flow of occurrences and events, very few of which, although repeatedly interwoven, seem to fall together coherently'.[5] As Kalberg explains, it was precisely because of the inherent complexity of social reality and the impossibility of arriving at full knowledge, however exhaustive the enquiry, that Weber suggested a daring innovation:

> Weber propounded the use of the ideal type to confront this conundrum. This purely analytic tool enables a purchase on reality through its simplification. Far from arbitrary, however, the procedures for doing so involve a deliberate *exaggeration of the essence* of the phenomenon under study and its reconstruction in a form with greater internal unity than ever appeared in empirical reality [emphasis in original].[6]

Weber applied his ideal types to the study of authority and religion, thereby generating nearly a century of emulation and contestation as his types were recognized, refined, revised or rejected. Of course I am not so big-headed as to compare myself with Weber, but proposing a set of ideal types of diasporas has undoubtedly yielded a considerable creative literature, mostly approving and sometimes usefully critical. The key point for a student is not to take an ideal type too literally, but to assume that deviation is normal because the real interrogates and deflates the ideal. The ideal is a yardstick, an abstraction and a simplification, a means of showing up similarities and differences in trying to encompass an array of possibilities that would otherwise have little form or shape. Used as a heuristic device in this way, a typology will help to delineate, analyse and compare many diasporic phenomena. However, in looking at any example, there is no need to force reality to conform in every respect to given ideal types. A creative imagination is always preferable to a dogged application of a formula.

COMPARING DIASPORAS: WITTGENSTEIN'S ROPE

To compare diasporas let me, in an abbreviated form, summarize what was set out more elaborately earlier in the book (see especially Table 1.1, p.17). Normally, diasporas exhibit several or most of the following features:

1. dispersal from an original homeland, often traumatically;
2. alternatively, the expansion from a homeland in search of work, in pursuit of trade or to further colonial ambitions;

3. a collective memory and myth about the homeland;
4. an idealization of the supposed ancestral home;
5. a return movement or at least a continuing connection;
6. a strong ethnic group consciousness sustained over a long time;
7. a troubled relationship with host societies;
8. a sense of co-responsibility with co-ethnic members in other countries; and
9. the possibility of a distinctive creative, enriching life in tolerant host countries.

These nine features are analogous to Wittgenstein's fibres of meaning. We need now to compare diasporas along the length of each fibre, bearing in mind that they entwine with one another and, in so doing, strengthen the diasporic 'rope'. I shall, after a detailed comparison of the first two fibres (dispersal and expansion), deal with the remaining seven strands in a more abbreviated way.

Dispersal

Though many diasporas are seen to be born of flight rather than choice, in practice voluntary and involuntary migration are not that easy to separate.[7] None the less, there are clearly a number of mass displacements that events wholly outside the individual's control occasion – wars, 'ethnic cleansing', natural disasters, pogroms, and the like. When we are talking of a trauma afflicting a group collectively, it is perhaps possible to isolate those events in which the suddenness, scale and intensity of exogenous factors unambiguously compel migration or flight.

Historically, Jews were dispersed to such an extent that their diaspora population massively outnumbered the original homeland population. Current estimates suggest that, with the establishment and repopulation of the State of Israel, together with demographic changes, the Israeli population is about one-third of the worldwide population of 14 million. By contrast, the number of people of African descent living outside the continent currently amounts to about 40 million people, about a tenth of the black African population. On the list of newer claimants to the designation diaspora, the Palestinians were nearly totally dispersed. Some 780,000 were expelled from the territory the Israeli army controlled, while a further 120,000 Palestinians were later classified as refugees because they had lost their land and livelihoods, though not their homes.[8]

The cases of the Irish and Lebanese are also dramatic in terms of the numbers of people affected. It is part of Irish folklore, for example, bitterly to recall both the brutality of English occupation and the ordeal of the famine. The Irish lost 25 per cent of their homeland population between 1845 and 1851, the years of the potato famine. Lebanon also experienced very heavy population losses – again about 25 per cent of the population before 1914 and a similar *tranche* consequent on the civil war of the 1970s.[9] The various current interventions by Syria and Israel and the conflicts between Hezbollah, other Islamicist forces and the Lebanese government have triggered further large outflows.

The remaining diasporas can be understood as arising from a mixture of underlying causes (such as poverty, insecure land tenure and overpopulation), which are combined with a variety of more immediate precipitating factors that serve to accelerate the basic movement or give to it a particular character and direction. In the case, for example, of Chinese indentured labour, Richardson suggests that migration was caused by a serious disequilibrium between population and land resources in north China, economic dislocation because of Western penetration of the economy, dynastic and social collapse and, in particular areas, the effect of the rebellion and banditry in the countryside. Such complex, multi-causal pictures can be replicated for other modern diasporic movements.[10] It should also be remembered that, though migration losses were heavy in absolute terms in the case of some of the newer diasporas, with hundreds of thousands, even millions, of people leaving, they rarely constituted a serious drain on the capacity for internal reproduction. In the case of the larger population groups (for example, the Chinese and Indians), the proportion of overseas emigrants to the home population was very small.

Expansion through work, trade or empire

The second fibre of the diaspora rope is that of migration for the purposes of work, trade or colonization. Consider the case of labour diasporas. As I suggested in Chapter 4, few workers – whether they are Indians in the plantation colonies, Haitians in New York or North African construction workers in France – intend to remain unskilled for ever: many hope to move into self-employment. The issue of whether the many groups that might be mobilized as labour diasporas attain or remain within that classification turns on a number of factors.

The most important variable is the extent of social mobility in the host society. Many of the Europeans that arrived in the USA between 1870 and 1914 were manual labourers destined to work in the mass industries of the period. Most were able to escape this status over two or three generations, leaving much of the 3D (dirty, dangerous and difficult) work to new entrants to the USA, to African-Americans and to undocumented Mexicans. In short, they lost their status as labour diasporas. A labour diaspora might, however, arise if an unskilled immigrant group is locked for some time into a subordinate status through lack of opportunity or prejudice. This is not that common a phenomenon, so, insofar as a group returns home (to recommence peasant proprietorship or commence petty entrepreneurship) or enters the middle class, a labour diaspora is normally a transitional type. That is not to say of course that there are not a large number of 3D jobs in many societies; it is rather to assert that they are filled by successive cohorts of 'new helots' or 'new untouchables' from a variety of source countries.[11] Low status jobs also go to labour migrants who circulate or oscillate between their home countries and their places of work abroad. These rotating workers are better considered as transnationals, rather than a labour diaspora, for they are not permanently dispersed.[12]

In the case of trade diasporas, these often arose without the approval of the authorities in the home countries. Chinese traders, for example, had to tolerate dismissive official attitudes. In the Confucian system of thought the merchant was at the bottom of a four-tier hierarchy, beneath the literati, the artisan and even the peasant. Wang points out that this low status was unique to China. Indian merchants occupied a low status in Hindu culture, but they were never at the bottom of the heap, while in the Christian and Muslim ecumenes traders often attained positions close to the seats of power.[13]

Despite this disadvantage, the Chinese in Southeast Asia remain one of the prototypical examples of a trading diaspora. Wang suggests that the long-distance trade *within* China provided a model for the overseas Chinese. By retaining their connections or 'registration' with their home towns they were able to draw on kin support, inviting kinsfolk to act not only as fellow traders but as artisans and workers in their various enterprises. More and more agents or young family members were fed into the network to stabilize existing businesses and to start new ventures. They generally remained on the political margins in the countries to which they emigrated. Chinese communities were rarely given the vote and were often regarded as aliens.[14]

Whereas the trade diasporas just discussed were not state-directed, but depended rather on the initiative of families and individuals, the modern European explorer-traders – Vasco da Gama, Marco Polo and Christopher Columbus, Bartholomew Diaz and the rest – opened up trade routes on behalf of monarchs. Venture capital and the big European trading companies followed, but found themselves constrained or persuaded that they needed to occupy enclaves (for instance Goa, Shanghai, Hong Kong, Manila and the Cape) to secure their trade routes. As night follows day, the European trade diasporas turned into imperial diasporas. Flag followed trade, with the general outcome of conquest, occupation and the subordination of the indigenous peoples.

In this book I have concentrated particularly on the case of the British imperial diaspora – one that was by far the most successful – but the Netherlands, Spain, France and Portugal were not far behind. Limping along in the rear were Germany and Italy, both of which also cherished imperial dreams. These imperial adventures moved from guaranteeing trade flows to using the export or population to establish hegemony on the ground. The British dominions of Australia, Canada, the USA, New Zealand, South Africa and Rhodesia all demonstrated the aptness of the designation 'dominion'.

The European diasporas were 'diasporas by design', a model that was to gain new currency in the global age. Rather than following the Europeans into occupation and political domination – the possibility of which was cut off by their defeat in the Second World War – the Japanese used their immense industrial power to extend their power abroad. The personnel who service the banks, insurance companies, import–export houses and transnational corporations are an updated version of the trading and imperial diasporas of old. To the Japanese diasporas by design has been added the case of contemporary Indian business and professional migration. Once discouraged as a 'brain drain', destructive to India's interests, the state and big business now deliberately train professionals, particularly in the IT industry, to emigrate to countries like the USA. The training received, the remittance income sent (see below) and the synergies with India's own industry have made this an astute strategy.

Other fibres of the diasporic rope

I have described in some detail the characteristics of the first two fibres that are interlaced along the diasporic rope. Seven more fibres remain. I am tempted *pari passu* to follow each one along its full length, drawing together salient comparisons as I go. However, this has the serious danger both of being too prolix and of repeating material that has already found expression in earlier chapters. So let me deal with the remaining seven strands in a more abbreviated way.

First, *a collective memory and myth about the homeland*. The idea of a shared origin and birthplace is a common feature of diasporas. The Jews say they are the 'chosen people', all descended from Abraham. The Armenians claim they are descended from Haik and that Noah's ark ended up on top of Mount Ararat, where the earth was reborn. The Lebanese proclaim they are Phoenicians. The Indian diaspora – or at least that part of it that is Hindu – looks back to the complex of gods and goddesses (notably Vishnu, Shiva, Shakti) who gave birth to the sacred land of India and the River Ganges. The myth of a common origin acts to 'root' a diasporic consciousness and give it legitimacy.[15] The more ancient and venerable the myth, the more useful it is as a form of social distancing from other ethnic groups and a means of affecting an air of difference, perhaps superiority, even in the teeth of dispossession and discrimination.

Second, *an idealization of the supposed ancestral home*. The myths of a common origin are often territorialized, while highly romantic fantasies of the 'old country' are fabulated and avowed. The 'promised land' of the Jews flowed with milk and honey. The aged cedars and scent of mint on Mount Lebanon can be used to brush away the smell of the corpses produced in the recent civil war. The impressive buildings of Zimbabwe stand as a testament to the notion that Africans once had superior civilizations and great empires: a direct refutation of their often low social status in the diaspora. The Assyrians in London and Chicago talk of their link to the great civilization in Mesopotamia, while their arch rivals, the Armenians, mount expensive archaeological expeditions to uncover *their* palaces and shrines. We have also observed that in some cases homeland has given way to a looser notion of 'home'. This can be displaced, as in the cases of the Sindhis and Parsis of Bombay, or deterritorialized through cultural links, as in the Caribbean case, and the substitution of sacred monuments, rivers, icons and shrines, as in the case of diaspora religions.

My third fibre is the presence of *a return movement or intermittent visits* to home. The contrast between the current condition of the diaspora and its imagined past is resolved by actual return or help given to return movements by the diaspora. Philhellenism, Zionism, Garveyism, Pan-Africanism, the attempts to create Khalistan and to remake Greater Armenia – all these are represented by the political vanguards of the diasporas as the only certain means to overcome their precarious and isolated existence in exile. Improvement schemes for homelands also were common in other diasporas. Although born in China, Sun Yixian (Sun Yat-sen) developed his political consciousness in Hong Kong and in the Chinese community in Hawaii. His Society for the Revival of China was a crucial instrument in the promotion of a modern Chinese nationalism. His career is interestingly paralleled by that of Mazzini; again born in Genoa, but finding an echo for his ideas of Italian unity, republicanism and nationalism mainly in the Italian diaspora.

With the increased possibilities for travel in the global age and the frequent discrepancy between favoured lifestyles in the diaspora and less secure ones at home, diasporas have nowadays retained their connections to home by means of virtual re-creations of home and intermittent visits rather than via a return movement.

Fourth, *a strong ethnic group consciousness sustained over a long time*. Marienstras, who correctly argued that 'time has to pass' before we can know that any community that has migrated 'is really a diaspora', strongly emphasized this historical dimension of diaspora formation.[16] In other words, one does not immediately announce the formation of a diaspora at the moment of arrival. A strong attachment to the past, or a block to assimilation in the present and future, must exist to permit a diasporic consciousness to be mobilized or be retained. It is possible to gauge the magnitude of contemporary dispersals, the incipient diasporas arising from civil wars, failed states, environmental disasters, post-colonial crises and the break-up of old political structures from the latest available UN figures on refugees (Table 9.1). Again, I add, these data are simply indicative of populations that may or may not become diasporas. Return, assimilation or the further fragmentation of such populations are just as likely outcomes as the emergence and development of a diasporic identity.

A fifth fibre is *a troubled relationship with the host society*. This feature of a diaspora is, unfortunately, all too common and there is barely a group mentioned that did not at some stage experience discrimination in the countries of their migration. The major exceptions to this rule are those diasporas that were, in effect, settler colonies. The British in the dominions and North America, and the Portuguese in Brazil were able to establish their own hegemony in language, law, property rights and political institutions, thereby forcing the indigenees onto the defensive.

Table 9.1 **Refugee population by region, 2006**

Central Africa and Great Lakes	1,119,400
East and Horn of Africa	872,300
Southern Africa	187,800
West Africa	261,800
Total Africa★	2,421,300
Central Asia, South West Asia, North Africa and Middle East	3,811,800
Americas	1,035,900
Asia and Pacific	875,100
Europe	1,773,700
TOTAL	9,877,800

★Excluding North Africa.
Source: UNHCR, *Global Trends 2006* (Geneva: United Nations High Commission for Refugees, 2007) available at http://www.unhcr.org/statistics/STATISTICS/4676a71d4.pdf

Elsewhere, the rule is pretty unwavering. The Chinese in Malaya, Indians in Fiji, Poles in Germany, Italians in Switzerland, Japanese in Peru, Irish in England, Palestinians in Kuwait, Caribbean peoples in Europe, Sikhs in Britain, Turks and Roma in Germany and Kurds in Turkey have all experienced antagonism and legal or illegal discrimination. A number have become the objects of violent hatred in their countries of settlement. What makes this form of inter-ethnic tension different from the general case is that in some measure these groups can look outside their immediate communities (for comfort, comparison and identification) to co-ethnic communities elsewhere and to the possibility of returning to a real or imagined homeland.

Sixth, *a sense of co-responsibility with co-ethnic members in other countries.* The sense of unease or difference that diaspora peoples feel in their countries of residence is paralleled by a tendency to identify instead with fellow members of their diaspora in other countries. None the less, there is often a great deal of tension in the relationship between scattered co-ethnic communities. A bond of loyalty to the country of refuge or settlement competes with ethnic solidarity, while there is frequently a considerable reluctance by those who have stepped quite far down the path of assimilation to accept too close a link with a despised or low-status ethnic group abroad, even if it happens to be one's own. It is perhaps predictable that those who have clawed their way to the top should pull up the ladder behind them.

The seventh and final fibre of the diaspora rope is *the possibility of a distinctive creative, enriching life in tolerant host countries.* Even victim diasporas can find their experiences in modern nation-states enriching and creative as well as enervating and terrifying. The Jews' considerable intellectual and spiritual achievements in the diaspora simply could not have happened in a narrow tribal society like that of ancient Judea. The Armenians and Irish thrived materially and politically in the 'land of opportunity', the USA. The Palestinians are characteristically more prosperous and better educated than the locals in the countries of their exile. Despite their bitter privations, Africans in the diaspora have produced influential musical forms like spirituals, jazz, blues, rock and roll, calypso, samba and reggae, initiated major innovations in the performing arts and generated a rich vein of literature and poetry. The Sindhis have turned their backs on their sorrowful period during the partition of India and prospered greatly in Bombay and much further afield.

DIASPORAS AS AGENTS OF DEVELOPMENT

It is time now to turn away from established methods to new themes for study. Scholars of diasporas have always been aware that diasporic connections led to profound changes at points of origin. Failing agricultural pursuits were given a renewed lease of life; family and kin were supported in their old age and in poverty, and sometimes more dramatic and far-reaching changes were initiated. While long recognized in the academic literature, development agencies, NGOs and richer countries seeking to target their development aid have only recently recognized these effects. For example in 2004, the UK government's Department for International Development (DfID) commissioned a team to see how UK-based diasporas could contribute towards development and poverty reduction in their home countries. Having surveyed Ghanaian, Nigerian, Indian, Sri Lankan Tamil, Somali and Chinese diasporas in Britain, the authors of the report concluded that DfID and other development agencies should (a) secure the rights of migrants, (b) cut the cost of money transfers, (c) encourage migrants to invest in community initiatives in their home countries and (d) engage with pro-poor drivers of change at home.[17] The department was quick off the mark and launched a 'send money home' website (http://www.sendmoneyhome.org/) supported by 500,000 leaflets directed to various incipient and established diasporas in the UK.

By trying to structure and lend legitimacy to these links, development agencies were recognizing that 'remittances' (recorded money migrants send to home countries abroad) are a large and rapidly growing part of international financial flows. In 2005 US$188 billion was transferred to poor countries and the sum was expected to grow by US$11 billion in 2006, while total remittances to rich and poor countries amounted to US$268 billion. These figures arise from a World Bank report, the authors of which also point out that these sums only reflect officially-sanctioned transfers. They add that: 'unrecorded flows through informal channels may add 50 per cent or more to recorded flows. Including these unrecorded flows, the true size of remittances, is larger than foreign direct investment flows and more than twice as large as official aid received by developing countries.'[18] The distribution of these remittances, by region, is shown in Table 9.2.

Table 9.2 **Global flows of international migrant remittances (US$ billion)**

INFLOWS	2001	2002	2003	2004	2005	2006*	% Change 2001–06
All developing countries	96	117	145	163	188	199	107
East Asia and the Pacific	20	29	35	39	44	45	125
Europe and Central Asia	13	14	17	23	31	32	149
Latin America and the Caribbean	24	28	35	41	48	53	119
Middle-East and North Africa	15	16	21	23	24	25	64
South Asia	19	24	31	30	35	36	86
Sub-Saharan Africa	5	5	6	7	7	7	62
World	147	170	205	230	257	268	83

* Estimate.
Source: Sanket Mohapatra, Dilip Ratha and Zhimei Xu, *Migration and Development*, Brief 2, Development Prospects Group, Migration and Remittances Team 1, Remittance Trends (Washington, DC: World Bank, 2006).

The recognition of the role that diasporas can play in development in their home areas has become something of a fashion in development agencies. Not only have they acknowledged that the existing volumes of funds transferred are immense, they see channelling aid through diasporas as preferable to sending aid to governments in poor countries, some of which are ineffective at best and corrupt at worst. For diaspora scholars a new field of applied studies has opened out. How are migration and development linked through diasporas? What are the best means to transfer funds and expertise? Which schemes work and do not work and for what reasons? Can one replicate good practice across different diasporas facing different circumstances in their home countries? Can diasporas link to other internal civil society organizations such as churches or hometown associations? Can one imagine a benign synergy between rich and poor countries ('co-development') in which labour, training and capital flows are traded without disadvantage to either partner?[19]

THE ROLE OF DIASPORAS IN INTERNATIONAL POLITICS

Another important topic in diaspora studies is the changing role of diasporas in international politics. Gabriel Sheffer initiated the pioneering work on this theme and continues to be the major political scientist working in the field.[20] In examining the contours of diasporic politics, Sheffer makes an important distinction between stateless and state-linked diasporas:

> Whereas stateless diasporas often choose separatist or irredentist strategies in regard to their homelands, most state-linked entities tend to opt for communalism in their host countries. Different choices

from among those divergent strategies will dictate different patterns of loyalties as well as differences in allocation of resources, organization, political behaviour and relationships with relevant social and political actors.[21]

This distinction immediately flags up the possibility and even likelihood that stateless diasporas will establish organizations to collect money and weapons to help armed struggle at home and mount campaigns for the recognition of irredentist states. Without pronouncing on the justness or otherwise of their causes, we can note the destabilizing role of the Sri Lankan Tamil diaspora in their support of the Tamil Tigers, the persistent efforts of the Kurdish diaspora to establish a Kurdish state and the success of the Croatian diaspora in helping to establish an independent Croatian state.

Of course these diasporas were not the only players involved. The bipolar shape of international politics disintegrated after the Cold War and states, NGOs, powerful corporations, networks and religions all compete for power and influence in a more complex, pluralist world. Within this lattice work of competing interests, diasporas have emerged as key players in the often precarious politics of their homeland states. The key finding of a recent collection of studies on diasporas in conflict is that they can be a force for stability ('peace-makers') as well as a force that amplifies and even creates conflict ('peace-wreckers'). As Smith and Stares remark: 'Diasporic involvement in conflict still needs to be studied, but what can be said is that diasporas play "significant and varied roles" in the whole range of activities in the conflict cycle.'[22] One interesting case is that of the Eritrean diaspora, which played the role of peace-wrecker and peace-maker, though its contribution to post-conflict reconstruction efforts has been less recognized.[23]

Also largely unrecognized is that the aftermath of 9/11 radically shifted the international politics of certain diasporas. In the political atmosphere in the USA that followed Al-Qaeda's attack, 'playing footsie' with terrorists was definitely off the political agenda. The Tamil diaspora in the USA distanced itself from the Tamil Tigers. Financial support given to the Irish Republican Army in Northern Ireland by the American Irish diaspora dried up (thus forcing republicans to the negotiating table). Even the longstanding State Department support for armed intervention in Cuba led by Cuban exiles was withdrawn and (informally leaked) official US policy, though no more friendly to the communist regime in Cuba, is to sit it out until Fidel Castro dies.

NEGATIVE REACTIONS TO THE GROWTH OF DIASPORAS

The sudden proliferation and recognition of diasporas have triggered a considerable degree of apprehension among Western academics and commentators, who have expressed a heightened consciousness that diasporas can represent a threat to the nation-state and the liberal-democratic order. American historians, writers, government officials and opinion-makers, who have been highly critical of any policies to recognize diversity and cultural plurality, have articulated a number of these concerns. Hu-DeHart describes these commentators collectively as 'triumphalists'. They merit this designation, she maintains, in championing a traditional view of American history that proclaims the triumph of Western civilization and American culture. She quotes George Will (a leading newspaper columnist) to this effect: 'America is predominantly a product of the Western tradition and is predominantly good because that tradition is good.'[24]

This position is strongly associated with neo-conservative opinion in the USA. The neo-conservative and conservative right in the USA and Europe has seized the political moment the terrorist threat afforded to question both the extent of migration and the degree of recognition afforded to migrants' home cultures, religions, languages and social practices. The attack on diversity and difference has been particularly fierce in the USA. Perhaps the most powerful academic voice on this question has been that of Samuel P. Huntington, a professor of politics at Harvard and the director of security planning for the National Security Council in the Carter administration. In his *cri de coeur* titled *Who are we?* he angrily denounces those in the USA who had discarded earlier notions that the USA was a 'melting pot' or 'tomato soup' and proposed instead that it was more like a 'mosaic' or 'salad bowl' of diverse peoples. He insists on the primacy of the English-speaking, Protestant eastern seaboard and deplores the 'deconstructionists' who sought to 'enhance the status and influence of subnational racial, ethnic, and cultural groups', which, he claims, had deleterious effects on democratic values and liberties:

> They downgraded the centrality of English in American life and pushed bilingual education and linguistic diversity. They advocated legal recognition of group rights and racial preferences over the individual rights central to the American Creed. They justified their actions by theories of multiculturalism and the idea that diversity rather than unity or community should be America's overriding value. The combined effect of these efforts was to promote the deconstruction of the American identity that had been gradually created over three centuries.[25]

However, even liberal historians like Arthur Schlesinger Jr have nailed their colours to the mast of a single national identity: 'The US escaped the divisiveness of a multi-ethnic society by a brilliant solution: the creation of a brand new identity. The point of America was not to preserve old cultures but to forge a new, American culture.'[26] Suddenly language rights, educational provisions

171

and the judicial system have become open to question. As Dickstein, probably more in sadness than in anger, argues:

> Once minority groups had been desperately eager to join the main-stream, to become assimilated. They were looking for simple justice not for ultimate approval. Now, an angry, even self-destructive separatism, an assertion of group pride at the expense of practical goals, often replaced the old desire for legal equality. Minorities no longer looked to be admitted to the club; instead they insisted on changing the rules.[27]

The debate about the dangers of multiculturalism is paralleled by an even more feverish debate about the dangers that diasporas present in their heedless efforts to have homelands of their own. Where the homeland does not exist, violence, usually terrorism is common. Illustrative cases are the claims by the IRA (Irish Republican Army) for a united Ireland, Hamas's and Hezbollah's insistence on a Palestine reconstituted by violence, the formation of militant Sikh groups demanding the Kalsa raj (a Sikh sovereign state) in the wake of the Indian troops' attack on the Golden Temple, and the terrorist section of the PKK (Kurdish Workers' Party) fighting for a sovereign Kurdistan. Though these examples provided concern, the thought that angry sections in Muslim communities abroad might embrace militant versions of political Islam ('jihadists') is viewed with considerable alarm, particularly in Western political circles. This notion of an Islamic threat to Western economic and political interests has gained strong credibility in the wake of the terrorist attacks in New York, Madrid and London commencing on 11 September 2001.

FINAL REMARKS

While such terrorist challenges have by no means totally undermined the power of the nation-state, they have none the less provided formidable security threats and diasporas are looked upon with suspicion as well as approval. How should contemporary nation-states react to the growing number and strength of diasporas? Ever since their state structures first cohered (starting in Europe around the sixteenth century), the leaders of nation-states have sought to have it all their own way. They have coped with ethnic diversity by demanding exclusive citizenship, border control, linguistic conformity and political obedience. Moreover, the nation-state was offered as an object of devotion. Its citizens were enjoined to love their country, to revere its institutions, to salute its flag, to support its sporting teams, and to fight and die for it in war.

In the face of powerfully defended nationalist sentiments it has, until recently, been difficult for diasporic groups to express their true attitudes to the nation-states in which they found themselves. I use the expression 'found themselves' because many migratory movements (as in transatlantic slavery, the recruitment of indentured labour, or forced migration arising from civil war) involved coercion. There is an inverse relationship between the amount of compulsion involved and the likelihood of anticipatory socialization to the new environment having taken place. In such contexts, ethnic or transnational communities will persist or be recreated. Now, it cannot be denied, many newer diasporas want to have their cake and eat it. They want not only the security and opportunities available in their countries of settlement, but also a continuing relationship with their country of origin and co-ethnic members in other countries. For such diasporas the nation-state is being used rather than revered.

Perhaps this is the case because unlike adherence to an ethnicity, religion or diaspora, the nation-state is often too large and too amorphous an entity to be the object of intimate affection. One can marry a spouse of one's own kind and feel the warm embrace of kinship; one can kneel in common prayer with one's co-religionists; one can affect easier friendships with those of a common background. Bonds of language, religion, culture and a sense of a common history and perhaps a common fate impregnate a diasporic relationship and give to it an affective, intimate quality that formal citizenship or even long settlement frequently lack.

The pessimists claim that certain values and ways of life that are imported are simply incompatible with the way in which Western liberal democracies (in particular) have evolved. To take one important example, the separation of church and state was resolved through bitter religious wars in Europe and the acceptance of secularism at the time of the founding of the large immigrant-importing states like the USA, Canada and Australia. The difference between the public and private domains is, however, fundamentally challenged by theocratic ideas (not only articulated by Muslims, but notably by them) that deny any domain differences between private worship, the provision of education and the governance of the state. Others are far from happy about the relative immunity of diasporas from the disciplines and duties of citizenship in a modern nation-state. For them, the nation-state is not an oppressive form of social organization, but one that protects free expression, political diversity, cultural pluralism and social tolerance. To abandon such features in the face of militant ethnic demands could be a disastrous reverse for the civilizing progress initiated by the Enlightenment. Diasporas articulate their demands in terms of human rights or 'group rights'. More exactly, the loudest mouths in the diaspora communities articulate these demands, often leaving little room for the dissenter, the individualist and the person who does not wish to affirm any special ethnic identity.

The optimists aver that liberal democracies can construct 'an egalitarian multicultural society' where

> it is possible, without threat to the overall unity of the national society, to recognize that minorities have a right to their own language in family

and community contexts, the right to practise their own religion, the right to organize domestic and family relations in their own way, and the right to maintain communal customs.[28]

Moreover, diasporas perform a vital social role. They bridge the gap between the individual and society, between the local and the global, between the cosmopolitan and the particular. Diasporas can be used to spread liberal democratic values to their home countries.[29] As we have seen above, diasporas can act as agents of benign development in their home countries; they can act also as peace makers helping in the reconstruction of their places or origin when they have been torn apart by conflict. Moreover, the sense of uprootedness, disconnection, loss and estrangement, which the traditionally-recognized diasporas hitherto morally appropriated, may now signify something more general about the human condition. Why not celebrate the creative, enriching side of living in 'Babylon', the radiance of difference?

To mediate between these contrasting views is as yet impossible, for the ultimate answer will turn on the capacity of nation-states to manage diversity while permitting free expression and the degree of social cohesion sufficient to ensure legitimacy for the state and its principal institutions. One of the most important features of modernity was that the leaders of powerful, hegemonic nation-states sought to make exclusive citizenship a *sine qua non*. The world is simply not like that any more; the scope for multiple affiliations and associations that has been opened up outside and beyond the nation-state has also allowed a diasporic allegiance to become both more open and more acceptable. There is no longer any stability in the points of origin, no finality in the points of destination and no necessary coincidence between social and national identities.[30] What nineteenth-century nationalists wanted was a 'space' for each 'race', a territorializing of each social identity. What they have got instead is a chain of cosmopolitan cities and an increasing proliferation of subnational and transnational identities that cannot easily be contained in the nation-state system. Will the rash of new diasporas provide an enduring, additional or alternative focus of loyalty and identification to the fealty demanded by the nation-state or traditional religions? Or will they melt away in the face of even more powerful forces like the juggernauts of internationalization and globalization?

A LITERATURE GUIDE

Unlike the entries at the end of previous chapters, this guide will cover the study of diasporas more generally and is not solely focused on this chapter.

Ethnic and religious diasporas

The major social science and historical literature on diasporas is organized along ethnic and religious lines. The following cover a selected number of examples published in the last decade. For ease of reference, they are listed in the alphabetical order of the ethnic group. The reference also appears alphabetically in the list of references.

Africans (Indian Ocean)	Ronald Segal, *Islam's black slaves: the history of Africa's other black diaspora* (London: Atlantic, 2001)
Africans (post-colonial)	Khalid Koser (ed.) *New African diasporas* (London: Routledge, 2003)
Armenians	Khachig Tölölyan, *Redefining diasporas: old approaches, new identities: the Armenian diaspora in an international context* (Occasional paper, London: Armenian Institute 2002)
Basques	Gloria Totoricagüena, *Basque diaspora: migration and transnational identity* (Las Vegas: Center for Basque Studies at the University of Nevada, 2004)
Chinese and Indians	Wong Siu-lun (ed.) *Chinese and Indian diasporas: comparative perspectives* (Hong Kong: Centre of Asian Studies, University of Hong Kong, 2004)
Hindus	Steven Vertovec, *The Hindu diaspora: comparative patterns* (London: Routledge, 2000)
Irish	Patrick O'Sullivan, *The Irish world wide: history, heritage, identity*, 6 vols (Leicester: Leicester University Press, 1992–97) *Patterns of migration*; II: *Irish in the new communities*; III: *the creative migrant*; IV: *Irish women and Irish migration*; V: *Religion and identity*; VI: *The meaning of the famine*.
Israelis	Steven J. Gold, *The Israeli diaspora* (London: Routledge, 2002)
Italians	Donna R. Gabaccia, *Italy's many diasporas* (London: UCL Press, 2000)
Kurds	Östen Wahlbeck, *Kurdish diasporas: a comparative study of Kurdish refugee communities* (Basingstoke: Palgrave Macmillan, 1999)
Palestinians	Helena Lindholm Schulz, *The Palestinian diaspora: formation of identities and the politics of homeland* (London: Routledge, 2003)
Russians	Hilary Pilkington, *Migration, displacement and identity in post-Soviet Russia* (London: Routledge, 1998)
Sikhs	Darshan Singh Tatla, *The Sikh diaspora: the search for statehood* (London: UCL Press, 1999)
Somalis	Rima Berns McGown, *Muslims in the diaspora: the Somali communities of London and Toronto* (Toronto: University of Toronto Press, 1999)
South Asians (defined by religion)	Harold Coward, John R. Hinnells and Raymond Brady Williams (eds) *The South Asian religious diaspora in Britain, Canada, and the United States* (Albany, NY: State University of New York Press, 2000)

South Asians (general)	Judith M. Brown, *Global South Asians: introducing the modern diaspora* (Cambridge: Cambridge University Press, 2006)
Ukrainians	Vic Satzewich, *The Ukrainian diaspora* (London: Routledge, 2002)
Zoroastrians	John R. Hinnells, *The Zoroastrian diaspora: religion and migration* (Oxford: Oxford University Press, 2005)

Refugees

David J. Griffiths, *Somali and Kurdish refugees in London: new identities in the diaspora* (Aldershot: Ashgate, 2002)

Christopher McDowell, *A Tamil asylum diaspora: Sri Lankan migration, settlement and politics in Switzerland* (Oxford: Berghahn Books, 1996)

Nicholas Van Hear, *New diasporas: the mass exodus, dispersal and regrouping of migrant communities* (London: UCL Press, 1998)

Politics and international relations

Edward Alexander and Paul Bogdanor (eds) *The Jewish divide over Israel: accusers and defenders* (New Jersey: Transaction Publishers 2006)

Gabriel Sheffer *Diaspora politics: at home abroad* (Cambridge: Cambridge University Press, 2003)

Hazel Smith and Paul Stares (eds) *Diasporas in conflict: peace-makers and peace-wreckers* (Tokyo: United Nations University Press, 2007)

French

The excellent work done by French scholars in recent years has been underexposed in the Anglophone world. Here are a few examples.

Lisa Anteby-Yemini, William Berthomière and Gabriel Sheffer (eds) *Les diasporas: 2000 ans d'histoire* (Rennes: Presses Universitaires de Rennes, 2005). (This contains some contributions in English.)

William Berthomière and Christine Chivallon (eds) *Les diasporas dans le monde contemporain* Paris: Karthala and Maison des Sciences de l'Homme (Bordeaux, Pessac, 2006) (This contains some contributions in English.)

Chantal Bordes-Benayoun and Dominique Schnapper, *Diasporas et nations* (Paris: Odile Jacob, 2006)

Christine Chivallon, *La diaspora noire de Amériques: expériences et theories à partir de la Caraïbe* (Paris: CNRS Editions, 2004)

Humanities and cultural studies

With the proliferation of different theories of diaspora, the concept has found a place in studies of language, gender, sexuality, visual, material and performing culture, and other areas in the humanities. Here are a few examples.

Gayati Gopinath *Impossible desire: queer diasporas and South Asian public cultures* (Durham, NC: Duke University Press, 2005)

Virinder S. Kalra, Raminder Kaur and John Hutnyk, *Diaspora and hybridity* (London: Sage, 2005)

Nicholas Mirzoeff, *Diaspora and visual culture: representing Africans and Jews* (London: Routledge, 2000)

Vijay Mishra *The literature of the Indian diaspora: theorizing the diasporic imaginary* (London: Routledge, 2007)

General works and readers

Stéphane Dufoix, (forthcoming) *Diasporas* (Berkeley: University of California Press)

Jana Evans Braziel and Anita Mannur, *Theorizing diaspora: a reader* (Oxford: Blackwell, 2003)

Andre Levy and Alex Weingrod (eds) *Homelands and diasporas: holy lands and other spaces* (Stanford: Stanford University Press, 2004)

Steven Vertovec and Robin Cohen (eds) *Migration, diasporas and transnationalism* (Cheltenham: Edward Elgar, 1999)

QUESTIONS TO THINK ABOUT

- What did Weber mean by an 'ideal type'? Does the use of a Weberian typology help or hinder in the study of diasporas?
- Why do some observers see diasporas in a negative light? Do you agree with their views?
- How successful are diasporas as agents of development compared with development aid and states in poor countries?

NOTES

1 FOUR PHASES OF DIASPORA STUDIES

1 William Safran, 'Diasporas in modern societies: myths of homeland and return', *Diaspora*, 1(1) (1991), 83.

2 This number is very approximate and includes subsets of earlier groups – thus, for example, Nigerian, Zimbabwean, Ghanaian diasporas as new segments of the African diaspora – as well as new claimants. As early as 1998, the editor of the journal *Diaspora* announced at a conference that he had already published articles concerning 38 different diasporas.

3 I have used the expression 'social constructionist' to signify a mode of reasoning, closely associated with postmodernism, which suggests that reality is determined by social interaction (or intersubjectivity), rather than by objectivity (the acceptance of a natural or material world) or by subjectivity (a world determined by individual perceptions). The perspective tends to favour voluntarism and collective human agency over structure, history and habituation.

4 David J. Goldberg and John D. Raynor, *The Jewish people: their history and their religion* (Harmondsworth: Penguin, 1989) pp. 46–8.

5 See the various case studies in Khalid Koser (ed.) *New African diasporas* (London: Routledge, 2003).

6 Christine Kinealy, *The great calamity: the Irish famine, 1845–52* (London: Gill & Macmillan, 1995).

7 Helena Lindholm Schultz, *The Palestinian diaspora: formation of identities and politics of homeland* (London: Routledge, 2003) p. 1.

8 Safran, 'Diasporas in modern societies'.

9 All phrases in quotation marks from Safran, 'Diasporas in modern societies', pp. 83–4.

10 I have previously dealt with the ambiguities Caribbean peoples present under the interrogative title of Robin Cohen, 'A diaspora of a diaspora? The case of the Caribbean', *Social Science Information*, 31(1), (1992), 193–203. See also Chapter 7 in this book.

11 Safran, 'Diasporas in modern societies, pp. 83–4.

12 Willian Safran, 'The Jewish diaspora in a comparative and theoretical perspective', *Israel Studies*, 10(1), (2005a), 37.

13 M. Grunwald *History of the Jews in Vienna* (Philadelphia: Jewish Publication Society of America, 1936); B. J. Israel, *The children of Israel: the Bene Israel of Bombay* (Oxford: Basil Blackwell, 1971).

14 Jacob Neusner, *Israel in America: a too-comfortable exile?* (Boston: Beacon, 1985).

15 The African political scientist, Ali A. Mazrui, *Cultural forces in world politics* (London: James Currey, 1990) p. 132, pointed out that the 15 million Jews worldwide (0.2 per cent of the world's population) provided about 25 per cent of Nobel Prize winners. The winners

are overwhelmingly from the diaspora, though there have been some notable Israeli laureates. An up-to-date list is maintained by the Israel Science and Technology page (http://www.science.co.il/Nobel.asp).

16 Pnina Werbner, 'The place which is diaspora: citizenship, religion and gender in the making of chaordic transnationalism', *Journal of Ethnic and Migration Studies*, 28(1), (2002), 120.

17 I am indebted to Werbner for this expression. See Pnina Werbner 'The place which is diaspora', 121–2.

18 In the first edition of this book I used the expression 'cultural diaspora', which has caused some confusion; 'deterritorialized' is a much better adjective. See Chapter 7.

19 Quoted in Stéphane Dufoix, *Diasporas* (Berkeley: University of California Press, forthcoming). I have done a little editing for punctuation.

20 Dufoix, *Diasporas*.

21 Gayati Gopinath, *Impossible desire: queer diasporas and South Asian public cultures* (Durham, NC: Duke University Press, 2005).

22 http://reporter.leeds.ac.uk/508/s9.htm. Press release 6 June 2005.

23 Rogers Brubaker, 'The "diaspora" diaspora', *Ethnic and Racial Studies*, 28(1), (January 2005), 3. Brubaker's observation recalls the telling line in Gilbert and Sullivan's operetta, *The Gondoliers*, namely that 'When everyone is somebody, then no one's anybody.'

24 Brubaker 'The "diaspora" diaspora', *Ethnic and Racial Studies*, 28(1), 1.

25 It might be worth recalling Marx's crucial insight that 'Men [read 'people'] make their own history, but they do not make it as they please; they do not make it under circumstances chosen by themselves, but under circumstances directly encountered, given and transmitted from the past. The tradition of all the dead generations weighs like a nightmare on the brains of the living.' See Karl Marx, 'The eighteenth Brumaire of Louis Napolean', in Lewis S. Feuer (ed.) *Marx and Engels: basic writings on politics and philosophy* (New York: Anchor Books, 1959) p. 321.

26 Avtar Brah, *Cartographies of diaspora: contesting identities* (London: Routledge, 1996) p. 180.

27 Brah, *Cartographies of diaspora*, p. 192.

28 Floya Anthias, 'Evaluating "diaspora": beyond ethnicity', *Sociology*, 32(3), (1998) includes the first edition of this book in her charge, though I thought it was clear that I was arguing for a more complex notion of origin (see Chapters 3 on Africans and 6 on Sikhs, which are similar to the edition she cites). I also concur that 'belonging' is not a given, but has to be established, mobilized and defended in social, cultural and political practices. I accept this was not as evident as it should have been in the first edition and I have revised a number of passages pertaining to this point in this edition. My views are clarified at length in Robin Cohen, *Frontiers of identity: the British and the Others* (London: Longman, 1994) Chapters 1 and 7.

29 Anthias, 'Evaluating diaspora', 577.

30 Yasemin Nugoğlu Soysal, 'Citizenship and identity: living in diasporas in post-war Europe?' *Ethnic and Racial Studies*, 23(1), (2000), 1–2. Nearly all diaspora theorists had in fact pointed out that diaspora was a concept that long predated the nation-state and that diasporic formations were constantly in tension with nation-states. See, for example, Robin Cohen 'Diasporas and the nation-state: from victims to challengers', *International Affairs*, 72(3), (July 1996), 507–20.

31 Soysal, 'Citizenship and identity', pp. 2–3.

32 Soysal, 'Citizenship and identity', p. 13.

33 Khachig Tölölyan, 'Restoring the logic of the sedentary to diaspora studies', in Lisa Anteby-Yemeni, William Berthomière and Gabriel Sheffer (eds) *Les diasporas: 2000 ans d'histoire* (Rennes: Presse Universitaires de Rennes, 2005) pp. 138–9.

34 Brubaker, 'The "diaspora" diaspora', p 5.

35 Brubaker, 'The "diaspora" diaspora', pp. 5–7.
36 William Safran, 'The tenuous link between hostlands and homeland: the progressive dezionization of western diasporas', in Lisa Anteby-Yemeni, William Berthomière and Gabriel Sheffer (eds) *Les diasporas: 2000 ans d'histoire* (Rennes: Presse Universitaires de Rennes, 2005) pp. 193-208. Cf. my discussion of the relationship between Israel and the Jewish diaspora in Chapter 6 of this book.
37 Safran, 'The tenuous link', pp. 199–200.
38 See Steven J. Gold, *The Israeli diaspora* (London: Routledge, 2002).
39 Martin Sökefeld, 'Mobilizing in transnational space: a social movement approach to the formation of diaspora', *Global Networks*, 6(3), (July 2006), 265–84.
40 David Chariandy, 'Postcolonial diasporas', *Postcolonial Text*, 2(1), (2006), http://postcolonial.org/index.php/pct/article/view/440/159 (online journal with no page numbers).
41 Chariandy, 'Postcolonial diasporas'. As I have indicated earlier in this chapter, while I think he is right in identifying the political agenda of such writers as an attempt to foster progressive post-colonial politics, there are serious dangers in bending the concept of diaspora to serve a particular political end. I have benefited from an email exchange with David Chariandy, for which I thank him.
42 For one exposition of the term 'creolization', see Robin Cohen, 'Creolization and cultural globalization: the soft sounds of fugitive power', *Globalizations*, 4(3), (September 2007), 1–16.
43 Anthias, 'Evaluating diaspora', p. 557. See also Akenson cited in Vic Satzewich, *The Ukrainian diaspora* (London: Routledge, 2002) p. 14; Chariandy, 'Postcolonial diasporas'; and Soysal, 'Citizenship and identity'.
44 Richard Marienstras, 'On the notion of diaspora', in Gérard Chaliand (ed.) *Minority peoples in the age of nation-states* (London: Pluto Press, 1989) p. 25. See also Brubaker 'The "diaspora" diaspora', p. 7.
45 See Safran, 'The Jewish diaspora in a comparative and theoretical perspective', p. 37 for a similar list, which I admire and from which I have drawn. The differences between us, which were more marked in the past, are not fundamental, but are largely matters of nuance.
46 A number of reference books will explain this. See, for example, the entry under Weber in Adam Kuper and Jessica Kuper (eds) *The social science encyclopaedia* (London: Routledge, 1999) pp. 906–10. See also Chapter 9 of this book.

2 CLASSICAL NOTIONS OF DIASPORA

1 I am grateful to Martin Baumann, 'Diaspora: genealogies of semantics and transcultural comparison', *Numen*, 47(3), (2000), 313–14 for clarifying this. Stefan Helmrich, 'Kinship, nation and Paul Gilroy's concept of diaspora', *Diaspora*, 2(2), (1992), 243–9, notes that the patriarchal connection to the word is quite strong, the scattering or sowing of seeds being closely related in Judeo–Christian and Islamic cosmology to male sperm.
2 Again Baumann's 'Diaspora', 316–17, carries conviction. Marienstras, 'On the notion of diaspora', p. 120 erroneously maintains that there is a rigid distinction by Jewish thinkers between *galût*, implying forced dispersal, and diaspora, implying free and voluntary migration. Would that life were so simple! Though *galût* always implies a negative origin and condition, as explained above the word diaspora is used similarly in the Jewish tradition.
3 James Clifford, 'Diasporas', *Current Anthropology*, 9(3), (1994), 303.
4 Barbara Kirshenblatt-Gimblett, 'Spaces of dispersal', *Cultural Anthropology*, 9(3), (1994), 340.
5 Jonathan Boyarin, 'Powers of diaspora', paper presented to a panel on diaspora at the International Congress of the Historical Sciences, Montreal, 27 August–3 September 1995, p. 5.

6 David J. Goldberg and John D. Raynor, *The Jewish people: their history and their religion* (Harmondsworth: Penguin, 1989) pp. 46–8.

7 Arnold Ages, *The diaspora dimension* (The Hague: Martinus Nijhoff, 1973) p. 10.

8 Goldberg and Raynor, *The Jewish people*, p. 53.

9 Ages, *The diaspora dimension*, pp. 3–7.

10 Galit Hasan-Rokem and Alan Dundes (eds) *The wandering Jew: essays in the interpretation of a Christian legend* (Bloomington, IN: Indiana University Press, 1986).

11 Pinsker, cited in Myron Weiner, 'Labour migrations and incipient diasporas', in Gabriel Sheffer (ed.) *Modern diasporas in international politics* (London: Croom Helm, 1986) p. 135.

12 See Weiner, 'Labour migrations and incipient diasporas', pp. 47–74.

13 Ages, *The diaspora dimension*, p. 9.

14 *Encyclopaedia Judaica* (Jerusalem: Keter Publishing House, 1971) vol. 13, p. 571.

15 *Marranos* are 'swine'. The word derives from the Arabic *moharram* meaning 'forbidden'. The term is obviously pejorative. The word *conversos* is more polite, but misleading because it has been established that many of the *Marranos* had little intention of fully converting.

16 This rather sick association of music with misfortune prefigured the even more morbid occasions when Jews had to listen to the strains of Wagner while marching towards the gas ovens in the Nazi concentration camps.

17 Francesca M. Wilson, *They came as strangers: the story of refugees to Great Britain* (London: Hamish Hamilton, 1959) pp. 168–9.

18 Edward Said, *Orientalism: Western conceptions of the Orient* (Harmondsworth: Penguin, 1991) pp. 26–7.

19 Amin Maalouf, *The Crusades through Arab eyes* (London: Al Saqi, 1984) p. ii.

20 Bernard Lewis, *The Arabs in history* (London: Hutchinson University Library, 1970) pp. 40–1.

21 Goldberg and Raynor, *The Jewish people*, p. 92.

22 Philip K. Hitti, *History of the Arabs: from the earliest times to the present* (London: Macmillan, 1974) pp. 533–4.

23 Hitti, *History of the Arabs*, pp. 356–7.

24 Solomon Dob Fritz Goitein, *A Mediterranean society: the Jewish communities of the Arab world as portrayed in the documents of the Cairo Geniza* (Berkeley: University of California Press, 1971) p. 407.

25 Clifford, 'Diasporas', p. 305.

26 Albert Hourani, *Arabic thought in the liberal age, 1798–1939* (Cambridge: Cambridge University Press, 1983) p. 30.

27 Marion Woolfson, *Prophets in Babylon: Jews in the Arab world* (London: Faber & Faber, 1980) p. 86.

28 Hourani, *Arabic thought in the liberal age*, p. 57.

29 Albert Hourani, *A history of the Arab peoples* (Cambridge, MA: The Belknap Press of Harvard University Press, 1991) pp. 288–9.

30 Ashkenaz was Noah's great-grandson. According to the Bible, after the flood had subsided 'the peoples of the coasts and islands separated into their own countries, each with their own language, family by family, nation by nation' (Genesis 10: 1–5).

31 Arthur Koestler, *The thirteenth tribe: the Khazar empire and its heritage* (London: Hutchinson, 1976) pp. 180–200 has some rather eccentric and some ridiculous passages on racial differences, including diagrams of Jewish noses, but it is difficult to refute his main point. On a global scale Jews resemble each other hardly at all, while they often resemble their surrounding peoples much more closely. Phenotypically, Ashkenazim are evidently of a different origin from Sephardim.

32 The Pale of Settlement was the area covering modern-day Belarus, Lithuania, Poland, Moldova, Ukraine and western Russia. Except for some minor exceptions, the Russian imperial authorities forced Jews to live in the Pale. Although students

should be careful about citing an unrefereed source, in this case the Wikipedia entry (http://en.wikipedia.org/wiki/Pale_of_Settlement) is informative and authoritative.

33 Albert S. Lindemann, *The Jew accused: three anti-Semitic affairs: Dreyfus, Beilis, Frank, 1884–1915* (Cambridge: Cambridge University Press, 1993) pp. 132–3.

34 Weizman cited in Lindemann, *The Jew accused*, p. 145. The revolutionary tradition nurtured in Eastern Europe was often carried abroad by the Jewish emigrants. In the USA, Jews were prominent in the anarchist and labour movements (see N. Levin, *While Messiah tarried: Jewish socialist movements, 1871–1917*, New York: Schocken, 1977). In South Africa, the Communist Party was founded by Jewish emigrants in 1921. Their long struggle finally paid off when, in 1994, the party's most prominent leader, Lithuanian-born Joe Slovo, became minister of housing in the post-apartheid government, just a few months before his death.

35 Daniel Halévy, an eminent French writer, concurred. He thought it essential to escape the confines of a traditional religion: 'How happy I am to have left that hell, to have escaped from Judaism.' Many other emancipated European Jews shared this sentiment. The German poet Heinrich Heine, who also had Jewish ancestry, was equally blunt. Judaism was not a religion but a misfortune: 'Those who would say Judaism is a religion would say that being a hunchback is a religion' (quotes from Lindemann, *The Jew accused*, pp. 62, 15).

36 Lindemann, *The Jew accused*, pp. 35–93.

37 A reliable account is provided by Michael R. Marrus, *The politics of assimilation: the French Jewish community at the time of the Dreyfus affair* (Oxford: Clarendon Press, 1980).

38 Herzl cited in Goldberg and Raynor, *The Jewish people*, p. 166.

39 This is not to say that only such political leaders could arrive at the same conclusion. In his careful examination of the Jews of France, Germany and Russia, Arnold Ages, *The diaspora dimension*, ultimately concludes that Jews who sought contentment in these countries were living an impossible dream, one that in the German case was shattered finally by Nazism. He avers (pp. 169–72) that American Jews are also doomed to go through the same cycle of acceptance–integration–superpatriotism–rejection, though this part of his argument is thinly developed.

40 See Michael R. Marrus, *Vichy France and the Jews* (New York: Basic Books, 1981) and Robert O. Paxton, *Vichy France: old guard and new order* (New York: Colombia University Press, 2001).

3 VICTIM DIASPORAS

1 Mohammed A. Bamyeh 'The Palestinian diaspora', in Hazel Smith and Paul Stares (eds) *Diasporas in conflict: peace-makers or peace-wreckers* (Tokyo: United Nations University Press, 2007) p. 90. See also Walid Khalidi, *Before their diaspora: a photographic history of the Palestinians, 1876–1948* (Washington, DC: Institute for Palestine Studies, 1984); and Schultz, *The Palestinian diaspora*.

2 Indeed, the Jewish diaspora was itself initially dispersed to Mediterranean Africa. Oral tradition also has it that the Ethiopian Jews (the term 'Falashas' is derogatory) were descendants of a love affair between King Solomon and Queen Sheba. Though this story is somewhat fanciful, part of the Jewish people and therefore its diaspora is African in origin, and not merely in the remote sense that we are all ultimately of African origin (Daniel Friedmann with Ulysses Santamara, *Les enfants de la reine de Saba: les Juifs d'Éthiopie (Falachas) – histoire, exode, intégration*, Paris: Éditions Métailié, 1994). Another intriguing connection is that of the Buba clan of the Bemba people (in southern Africa), who are phenotypically African, have an irrefutable DNA connection to the Cohanim (the Jewish priestly caste, often carrying the surname Cohen). See Nicholas Wade, 'Group in Africa has Jewish roots, DNA indicates', *New York Times*, 9 May 1999.

3 George Shepperson, 'African diaspora: concept and context', in Joseph E. Harris (ed.) *Global dimensions of the African diaspora* (Washington, DC: Howard University Press, 1993, second edition) pp. 41–9.

4 R. Hrair Dekmejian, 'Determinants of genocide: Armenians and Jews as case studies', in R. G. Hovannisian (ed.) *The Armenian genocide in perspective* (New Brunswick, NJ: Transaction Publishers, 1991) p. 86.

5 Dekmejian, 'Determinants of genocide', p. 94.

6 Cited in Ronald Segal, *The black diaspora* (London: Faber & Faber, 1995) p. 28.

7 Segal, *The black diaspora*, p. 31.

8 J. O. Hunwick, 'African slaves in the Mediterranean world: a neglected aspect of the African diaspora', in Joseph E. Harris (ed.) *Global dimensions of the African diaspora* (Washington, DC: Howard University Press, 1993) p. 289. The numbers involved are not definitive, but two common estimates are ten million for the Atlantic trade and about seven million for the Indian Ocean trade.

9 Shepperson, 'African diaspora', p. 46.

10 I do not use the word 'myth' in the popular sense of 'an unlikely legend or untruth' but in an anthropological and sociological sense. Myth alludes to collectively-generated explanations and understandings that are widely believed and articulated. As Guerin C. Montilus, 'Guinea versus Congo lands: aspects of the collective memory in Haiti', in Joseph E. Harris (ed.) *Global dimensions of the African diaspora* (Washington, DC: Howard University Press, 1993) p. 159 grandly puts it, myth 'is the resurgence of societal thought and consciousness through space and time serving to structure and rebuild experience'.

11 See Montilus, 'Guinea versus Congo lands', pp. 160–4. In trying to create a 'research agenda' for the study of the African diaspora, scholars are increasingly emphasizing 'the study of slave rebellions, uprisings, and even possibly revolutionary networks' (Ruth Simms Hamilton, *Creating a paradigm and research agenda for comparative studies of the worldwide dispersion of African peoples*, East Lansing, MI: African Diaspora Research Project, Michigan State University 1990, p. 6).

12 See Christopher Fyfe's classic, *A history of Sierra Leone* (London: Oxford University Press, 1962). A popular account, focusing on African returnees who had fought on the British side during the American war of independence, is provided by Simon Scharma, *Rough crossings: Britain, the slaves and the American revolution* (London: BBC Books, 2005).

13 S. Y. Boadi-Siaw, 'Brazilian returnees of West Africa', in Joseph E. Harris (ed.) *Global dimensions of the African diaspora* (Washington, DC: Howard University Press, second edition, 1993) pp. 421–37.

14 S. J. Lemelle *et al.*, *Imagining home: class, culture and nationalism in the African diaspora* (London: Verso, 1994).

15 Both citations in Bernard Makhosezwe Magubane, *The ties that bind: African-American consciousness of Africa* (Trenton, NJ: Africa World Press, 1987) p. 163.

16 This usage is closer to the Greek meaning, which translates as 'burnt face' and to the seventeenth-century English understanding, which equated 'Ethiopian' with 'black'.

17 Ken Post, *Arise ye starvelings: the Jamaican labour rebellion of 1938 and its aftermath* (The Hague: Martinus Nijhoff, 1978) p. 172.

18 Adrian Boot and Michael Thomas, *Jamaica: Babylon on a thin wire* (London: Thames & Hudson, 1976) p. 78.

19 Joe E. Thomas (cited Magubane, *The ties that bind*, p. 167).

20 A very detailed description of the military campaign to restore the Emperor is provided in David Shirreff, *Barefeet and bandoliers: Wingate, Sandford, the Patriots and the part they played in the liberation of Ethiopia* (London: The Radcliffe Press, 1995).

21 Richard Wright, *American hunger* (New York: Harper & Row, 1944) p. 28.

22 Cited in Roy Ottley, *Black odyssey: the story of the Negro in America* (New York: Charles Scribner & Sons, 1948) p. 235.

23 DuBois cited in Magubane, *The ties that bind*, pp. 149–50.

24 Padmore's break with international communism is explained in his informative *mea culpa* published under the title of *Pan-Africanism or communism* (New York: Doubleday, 1972, first published 1949).

25 It is fairly well known that Elvis Presley 'ripped off' black music and exploited his relatively greater acceptability to white audiences by distancing himself from the music's origins. Needless to say, the shrine to the chubby singer at his former residence, Graceland, is not replete with African-American mourners.

26 The words of Marley's 'Redemption Song' express diasporic sentiments poignantly. See also James Lincoln Collier, *The making of jazz: a comprehensive history* (London: Macmillan, 1978); Paul Oliver, *Savannah syncopators: African retentions in the blues* (London: Studio Vista, 1970) and Segal, *The black diaspora*, pp. 375–95.

27 Vahan M. Kurkjian, *A history of Armenia* (New York: Armenian General Benevolent Union of America, 1964) p. 49.

28 David Marshall Lang, *Armenia: cradle of civilisation* (London: George Allen & Unwin, 1978) p. 9. I do not wish to oppose this statement in a narrow didactic manner, but simply note that we have already come across claims for primacy on behalf of Judea, Greece, Rome, Islam, Egypt, Mesopotamia (Sumaria and Babylon) as well as Armenia. Such claims have something to do with the idea of the 'known world'. The list just provided, for example, leaves out some rather significant Asian claimants like China and India, not to mention the Incas and Aztecs. The great world historian, Arnold Toynbee, *A study of history* (London: Oxford University Press, 12 vols, 1934–61), started with a list of 21 civilizations in the first edition of his multi-volume *Study of history*, but by the time the posthumous one-volume summary of his work was published, he was prepared to admit 'up to at least thirty-one, besides a few more that were abortive' (Arnold Toynbee with Jane Caplan, *A study of history*, London: Oxford University Press, 1988, revised abridged edition first published 1972, p. 11). An increased appreciation of the spiritually rich and ecologically friendly ways of life of the native Americans, San, Inuit, Maoris, Aborigines and other indigenous peoples have, in any case, questioned the value of the 'great civilizations' approach to history.

29 Emperor Maurice quoted in Lang, *Armenia*.

30 Garbis Armen *et al.* (eds) *Historical atlas of Armenia* (New York: Armenian National Education Committee, 1987) pp. 6–24.

31 Richard G. Hovannisian 'The historical dimensions of the Armenian question, 1878–1923', in Richard G. Hovannisian (ed.) *The Armenian genocide in perspective* (New Brunswick, NJ: Transaction, 1981) p. 29.

32 Robert Melson, *Revolution and genocide: on the origins of the Armenian genocide and the holocaust* (Chicago: University of Chicago Press, 1992) pp. 146–7.

33 David Marshall Lang and Christopher J. Walker, *The Armenians* (London: Minority Rights Group, MRG Report No. 32, fifth edition, 1987) p. 8.

34 Arnold Toynbee (ed.) *The treatment of Armenians in the Ottoman empire, 1915–16* (London: Her Majesty's Stationary Office, 1916).

35 Quoted by Gerard Chaliand and Yves Ternon, *The Armenians: from genocide to resistance*, translated by Tony Berrett (London: Zed Books, 1983) p. 46.

36 This is not to deny that there were small bands of Armenian nationalists who wanted to oppose the Ottomans by revolutionary means. However, I do not wish to imply support for the justice commandos of the Armenian genocide or for the Armenian Secret Army for the Liberation of Armenia, which commenced terrorist operations against Turkish targets in the 1970s.

37 The most analytically ambitious comparison is made by Robert Melson, *Revolution and genocide*, who creates a 'scale of genocide' from 'massacre or pogrom' to 'partial genocide' to 'total genocide' to 'the holocaust' or 'final solution'. According to Melson (p. 29),

the difference between the last and the second last categories is that some members of the victim group may save themselves by abandoning their identity, as apparently happened to some Armenians who embraced Islam. If we need to make this distinction at all I would, with Zygmunt Baumann, *Modernity and the holocaust* (Cambridge: Polity, 1989), focus more on the differential technological capacities and totalitarian characters of the perpetrator states concerned.

38 Christopher J. Walker, *Armenia: survival of a nation* (London: Croom Helm, 1980) p. 243.
39 Levon Boyajian and Haigaz Grigorian, 'Psychosocial sequelae of the Armenian genocide', in R. G. Hovannisian (ed.) *The Armenian genocide in perspective* (New Brunswick, NJ: Transaction Publishers, 1991) pp. 177–85.
40 William Saroyan, *Here comes, there goes, you know who: an autobiography* (London: Peter Davis, 1962) pp. 87–8.
41 Leo Hamilian, 'The Armenian genocide and the literary imagination', in Richard G. Hovannisian (ed.) *The Armenian genocide in perspective* (New Brunswick, NJ: Transaction, 1981) p. 155 refutes the claim that Michael Arlen forgot his past. He recalls Arlen describing a chance encounter with the Nazi, Goebbels, whom he observed from the veranda of his hotel in Athens in 1940. He spat on Goebbels's 'superb silk hat' as he passed below him and wrote afterwards: 'It made me mad. It always makes me mad when people get away with murder and grin happily ever after. I wanted to throw a brick down at him ... I wanted to knock his hat off. I wanted to forget that I was a naturalized Englishman and become an Armenian again. I wanted to be a Jew and revenge all Jews.'
42 Boyajian and Grigorian, 'Psychosocial sequelae of the Armenian genocide', p. 183.
43 Martine Hovanessian, *Le lien communautaire: trois générations d'Arméniens* (Paris: Armand Colin, 1992).
44 Cf. Stuart Hall, 'Ethnicity, identity and difference', *Radical America*, 23(4), (1991), 9–20.
45 Lang, *Armenia*, pp. 290–1.
46 Cited Lang and Walker, *The Armenians*, p. 9.
47 *Financial Times*, 16 September 1994.
48 Khachig Tölölyan 'The Armenian diaspora and the Karabagh conflict', in Hazel Smith and Paul Stares (eds) *Diasporas in conflict: peace-makers and peace-wreckers* (Tokyo: United Nations University Press, 2007) pp. 106–28.
49 For example, G. Azarpay, *Urartian art and artefacts* (Berkeley: University of California Press, 1968); Lang, *Armenia*; and Sirarpie Der Nersessian, *The Armenians* (London: Thames & Hudson, 1969).
50 Cited Roland Grigor Suny, *Looking toward Ararat: Armenia in modern history* (Bloomington, IN: Indiana University Press, 1993) p. 22.
51 Tölölyan, 'The Armenian diaspora', p. 111.

4 LABOUR AND IMPERIAL DIASPORAS

1 By 1914 nearly one million Italians lived in Argentina while one and a half million lived in the USA, most of them workers. Samuel L. Baily, 'The adjustment of Italian immigrants in Buenos Aires and New York, 1870–1914', in Dirk Hoerder and Leslie Page Moch (eds) *European migrants: global and local perspectives* (Boston: Northeastern University Press, 1995) pp. 282–308; and Donna Gabaccia, 'Clase y cultura: los migrantes Italianos en los movimientos obreros en el mundo, 1876–1914, *Estudios Migratorios Latinoamericanos*, 7(22) (1992), 425–51. These sources show the complexity of the migration process that underlay these figures. Many were content to come on a one-way ticket. Others returned home. And a significant group moved back and forth between Italy and the Americas. The temporary migrants were prepared to stay in the cheapest housing to maximize their savings and remittances. In terms of their occupational profile, data from Argentina can be cited. By 1887, Italians constituted 32 per cent of the population of Buenos Aires,

53 per cent of the industrial workers and 39 per cent of the workers in commercial enterprises (Baily, 'The adjustment of Italian immigrants', p. 284). For Turks and North Africans see Stephen Castles and Godula Kosack, *Immigrant workers and class structure in western Europe* (Oxford: Oxford University Press, second edition, 1985); Robin Cohen, *The new helots: migrants in the international division of labour* (Aldershot: Gower, 1987) pp. 111–44; and Milton J. Esman, *Ethnic politics* (Ithaca: Cornell University Press, 1994) pp. 176–215.

2 Though in fact just such an appellation has been loosely applied *inter alia* to Mexicans, Puerto Ricans, Cubans, Germans and Poles in the USA and to many ethnic groups arriving in Europe or Australasia. I do not accord a 'diaspora' designation to such groups, rather I argue that it has to be demonstrated that some of the other general features of a diaspora (as discussed in Chapter 1) have to be shown to be present.

3 Weiner, 'Labour migrations and incipient diasporas', p. 48.

4 John A. Armstrong, 'Mobilized and proletarian diasporas', *American Political Science Review*, 20(2) (1976), 405 and passim.

5 H. Epstein, *Jewish labor in USA: an industrial, political and cultural history of the Jewish labor movement* (New York: Ktav, 1969); Nancy L. Green, 'The modern Jewish diaspora: Eastern European Jews in New York, London and Paris', in Dirk Hoerder and Leslie Page Moch (eds) *European migrants: global and local perspectives* (Boston: Northeastern University Press, 1995) pp. 263–81.

6 Donna Gabaccia, *Militants and migrants: rural Sicilians become American workers* (New Brunswick, NJ: Rutgers University Press, 1988).

7 Slavery and indenture created new forms of coerced labour, but many workers were unfree before they were transported. Indeed, seen on a global scale, unfree labour was the predominant form of labour control until much later than many might suppose. Even in Europe, Steinfield (cited in T. Brass *et al.*, *Free and unfree labour* (Amsterdam: International Institute for Social History, 1993) p. 8) suggests that free labour, conceived in the sense of the freedom to choose one's employer, did not become a dominant legal ideal until the late eighteenth century and not the dominant paradigm until the nineteenth.

8 Bhikhu Parekh, 'Some reflections on the Hindu diaspora', *New Community*, 20(4) (1994), 605.

9 Hugh Tinker, *A new system of slavery: the export of Indian labour overseas, 1830–1920* (London: Oxford University Press for the Institute of Race Relations, 1974).

10 Steven Vertovec, 'Indian indentured migration to the Caribbean', in Robin Cohen (ed.) *The Cambridge survey of world migration* (Cambridge: Cambridge University Press, 1995) pp. 57–62.

11 David Dabydeen and Brinsley Samaroo (eds) *India and the Caribbean* (London: Hansib in association with the Centre for Caribbean Studies, University of Warwick and the London Strategic Policy Unit, 1987) p. 281

12 This is the figure for Muslims in Trinidad given by Ceri Peach, 'Three phases of South Asian emigration', in Judith M. Brown and Rosemary Foot (eds) *Migration: the Asian experience* (New York: St Martin's Press in association with St Antony's College, Oxford, 1994) p. 43, citing Colin Clarke. The further complications of considering smaller groups – Jains, Parsis, Goans, Ismailis, Baluchis – are not even addressed here. However, it is worth drawing attention to the notable work by John R. Hinnells, 'The modern Zoroastrian diaspora', in Judith M. Brown and Rosemary Foot (eds) *Migration: the Asian experience* (New York: St Martin's Press in association with St Antony's College, Oxford, 1994) pp. 56–82 on the Zoroastrian/Parsee diaspora. The Parsee diaspora is of notable antiquity and endurance (paralleling the Jews in this respect), beginning in the sixth century BCE (see Chapter 8).

13 Parekh, 'Some reflections'.

14 Parekh, 'Some reflections', p. 607.
15 Reddock cited in Jo Beall, 'Women under indenture in colonial Natal, 1860–1911', in Colin Clarke *et al.* (eds) *South Asians overseas: migration and ethnicity* (Cambridge: Cambridge University Press, 1990) pp. 72–3.
16 They were also involved in trying to persuade women, apparently with some success, to return to their conventional roles, to become 'pure like Sita'.
17 Parekh, 'Some reflections', p. 612.
18 John D. Kelly, '*Bhaki* and postcolonial politics: Hindu missions to Fiji', in Peter van der Veer (ed.) *Nation and migration: the politics of space in the South Asian diaspora* (Philadelphia: University of Pennsylvania Press, 1995) pp. 43–72.
19 Parekh, 'Some reflections', pp. 613–14.
20 Krishna Datt, 'Indo-Fijian concerns', *Report on consultation on Fiji's constitutional review* (Suva, Fiji: International Alert and the School of Social and Economic Development, University of South Pacific, 1994) pp. 90–1.
21 Ravi Thiara, 'Indian indentured workers in Mauritius, Natal and Fiji', in Robin Cohen (ed.) *The Cambridge survey of world migration* (Cambridge: Cambridge University Press, 1995) pp. 63–8.
22 Vaughan Robinson, 'The migration of East African Asians to the UK', in Robin Cohen (ed.) *The Cambridge survey of world migration* (Cambridge: Cambridge University Press, 1995) pp. 331–6.
23 While I use the British as the exemplary case of an imperial diaspora here, I want to mention another example of the phenomenon that postdated the high point of British expansionism. I allude to the Russians, further discussed in Chapter 8, who were sent as soldiers or arrived as settlers in many of the non-Russian parts of the USSR, especially the Baltic states. Though not normally considered a diaspora, the designation may help to understand the politics of the post-Soviet period. As for the British, the label 'diaspora' is unusual, but far from unknown. For example, a conference on the theme of 'The Diaspora of the British' was convened at the University of Kent in 1981 and the collection of papers from this conference were subsequently published by London University's Institute of Commonwealth Studies (Anon., *The diaspora of the British*, London: Institute of Commonwealth Studies Collected Seminar Papers, 1982).
24 W. S, Shepperson, *British emigration to North America: projects and opinions in the early Victorian period* (Oxford: Basil Blackwell, 1957) pp. 6–7.
25 Cited by Eric Williams, *Capitalism and slavery* (London: André Deutsch, 1964) p. 10.
26 Sir John Seeley, *The expansion of England* (Cambridge: Cambridge University Press, 1895) pp. 357–8.
27 Cited in Shepperson, *British emigration to North America*, p. 18.
28 Cited by Sir John A. R. Marriott, *Empire settlement* (London: Oxford University Press, 1927) p. 7.
29 Marriott, *Empire settlement*, p. 14.
30 Cited in Shepperson, *British emigration to North America*, p. 67.
31 It is perhaps at first surprising that the trade unions supported emigration. However, they had to face up to the redundancies that steam power would bring and they thought it best to protect the jobs of the members they were likely to retain.
32 A point convincingly made by Eric Richards, 'How did poor people emigrate from the British Isles to Australia in the nineteenth century?' *Journal of British Studies*, 32(3) (1993), 253.
33 Quoted by Marriott, *Empire settlement*, p. 41.
34 More effective were the Empire Settlement Act of 1922, where the imperial and dominion governments shared the cost of the transport and care of the children, and the Migration and Settlement Act of 1925, which made provision for assisted passages to 450,000 emigrants.

35 A. James Hammerton, *Emigrant gentlewomen: genteel poverty and female emigration, 1830–1914* (London: Croom Helm, 1979) p. 177.

36 Cited in Hammerton, *Emigrant gentlewomen*, p. 115.

37 Cited in Hammerton, *Emigrant gentlewomen*, p. 57.

38 Marriott, *Empire settlement*, pp. 71 and 61.

39 Cited in Shepperson, *British emigration to North America*, p. 254.

40 Cited in Marriott, *Empire settlement*, pp. 76–7.

41 English rather than British here, as the sporting traditions of the Celtic fringe diverge radically. The Gaelic Athletic Association, for example, banned all non-indigenous games from 1887. Richard Holt, *Sport and the British: a modern history* (Oxford: Oxford University Press, 1990) maintained that sport provided the crucial function of promoting loyalty to the empire by colonial whites (and also by native elites). Cricket, athletics and rugby – the sports of the English public schools – were vigorously promoted in the empire and dominions. (Football was too 'working-class'.) Partly because of the presence of non-British whites, the French Canadians, these sports did not 'catch on' in Canada. On the other hand, despite John Buchan's disparaging remark that the Afrikaners of South Africa 'were not a sporting race', the Boers took to rugby with such avidity and determination that the mauling scrum became a crucial ritual through which their deep resentment against the British was expressed.

42 The British government has a considerable stake in the success of the post-apartheid settlement as further political destablization could lead the approximately one million people of British descent (so-called 'patrials') to claim their entitlement to settle (or 'repatriate') in the United Kingdom.

43 Cohen, *Frontiers of Identity*.

44 Perry Anderson, *English questions* (London: Verso, 1992) p. 32.

45 Stanley Cohen and Laurie Taylor, *Escape attempts: the theory and practice of resistance to everyday life* (London: Allen Lane, 1976).

46 Victor Lal, 'The Fiji Indians: marooned at home', in Colin Clarke *et al.* (eds) *South Asians overseas: migration and ethnicity* (Cambridge: Cambridge University Press, 1990) pp. 113–30.

47 Anthony Lemon, 'The political position of Indians in South Africa', in Colin Clarke *et al.* (eds) *South Asians overseas: migration and ethnicity* (Cambridge: Cambridge University Press, 1990) p. 131.

48 Cited by Aisha Khan, 'Homeland, motherland: authenticity, legitimacy and ideologies of place among Muslims in Trinidad', in Peter van der Veer (ed.) *Nation and migration: the politics of space in the South Asian diaspora* (Philadelphia: University of Pennsylvania Press, 1995) p. 85.

5 TRADE AND BUSINESS DIASPORAS

1 Abner Cohen, 'Cultural strategies in the organization of trading diasporas', in Claude Meillassoux (ed.) *The development of indigenous trade and markets in West Africa* (Oxford: Oxford University Press, 1971) pp. 266–81, discussed in Ina Baghdiantz McCabe, Gelina Harlaftis and Ioanna Pepelasis Minoglou (eds) *Diaspora entrepreneurial networks: four centuries of history* (Oxford: Berg, 2005) p. 29.

2 Philip Curtin, *Cross-cultural trade in world history* (Cambridge: Cambridge University Press, 1984) pp. 2–3.

3 For China, see also Gungwu Wang, *China and the Chinese overseas* (Singapore: Times Academic Press, 1991). Curtin, *Cross-cultural trade*, p. 2 acknowledges his debt to other scholars – in particular, Abner Cohen, Lloyd Fallers and Karl Y. Yambert – in developing his use of the term, but as there are no serious discrepancies between usages, Curtin remains the single most helpful source on trade diasporas. I have diverged from his

understanding in that he argues (pp. 230–40) that trade diasporas, strictly speaking, were supplanted between the period 1740 and 1860 by European commercial empires. Certainly, he is right in arguing that trading companies like the English East India Company or the Dutch VOC ushered in a new era where commerce, empire and military conquest went hand-in-hand. However, I would prefer to see these firms as precursors of the transnational corporations, with trade diasporas still continuing, though transmuting and refurbishing themselves as auxiliaries in the colonial era and as ethnic entrepreneurs in the global age.

4 Hugh Tinker, *The Banyan tree: overseas emigrants from India, Pakistan and Bangladesh* (Oxford: Oxford University Press, 1977) pp. 96–137; and Hugh Tinker, 'Indians in Southeast Asia: Imperial auxiliaries', in Colin Clarke *et al.* (eds) *South Asians overseas*, Cambridge: Cambridge University Press, 1990) pp. 39–56 uses the two expressions, apparently without a different intent. Though suggestive, his terms are not clearly defined or elaborated. I would prefer to confine the idea of an auxiliary diaspora to an emigrant group, or part of an emigrant group, which more definitely became intermediaries. Thus, I would suggest that whereas Indian traders were the auxiliary part of the South Asian diaspora, Indian plantation workers were not.

5 I exclude the Gurkhas who invariably returned to Nepal. They were nonetheless invaluable servants of the British Crown, having served in the colonial armies since 1815. Over a quarter of a million served in the two world wars.

6 Wang, *China and the Chinese overseas*, pp. 80–99.

7 Wang, *China and the Chinese overseas*, p. 98.

8 Raffles cited in Lynn Pan, *Sons of the yellow emperor: the story of the overseas Chinese* (London: Mandarin, 1991) p. 27.

9 A point forcibly made by Wang, *China and the Chinese overseas*, pp. 170–1 of the Singaporean case.

10 Pan, *Sons of the yellow emperor*, pp. 12–13, 21.

11 Gungwu Wang, *Community and nation: China, Southeast Asia and Australia* (St Leonards, Australia: Allen & Unwin for the Asian Studies Association of Australia, 1992) pp. 1–10.

12 Cited in Wang, *Community and nation*, p. 10.

13 By the same token, the connection between homeland and diaspora could be revived in response to changes at the political level. After President Nixon recognized the People's Republic in 1972, Chinese-Americans felt free to travel to China without being thought of as 'unAmerican'. Mainland China also began to encourage tourism, Western investment and an outreach policy to the diaspora. See C. P. Fitzgerald, *China and the overseas Chinese: a study of Peking's changing policy, 1949–1970* (Cambridge: Cambridge University Press, 1972).

14 Kwen Fee Lian, 'Migration and the formation of Malaysia and Singapore', in Robin Cohen (ed.) *The Cambridge survey of world migration* (Cambridge: Cambridge University Press, 1995) pp. 392–6.

15 Gangs of Chinese labourers were used on public works in various African countries, but the only significant permanent settlement was in Mauritius. After the disruption caused by the Boer War, 63,000 indentured Chinese were recruited to get the gold mines back into production, but after a political storm in Britain about the use of indentured workers for this purpose, they were repatriated (see Peter Richardson, 'Coolies, peasants, and proletarians: the origins of Chinese indentured labour in South Africa, 1904–1907', in Shula Marks and Reter Richardson (eds) *International labour migration: historical perspectives* (London: Maurice Temple Smith for the Institute of Commonwealth Studies, 1984), pp. 167–85). I should add that by 2007 Africa is very much in China's sights as a source of raw materials to keep the speed of China's breakneck economic growth going.

16 I speak here of the communities established before the Second World War and the Chinese Revolution. Thereafter, a great number of professionals started migrating,

particularly from Hong Kong, Taiwan and China to places like Canada, the USA and Australia. The changed class composition of the Chinese diaspora also allowed a modified version of the sojourner tradition to reassert itself (see Chapter 8).

17 Jing Hui Ong, 'Chinese indentured labour: coolies and colonies', in Robin Cohen (ed.) *The Cambridge survey of world migration* (Cambridge: Cambridge University Press, 1995) pp. 51–6.

18 Peter Kwong, *The new Chinatown* (New York: Hill & Wang, 1987) pp. 25–6.

19 Pan, *Sons of the yellow emperor*, pp. 305–6. The Exclusion Acts referred to by Pan were attempts to keep the Chinese out of the USA. The first Act was passed in 1882 in response to hysteria about the 'Yellow Peril'. See Miller (1969).

20 Kwong, *The new Chinatown*, p. 8.

21 Kwong, *The new Chinatown*, p. 45.

22 Constance Lever-Tracy, David Ip and Noel Tracy, *The Chinese diaspora and Mainland China: an emerging economic synergy* (Basingstoke: Macmillan, 1996).

23 'Lebanon' did not exist as an independent entity until 1946. The Ottoman province of Syria included the *wilayet* of Beirut and the *sanjak* of Lebanon. After the First World War, the French administered the area under a League of Nations mandate, setting up Great Lebanon, a designation that lasted from 1920 to 1946. Its Ottoman history meant that many Lebanese abroad were classified as 'Syrians', 'Syro-Lebanese', 'Ottomans' or 'Turks'. Their religious differences (Maronite, Greek Orthodox, Greek Catholic, Armenian Orthodox and Muslim), plus the arrival of Middle Eastern Jews and other Middle Eastern Arabs, led to some delicious classificatory pickles, particularly in the Americas. I illustrate this with a personal experience. While in the Caribbean, I (of Ashkenazi origins, but born in South Africa) was welcomed and accorded hospitality as a 'fellow Syrian' at the local Phoenician club, an offer I was only too happy to accept. For the purposes of this chapter I have used the category 'Lebanese' as a catch-all, except where it needs more explanation.

24 Kohei Hashimoto, 'Lebanese population movements, 1920–1939: towards a study', in Albert Hourani and Nadim Shehadi (eds) *The Lebanese in the world: a century of emigration* (London: I. B. Tauris for the Centre for Lebanese Studies, 1992) pp. 65–108.

25 Charles Issawi, 'The historical background of Lebanese emigration, 1800–1914', in Albert Hourani and Nadim Shehadi (eds) *The Lebanese in the world: a century of emigration* (London: I. B. Tauris for the Centre for Lebanese Studies, 1992) p. 31.

26 Alixa Naff, 'Lebanese immigration into the United States: 1880 to the present', in Albert Hourani and Nadim Shehadi (eds) *The Lebanese in the world: a century of emigration* (London: I. B. Tauris for the Centre for Lebanese Studies, 1992) p. 145.

27 All quotes from Albert Hourani and Nadim Shehadi (eds) *The Lebanese in the world: a century of emigration* (London: I. B. Tauris for the Centre for Lebanese Studies, 1992). For Bishmizzini villagers (p. 42); Lebanese in Brazil (p. 293); A Lebanese in Jamaica: (p. 343); Lebanese in the USA: (pp. 145–6, p. 147) and Lebanese in Montreal: (p. 27).

28 H. L. van der Laan, *The Lebanese traders in Sierra Leone* (The Hague: Mouton for the Afrika-Studiecentrum, Leiden, 1975) pp. 222–4, quote from p. 223.

29 Albert Hourani, 'Introduction', in Albert Hourani and Nadim Shehadi (eds) *The Lebanese in the world: a century of emigration* (London: I.B. Tauris for the Centre for Lebanese Studies, 1992) pp. 5–9

30 Hashimoto, 'Lebanese population movements', citing Chiha.

31 Hashimoto, 'Lebanese population movements', p. 66n.

32 Malouf cited in Hourani, 'Introduction', p. 11.

33 I was in Nigeria during the Biafra war and in Liberia at the beginning of *its* civil war. Though many international airlines suspended or interrupted their flights to West Africa, MEA, like the famed St Bernard dog coming to the rescue of distressed travellers, could always be trusted to get through to service the Lebanese diaspora (and many others

like me). Only the shelling of the airport in Beirut itself during the Lebanese civil war in the 1970s and 1980s temporarily scuppered the airline.

34 Guita G. Hourani and Eugene Sensinig-Dabbous, *Insecurity, migration and return: the case of Lebanon following the Summer 2006 war* (Florence: Robert Schuman Centre for Advanced Studies, European University Institute, 2007) pp. 53, 54.

35 See Reinhard Bendix, *Max Weber: an intellectual portrait* (London: Methuen, 1973) p. 150.

36 Chan Kwok Bun and Ong Jin Hui, 'The many faces of immigration entrpreneurship', in Robin Cohen (ed.) *The Cambridge survey of world migration* (Cambridge: Cambridge University Press, 1995) pp. 523–31.

37 Bendix, *Max Weber*, pp. 98–256.

38 Paul Kennedy, *African capitalism: the struggle for ascendency* (Cambridge: Cambridge University Press, 1988) pp. 141–3.

39 Joel Kotkin, *Tribes: how race, religion and identity determine success in the new global economy* (New York: Random House, 1992) pp. 129–30.

40 Arnold J. Toynbee, *A study of history*. Abridgement of vols 7–10 by D. C. Somervell (London: Oxford University Press under the auspices of the Royal Institute of International Affairs, 1957) p. 217.

41 Edna Bonacich, 'A theory of middlemen minorities', *American Sociological Review*, 38 (1973) 583–94. Her equally interesting work, Edna Bonacich, 'The costs of immigrant entrepreneurship', in Ivan Light and Edna Bonacich, *Immigrant entrepreneurs* (Berkeley: University of California Press, 1988) pp. 425–36; and Edna Bonacich, 'The other side of ethnic entrepreneurship: a dialogue with Waldinger, Aldrich, Ward and associates', *International Migration Review*, 27(3) (1993), 685–92, lays less emphasis on exploitation by others and more emphasis on self-exploitation. Her sympathetic description of Korean entrepreneurs in the USA points to their health problems, marital breakdowns and long hours of self- and family-exploitation. She is also less inclined to see the external dominant groups as consciously deploying a divide-and-rule strategy to pit ethnic groups against one another. Instead, she argues that ethnic competition is an unintended but, for the ruling groups, welcome consequence of migration and settlement.

6 DIASPORAS AND THEIR HOMELANDS

1 Walker Conner, 'The impact of homelands upon diasporas', in Gabriel Sheffer (ed.) *Modern diasporas in international politics* (London: Croom Helm, 1986) p. 16; Levy and Weingrod (eds) (2004)

2 Cited in Conner, 'The impact of homelands upon diasporas', p. 17.

3 See Cohen, *Frontiers of identity*, pp. 192–205.

4 For other examples see Aristide R. Zolberg, 'The formation of new states as a refugee generating process', *Annals of the American Academy of Political and Social Science*, 467 (1983), 24–38. Of course this does not provide a moral defence of any of these events: it merely shows that each is part of a wider phenomenon.

5 Quoted in Regina S. Sharif, *Non-Jewish Zionism: its roots in Western history* (London: Zed Books, 1983) p. 5.

6 Yosef Gorny, *The state of Israel in Jewish public thought: the quest for collective identity* (Basingstoke: Macmillan, 1994) pp. 41–2.

7 The literature on these themes is so voluminous that I do not pretend to have consulted it all. For those who wish to follow these debates in detail, the following appear to be relevant references: H. Arendt, *The Jew as pariah: Jewish identity and politics in the modern age* (New York: Grove Press, 1978); S. Avineri, *The making of modern Zionism* (New York: Basic Books, 1981); Yehuda Bauer, *The Jewish emergence from powerlessness* (Basingstoke: Macmillan, 1980); M. Endelman, 'The legitimization of the diaspora experience in recent Jewish historiography', *Modern Judaism*, 11(2) (1991), 195–209;

S. Gilman, *Jewish self-hatred: anti-Semitism and the hidden language of the Jews* (Baltimore: Johns Hopkins University Press, 1986); Joseph B. Gittler (ed.) *Jewish life in the United States: perspectives from the social sciences* (New York: New York University Press, 1981); S. Heilman, 'The sociology of American Jewry: the last ten years', *Annual Review of Sociology*, 8 (1982), 135–60; A. Liebman, *Jews and the left* (New York: Wiley, 1979); C. Liebman, *The ambivalent American Jew* (Philadelphia: Jewish Publication Society, 1976); Charles S. Liebman and Steven M. Cohen, *Two worlds of Judaism: the Israeli and American experiences* (New Haven: Yale University Press, 1990); F. Markowitz, 'Plaiting the strands of Jewish identity', *Comparative Studies in Society and History*, 32(1) (1990), 181–9; W. Reich, 'Israel and the diaspora', *Jewish Social Studies*, 49(3–4) (1987), 326–32; and David Vital, *The future of the Jews: a people at the cross-roads?* (Cambridge, MA: Harvard University Press, 1990). I have also relied on the lived reality of these debates among my own friends and family, together with the highly insightful accounts by David J. Goldberg, *The divided self: Israel and the Jewish psyche today* (London: I.B.Tauris, 2006); David Theo Goldberg and Michael Krauz (eds) *Jewish identity* (Philadelphia: Temple University Press, 1993); and Gorny, *The state of Israel*.

8 Some of the most important Zionist organizations, most still in existence, are the World Zionist Congress, the Jewish Agency, the Jewish National Fund, the United Jewish Appeal, the Zionist Organization of America and Zionist youth bodies such as *Habonim* (the builders).

9 Perhaps the most fundamental attack on the legacy of Ben-Gurion from inside the Zionist establishment is Avraham Burg's book *Defeating Hitler*, not yet published in English at the time of writing. Burg, a former Knesset speaker, former chairman of the World Zionist Organization and son of one of Israel's notable founders now (June 2007) argues that the Israeli state has become a 'brutal Sparta sliding towards Nazism'. See J. J. Goldberg 'Avraham Burg's new Zionism', www.forward.com/articles/avraham-burg-s-new-zionism, accessed 2 August 2007.

10 Gorny, *The state of Israel*, pp. 12–13.

11 Roger Waldinger, 'Review of Seymour Martin Lipset and Earl Raab *Jews and the new American scene*, Cambridge, MA: Harvard University Press, 1995', *New Community*, 22(1) (1996), 174.

12 Waldinger, 'Review'.

13 Daniel Boyarin, *A radical Jew: Paul and the politics of identity* (Berkeley: University of California Press 1994); Jonathan Boyarin, *Storm from paradise: the politics of Jewish memory* (Minneapolis: University of Minnesota Press, 1992); Daniel Boyarin and Jonathan Boyarin, 'Diaspora: generation and the ground of Jewish identity', *Critical Enquiry*, 19(4) (1993), 693–725; and Daniel Boyarin and Jonathan Boyarin, 'Powers of diaspora', paper presented at the International Congress of the Historical Sciences, Montreal, 27 August–3 September 1994.

14 Boyarin and Boyarin, 'Diaspora', p. 721.

15 Boyarin and Boyarin, 'Diaspora', p. 723.

16 In some Zionist thinking, *golah* (the diaspora) is contrasted to *galut* (the place of exile), but the expressions are also used interchangeably. For Zionists, neither condition is acceptable, but *galut* at least implies that there was no alternative. Zionists also distinguish between *yordim* (the fallen, who have chosen to live outside Israel) and *olim* (the redeemed who have ascended to a full Jewish national identity in the homeland). For more on these distinctions see Richard Shusterman, 'Next year in Jerusalem: postmodern Jewish identity and the myth of return', in David Theo Goldberg and Michael Krausz (eds) *Jewish identity* (Philadephia: Temple University Press, 1993) pp. 291–308.

17 Shusterman, 'Next year in Jerusalem', p. 299.

18 Named after an indigenous cactus plant, with the implications of virtue, rootedness and authenticity.

19 Steven J. Gold, *The Israeli diaspora* (London: Routledge, 2002) p. 230.
20 See Arthur W. Helweg, *Sikhs in England: the development of a migrant community* (Delhi: Oxford University Press, 1979) pp. 2–3.
21 Khushwant Singh, *A history of the Sikhs. Volume 2, 1839–1974* (Delhi: Oxford University Press, 1977, first edition) p. 3.
22 In all parts of the empire the British had the unvarying conviction that 'northerners' or 'hillsmen' made better soldiers than 'southerners' or those who lived on the coast. The latter were seen as corrupt and soft, the former as hardened and warlike. The generalization was dubious, but the Sikhs did indeed make remarkable soldiers, partly because of the soldier–saint ideal. The sight of an unyielding turbaned regiment of Sikhs struck fear into Asian, African and European enemies alike. In addition to the Sikhs, the British recruited Gurkhas, Jats, Dogras, Pathans, Rajputs and Garhwalis.
23 Also known as the Indian Mutiny and, to Indian nationalists, as the Indian National Rising.
24 Singh, *A history of the Sikhs, 1839–1974*, pp. 83–4.
25 Rozina Visram, *Ayahs, lascars and princes: Indians in Britain, 1700–1947* (London: Pluto Press, 1986) pp. 71–3.
26 James G. Chadney, *The Sikhs of Vancouver* (New York: AMS Press, 1984) pp. 26–7.
27 Cited in Singh, *A history of the Sikhs, 1839–1974*, p. 169.
28 Visram, *Ayahs, lascars and princes*, p. 192.
29 Darshan Singh Tatla, 'The politics of homeland: a study of ethnic linkages and political mobilisation amongst Sikhs in Britain and North America', PhD thesis, University of Warwick, 1993, pp. 171–2.
30 Cited Tatla, 'The politics of homeland', p. 173.
31 Verne A. Dusenbery, 'A Sikh diaspora', in Peter van der Veer (ed.) *Nation and migration: the politics of space in the South Asian diaspora* (Philadelphia: University of Pennsylvania Press, 1995) p. 24.
32 See Dilip Bobb and Asoka Raina, *The great betrayal: assassination of Indira Gandhi* (Delhi: Vikas, 1985).
33 Cited Tatla, 'The politics of homeland, pp. 187–8.
34 Singh, *My bleeding Punjab.*
35 See Gurharpal Singh, 'Review of Khushwant Singh *A history of the Sikhs. Volume 2, 1839–1988*, Delhi: Oxford University Press (second edition)', *Punjab Research Group: Newsletter of the Association for Punjab Studies in Great Britain*, 5, January 1993, p. 13.
36 David Jacobson, *Rights across borders: immigration and the decline of citizenship* (Baltimore: Johns Hopkins University Press, 1996) pp. 128–34.
37 Tom Nairn, *The break-up of Britain: crisis and neo-nationalism* (London: Verso, 1977) pp. 96–8.

7 DETERRITORIALIZED DIASPORAS

1 'Assumed to be', because as historians remind us in a number of cases complex patterns of oscillating migration were common long before the so-called 'transnational turn' in migration studies was discovered. In the case of Italians, for example, 26 million people departed (1876–1976), but 8.5 million remigrated (1905–1976). See Rudolph J. Vecoli 'The Italian diaspora 1876–1976', in Robin Cohen (ed) *The Cambridge survey of world migration* (Cambridge: Cambridge University Press, 1995) p. 114.
2 Clifford's brilliant article on this theme is the locus classicus, though he regards this as a normal rather than an exceptional outcome. James Clifford, 'Traveling cultures', in Lawrence Grossberg *et al.* (eds) *Cultural studies* (New York: Routledge, 1992) pp. 96–116.

3 I have adopted the expression 'deterritorialized diasporas' to replace 'cultural diasporas' used in the first edition of this book. The latter was insufficiently precise and led to some confusion.

4 I am grateful to my colleague at Warwick, Paola Toninato, who has educated me on the salience of Romani literature in fostering a diasporic consciousness. There is a vast literature on the Roma/Gypsies; one good specialist collection is at the University of Leeds. See http://www.leeds.ac.uk/library/spcoll/spprint/26600.htm

5 On a visit to the island (2007) I was pleased to learn that some 3000 people in Dominica claim to be Caribs and have a small degree of territorial autonomy. Many of the claimants are of mixed heritage, but the cultural identification with Carib ways is none the less impressively strong.

6 Stuart Hall, 'Cultural identity and diaspora', in Jonathan Rutherford (ed.) *Identity: community, culture, difference* (London: Lawrence & Wishart, 1990) pp. 222–37.

7 Stuart Hall, 'Cultural identity and diaspora', p. 235.

8 For further information, see Josh DeWind *et al.*, 'Contract labour in US agriculture: the West Indian cane cutters in Florida', in Robin Cohen *et al.* (eds) *Peasants and proletarians: the struggles of third world workers* (London: Hutchinson, 1979) pp. 380–96; and R. W. Palmer (ed.) *In search of a better life: perspectives on migration from the Caribbean* (New York: Praeger, 1990). Nancy Foner, 'West Indians in New York and London: a comparative analysis', *International Migration Review*, 13(2) (1979), 284–97; Nancy Foner, 'Race and colour: Jamaican migrants in London and New York', *International Migration Review*, 19(4) (1985), 708–27; and Constance R. Sutton and Susan R. Makiesky, 'Migration and West Indian racial and ethnic consciousness', in Helen I. Safa and Brian M. Du Toit (eds) *Migration and development: implications for ethnic identity and political conflict* (The Hague: Mouton, 1975) pp. 113–43 produced pioneering work comparing the fates and fortunes of African–Caribbean people in the USA and Britain.

9 Paul Gilroy, *'There ain't no black in the Union Jack': the cultural politics of race and nation* (London: Hutchinson, 1987); John Solomos, *Race and racism in contemporary Britain* (Basingstoke: Macmillan, 1989).

10 Ceri Peach, *West Indian migration to Britain: a social geography* (London: Oxford University Press, 1968).

11 I am well aware that stereotyping and channelling may produce successes in these areas and am not arguing, of course, that achievement in these fields alone is a remotely adequate measure of social mobility.

12 *Guardian*, 4 May 1996, p. 5.

13 Ceri Peach, 'Trends in levels of Caribbean segregation, Great Britain, 1961–91', paper presented at a Conference on Comparative History of Migration within the Caribbean and to Europe, Oxford Brookes University, Oxford, 22–4 September 1995.

14 Malcolm Cross and Han Entzinger (eds) *Lost illusions: Caribbean minorities in Britain and the Netherlands* (London: Routledge, 1988).

15 Malcolm Cross, '"Race", class formation and political interests: a comparison of Amsterdam and London', in Alec G. Hargreaves and Jeremy Leaman (eds) *Racism, ethnicity and politics in contemporary Europe* (Aldershot: Edward Elgar, 1995) p. 72.

16 Condon and Ogden, 'Questions of emigration', p. 38.

17 To be clear here, such is the level of acceptance of French culture that these 'roots' are not regarded as being located in Africa, but in Guadeloupe and Martinique. See Condon and Ogden, 'Questions of emigration', p. 46.

18 Helen M. Hintjens, *Alternatives to independence: explorations in post-colonial relations* (Aldershot: Dartmouth, 1995).

19 M. Al-Rasheed, 'The meaning of marriage and status in exile: the experience of Iraqi women', *Journal of Refugee Studies*, 6(2) (1993), 91–2; Victor Turner, *The ritual process, structure and anti-structure* (London: Routledge & Kegan Paul, 1969).

20 Paul Gilroy, *Small acts: thoughts on the politics of black cultures* (London: Serpent's Tail, 1993) p. 103.

21 Paul Gilroy, *The black Atlantic: modernity and double consciousness* (London: Verso, 1993).

22 The first number of a new journal, *Social Identities* 1(1) 175–220, provided the ultimate accolade to an academic author – publishing extended reviews by three reviewers of Gilroy's *Black Atlantic*. This is a useful source from which to begin an appreciation and critique of Gilroy's work. He promises a reply in a forthcoming issue of the journal.

23 Notably Melville J. Herskovitz, *Life in a Haitian valley* (New York: Alfred A. Knopf, 1937); Melville J. Herskovitz *et al.*, *Trinidad village* (New York: Alfred Knopf, 1947); Melville J. Herskovitz, *The New World Negro: selected papers in Afro-American studies* (Bloomington, IN: Indiana University Press, 1961).

24 Thus, for example, it presents no paradox to Trinidadians to boast that Prime Minister Eric Williams's famous exposition of *Capitalism and slavery* (1944) of the link between capitalism in Britain and slavery in the West Indies, was presented as a doctorate to the University of Oxford.

25 Gilroy, *The black Atlantic*; Gilroy, *Small acts*.

26 Stefano Harney, *Nationalism and identity: culture and the imagination in a Caribbean diaspora* (London: Zed Books, 1996).

27 *Daily Gleaner*, 12 February 1931.

28 I do not want to get diverted in my text into a sub-theme, but should mention that the main thesis of Carole D. Yawney, 'The globalization of Rastafari: methodological and conceptual issues', paper presented at the annual meeting of the Society for Caribbean Studies (UK) London, 5–7 July 1995, is that, with the globalization of Rastafarianism, the conservative dominance of the House of Nyahbinghi in Jamaica is being eroded, particularly in respect of gender relations.

29 Stuart Hall, 'Negotiating Caribbean identities', *New Left Review*, no. 209, January–February 1995, p. 14.

30 Caryl Phillips, *Crossing the river* (London: Picador, 1993) pp. 235–7.

31 Samuel Selvon, *The lonely Londoners* (Harlow: Longman, 1985) cited by Harney, *Nationalism and identity*, p. 103.

32 Gilroy, *Small acts*, p. 37.

33 *Daily Gleaner*, 1–7 May 1996.

34 Mehtab Ali Shah, *The foreign policy of Pakistan: ethnic impacts on diplomacy* (London: I.B.Tauris, 1997) p. 43.

35 Mark-Anthony Falzon, '"Bombay, our cultural heart": rethinking the relation between homeland and diaspora', *Ethnic and Racial Studies*, 26(4) (2003), 602–83.

36 Falzon, 'Bombay, our cultural heart', pp. 668, 669.

37 Quoted in Falzon, 'Bombay, our cultural heart', p. 662.

38 Falzon, 'Bombay, our cultural heart', p. 673.

39 Janet J. Ewald, 'Crossers of the sea: slaves, freedmen, and other migrants in the northwestern Indian Ocean, *c.* 1750–1914', *American Historical Review*, 105(1) (2000), Online version http://www.historycooperative.org/journals/ahr/105.1/ah000069.html

40 John R. Hinnells, *The Zoroastrian diaspora: religion and migration* (Oxford, Oxford University Press, 2005) Chapter 2.

41 Theodor Adorno, *Minima moralia* (London: Verso, 1974) p. 39

42 Susan Craig, 'Intertwining roots', *The Journal of Caribbean History*, 26(2) (1992), 215–27 (review article).

8 MOBILIZING DIASPORAS IN A GLOBAL AGE

1 Nicholas Van Hear, *New diasporas: the mass exodus, dispersal and regrouping of migrant communities* (London: UCL Press, 1998) pp.195–231.

2 Martin Albrow, *The global age* (Cambridge: Polity Press, 1996). Other aspects of globalization are discussed in Robin Cohen and Paul Kennedy, *Global sociology* (Basingstoke: Palgrave, 2007).

3 Kotkin, *Tribes*, pp. 134–5.

4 Sterling Seagrave, *Lords of the rim: the invisible empire of the overseas Chinese* (New York: G. P. Putnam & Sons, 1995) pp. 282–5.

5 Anon. (2006) *Total investment of Shenzhen Overseas Chinese Chamber of Commerce in China amounted to US$20 billion* http://english.hbdofcom.gov.cn/file/2006/5-9/9523.html. For a slightly outdated, but still valuable benchmark survey, see Lever-Tracy et al., *The Chinese diaspora*.

6 One might say that the authorities in countries like the USA, Canada and the UK have been hoist by their own petards. Because it became politically difficult to deny access on racial grounds, family reunification and *jus sanguinis* (the law of blood or descent) have been stressed in recent immigration laws, with a view to strengthening the dominant Anglo-Saxon groups. However, a number of minority groups, especially Asians in recent years, have successfully used the family reunification provisions for immigration purposes.

7 This practice is now covered by a growing literature on transnationalism, which I cannot cover here. The best introduction is Steven Vertovec, 'Conceiving and researching transnationalism', *Ethnic and Racial Studies*, 22(2) (1999), 447–62.

8 Wang Gungwu, 'Sojourning: the Chinese experience in Southeast Asia', Jennifer Cushman Memorial Lecture, mimeo, 1992, p. 3.

9 John Friedman, 'The world city hypothesis', *Development and Change*, 17(1) (1986), 69–83; Jeff Henderson and Manuel Castells (eds) *Global restructuring and territorial development* (London: Sage, 1987); Sassen-Koob (1990).

10 Peter Dicken, *Global shift: the internationalization of economic activity* (London: Paul Chapman Publishing, second edition, 1992) pp. 196–8.

11 Steven Vertovec and Robin Cohen, 'Introduction: conceiving cosmopolitanism', in Steven Vertovec and Robin Cohen (eds) *Conceiving cosmopolitanism: theory, context and practice* (Oxford: Oxford University Press, 2001) p. 5.

12 Stuart Hall, 'The local and the global: globalization and ethnicity', in Anthony D. King (ed.) *Culture, globalization and the world-system: contemporary conditions for the representation of identity* (Basingstoke: Macmillan, 1991) pp. 35–6.

13 John Armstrong, 'Mobilized and proletarian diasporas', pp. 396–7.

14 Yiddish for intuitive knowledge, being quick-witted or streetwise.

15 Kotkin, *Tribes*. The idea of 'global tribes' in the title of his book does not merit serious dissection because it is not used analytically, but is simply meant as a headline-grabbing device to evoke the powerful sense of ethnic solidarity among the five groups he depicts.

16 Kotkin, *Tribes*, pp. 255, 258.

17 Kotkin, *Tribes*.

18 'The journey' is a much neglected aspect of migrancy. Reflexive views on the old country, anticipatory socialization, the beginnings of business plans and the bonds of co-responsibility may all happen on the journey.

19 Kwong, *The new Chinatown*, p. 86.

20 Kwong, *The new Chinatown*, pp. 71–2.

21 Baumann, 'Diaspora', p. 319. The long quote within the block quote comes from a PhD thesis by Aiyenakun P. J. Arowele fully cited in Baumann's article. I am grateful to Martin Baumann, Steven Vertovec and Stéphane Dufoix who in various ways have 'put me right' on the connections between religious communities and diaspora.

22 Alain Epp Weaver (n.d.) *Constantinianism, Zionism, diaspora: toward a political theology of exile and return*, Occasional Papers, Number 28, Akron, Pennsylvania: Mennonite Central Committee, http://mcc.org/respub/occasional/28.html

23 Ninian Smart, 'The importance of diasporas', in S. Shaked, D. Shyulman and C. G. Stroumsa (eds) *Gilgut: essays on transformation, revolution and permanence in the history of religions* (Leiden: Brill, 1987) pp. 288–97.

24 This section draws on Robin Cohen and Paul Kennedy, *Global Sociology*, Chapter 16.

25 See A. D. Smither, 'The business of miracle working', *Independent* (London daily newspaper) 14 August 2004, p. 28.

26 Smart, 'The importance of diasporas', pp. 290–1.

27 Baumann, 'Diaspora', p. 323.

28 Smart, 'The importance of diasporas'.

29 Hinnells, 'The modern Zoroastrian diaspora', p. 79.

30 Steven Vertovec, 'Religion and diaspora', Working paper, Transnational Communities Programme, University of Oxford, WPTC-01-01, 2001, http://www.transcomm. ox.ac.uk/working%20papers/Vertovec01.PDF. See also the schema proposed by Kim Knott 'Bound to change? The religions of South Asians in Britain' in Steven Vertovec (ed.) *Aspects of the South Asian diaspora* (Delhi: Oxford University Press, 1991) pp. 86–111.

31 Vertovec, 'Religion and diaspora', pp. 13–34.

32 Roland Robertson, 'Religion and the global field', *Social Compass*, 41(1) (1994), 128.

9 STUDYING DIASPORAS

1 Stefan Helmrich, 'Kinship, nation and Paul Gilroy's concept of diaspora', *Diaspora*, 2(2) (1992), 243–49.

2 Liisa Malkki, 'National geographic: the rooting of peoples and the territorialization of national identity among scholars and refugees', *Cultural Anthropology*, 7 (1992), 24–44.

3 Thomas Browne, *Pseudodoxia epidemica* (London, 1646). Browne was preoccupied with trying to distinguish medical treatments that worked from those that were based on 'popular Errors, both in the wiser and common sort, Misapprehension, Fallacy, or false deduction, Credulity, Supinity, adherence unto Antiquity, Tradition and Authority'. He subtitled his book 'Enquiries into very many received tenents and commonly presumed truths'. Internet access to the sixth and last edition of *Pseudodoxia Epidemica* (1672) is provided at http://penelope.uchicago.edu/pseudodoxia/pseudodoxia.shtml.

4 All three insights are discussed in Rodney Needham, 'Polythetic classification: convergence and consequences', *Man* (NS) 10 (1975), 349–50.

5 Stephen Kalberg, 'Max Weber', in Adam Kuper and Jessica Kuper (eds) *The social science encyclopaedia* (London: Routledge, 1999) p. 907.

6 Kalberg, 'Max Weber', p. 907.

7 Relevant discussion can be found in Cohen, *The new helots*, pp. 33–42; Anthony H. Richmond, *Global apartheid: refugees, racism and the new world order* (Toronto: Oxford University Press, 1994); and Aristide Zolberg *et al.*, *Escape from violence: conflict and the refugee crisis in the developing world* (New York: Oxford University Press, 1989) pp. 258–82.

8 Janet Lippman Abu-Lughod, 'The displacement of the Palestinians', in Robin Cohen (ed.) *The Cambridge survey of world migration* (Cambridge: Cambridge University Press, 1995) p. 410.

9 Hourani and Shehadi, *The Lebanese in the world*.

10 Richardson, 'Coolies, peasants, and proletarians', pp. 177–9.

11 Cohen, *The new helots*; Nigel Harris, *The new untouchables: immigration and the new world order* (London: I. B. Tauris, 1995).

12 The pioneering account on transnational migration is Nina Glick Schiller, L. Basch and C. Blanc Szanton, 'From immigrant to transmigrant: theorizing transnational migration', *Anthropological Quarterly*, 68(1) (1995), 48–63. Quite often continuing relationships build up between a home village in a labour-exporting country and a sort of rotating community that develops at a particular place in a destination country. This process

is notably analysed by Peggy Levitt, *The transnational villagers* (Berkeley: University of California Press, 2001). The relationship between these rotating communities and the wider diasporic group with which they may share a religion or ethnicity is as yet an under-researched topic.

13 Wang, *China and the Chinese overseas*, p. 183.

14 Wang, *China and the Chinese overseas*, pp. 4–5.

15 Elliott P. Skinner, 'The dialectic between diasporas and homelands', in Joseph E. Harris (ed.) *Global dimension of the African diaspora* (Washington, DC: Howard University Press, 1993) pp. 11–40.

16 Marienstras, 'On the notion of diaspora', p. 25.

17 Nicholas Van Hear, Frank Pieke and Steven Vertovec *The contribution of UK-based diasporas to development and poverty-reduction*. Report of the ESRC Centre on Migration, Policy and Society, University of Oxford, April 2004, p. 25

18 Sanket Mohapatra, Dilip Ratha and Zhimei Xu, *Migration and Development*, Brief 2 Development Prospects Group, Migration and Remittances Team 1, Remittance Trends (Washington, DC: World Bank, 2007) p.3.

19 A comprehensive report directed to policymakers is Dina Ionescu, *Engaging diasporas at development partners for home and destination countries: challenges for policymakers* (Geneva: International Organization for Migration, 2007).

20 See, in particular, Gabriel Sheffer, *Modern diasporas in international politics* (London: Croom Helm, 1986); and Gabriel Sheffer, *Diaspora politics: at home abroad* (Cambridge: Cambridge University Press, 2003).

21 Gabriel Sheffer, *Diaspora politics*, p. 244.

22 Hazel Smith and Paul Stares (eds) *Diasporas in conflict: peace-makers and peace-wreckers* (Tokyo: United Nations University Press, 2007) p. 9.

23 Khalid Koser, 'African diasporas and post-conflict reconstruction: an Eritrean case study', in Hazel Smith and Paul Stares (eds) *Diasporas in conflict: peace-makers and peace-wreckers* (Tokyo: United Nations University Press, 2007) pp. 239–52.

24 Evelyn Hu-DeHart, 'Rethinking America: the practice and politics of multiculturalism in higher education', in Becky W. Thompson and Sangeeta Tyagi (eds) *Beyond a dream deferred: multicultural education and the politics of excellence* (Minneapolis: University of Minnesota Press, 1993) pp. 7–8.

25 Samuel P. Huntington, *Who are we? America's great debate* (London: Simon & Schuster, 2004) p. 142.

26 Cited in Hu-DeHart, 'Rethinking America', p. 8.

27 Morris Dickstein, 'After the Cold War: culture as politics, politics as culture', *Social Research*, 60(3) (1993), 535.

28 John Rex, 'Ethnic identity and the nation state: the political sociology of multi-cultural societies', *Social Identities*, 1(1) (1995), 30–1.

29 This view is notably advanced by Yossi Shain, *Marketing the American creed abroad: diasporas in the US and their homelands* (Cambridge: Cambridge University Press, 1999).

30 Cf. Khan, 'Homeland, motherland', p. 93.

REFERENCES

Adorno, Theoor (1974) *Minima moralia*, London: Verso

Ages, Arnold (1973) *The diaspora dimension*, The Hague: Martinus Nijhoff

Albrow, Martin (1996) *The global age*, Cambridge: Polity Press

Alexander, Edward and Paul Bogdanor (eds) (2006) *The Jewish divide over Israel: accusers and defenders*, New Jersey: Transnational Publishers

Al-Rasheed, M. (1993) 'The meaning of marriage and status in exile: the experience of Iraqi women', *Journal of Refugee Studies*, 6(2), 89–103

Anderson, Perry (1992) *English questions*, London: Verso

Anon. (1982) *The diaspora of the British*, London: Institute of Commonwealth Studies Collected Seminar Papers

Anon. (2006) *Total investment of Shenzhen Overseas Chinese Chamber of Commerce in China amounted to US$20 billion* http://english.hbdofcom.gov.cn/file/2006/5-9/9523.html

Anteby-Yemini, Lisa William Berthomière and Gabriel Sheffer (eds) (2005) *Les diasporas: 2000 ans d'histoire*, Rennes: Presses Universitaires de Rennes

Anthias, Floya (1998) 'Evaluating "diaspora": beyond ethnicity', *Sociology*, 32(3), 557–80

Arendt, H. (1978) *The Jew as pariah: Jewish identity and politics in the modern age*, New York: Grove Press

Arlen, Michael (1926) *The green hat: a romance for a few people*, London: W. Collins

Arlen, Michael J. (1976) *Passage to Ararat*, New York: Ballantine

Armen, Garbis *et al.* (eds) (1987) *Historical atlas of Armenia*, New York: Armenian National Education Committee

Armstrong, John A. (1976) 'Mobilized and proletarian diasporas', *American Political Science Review*, 20(2), 393–408

Avineri, S. (1981) *The making of modern Zionism*, New York: Basic Books

Azarpay, G. (1968) *Urartian art and artefacts*, Berkeley: University of California Press

Baily, Samuel L. (1995) 'The adjustment of Italian immigrants in Buenos Aires and New York, 1870–1914', in Dirk Hoerder and Leslie Page Moch (eds) *European migrants: global and local perspectives*, Boston: Northeastern University Press, pp. 282–308

Bamyeh, Mohammed A. (2007) 'The Palestinian diaspora', in Hazel Smith and Paul Stares (eds) *Diasporas in conflict: peace-makers and peace-wreckers*, Tokyo: United Nations University Press, pp. 90–105

Bauer, Yehuda (1980) *The Jewish emergence from powerlessness*, Basingstoke: Macmillan

Baumann, Zygmunt (1989) *Modernity and the holocaust*, Cambridge: Polity

Baumann, Martin (2000) 'Diaspora: genealogies of semantics and transcultural comparison', *Numen*, 47(3), 313–37

Beall, Jo (1990) 'Women under indenture in colonial Natal, 1860–1911', in Colin Clarke *et al.* (eds) *South Asians overseas: migration and ethnicity*, Cambridge: Cambridge University Press, pp. 57–74

Bendix, Reinhard (1973) *Max Weber: an intellectual portrait*, London: Methuen

Berthomière, William and Christine Chivallon (eds) (2006) *Les diasporas dans le monde contemporain*, Paris: Karthala and Maison des Sciences de l'Homme, Bordeaux, Pessac

Boadi-Siaw, S. Y. (1993) 'Brazilian returnees of West Africa', in Joseph E. Harris (ed.) *Global dimensions of the African diaspora*, Washington, DC: Howard University Press (second edition), pp. 421–37

Bobb, Dilip and Asoka Raina (1985) *The great betrayal: assassination of Indira Gandhi*, Delhi: Vikas

Bonacich, Edna (1973) 'A theory of middlemen minorities', *American Sociological Review*, 38, 583–94

Bonacich, Edna (1988) 'The costs of immigrant entrepreneurship', in Ivan Light and Edna Bonacich, *Immigrant entrepreneurs*, Berkeley: University of California Press, pp. 425–36

Bonacich, Edna (1993) 'The other side of ethnic entrepreneurship: a dialogue with Waldinger, Aldrich, Ward and associates', *International Migration Review*, 27(3), 685–92

Boot, Adrian and Michael Thomas (1976) *Jamaica: Babylon on a thin wire*, London: Thames & Hudson

Bordes-Benayoun, Chantal and Dominique Schnapper (2006) *Diasporas et nations*, Paris: Odile Jacob

Boyajian, Levon and Haigaz Grigorian (1991) 'Psychosocial sequelae of the Armenian genocide', in R. G. Hovannisian (ed.) *The Armenian genocide in perspective*, New Brunswick, NJ: Transaction Publishers, pp.177–85

Boyarin, Daniel (1994) *A radical Jew: Paul and the politics of identity*, Berkeley: University of California Press

Boyarin, Daniel and Jonathan Boyarin (1993) 'Diaspora: generation and the ground of Jewish identity', *Critical Enquiry*, 19(4), 693–725

Boyarin, Daniel and Jonathan Boyarin (1994) 'Powers of diaspora', paper presented at the International Congress of the Historical Sciences, Montreal, 27 August–3 September

Boyarin, Jonathan (1992) *Storm from paradise: the politics of Jewish memory*, Minneapolis: University of Minnesota Press

Boyarin, Jonathan (1995) 'Powers of diaspora', paper presented to a panel on diaspora at the International Congress of the Historical Sciences, Montreal, 27 August–3 September

Brah, Avtar (1996) *Cartographies of diaspora: contesting identities*, London: Routledge

Brass, T. *et al.* (1993) *Free and unfree labour*, Amsterdam: International Institute for Social History

Bridge, Carl and Kent Fedorowich (eds) (2003) *The British world: diaspora, culture and identity*, London: Frank Cass

Brown, Judith M. (2006) *Global South Asians: introducing the modern diaspora*, Cambridge: Cambridge University Press

Browne, Thomas (1646–72) *Pseudodoxia epidemica*, London, six editions

Brubaker, Rogers (2005) 'The "diaspora" diaspora', *Ethnic and Racial Studies*, 28(1), 1–19

Castles, Stephen and Godula Kosack (1985) *Immigrant workers and class structure in western Europe*, Oxford: Oxford University Press (second edition)

Césaire, Aimé (1956) *Return to my native land*, Harmondsworth: Penguin

Chadney, James G. (1984) *The Sikhs of Vancouver*, New York: AMS Press

Chaliand, Gerard and Yves Ternon (1983) *The Armenians: from genocide to resistance*, translated by Tony Berrett, London: Zed Books

Chan Kwok Bun and Ong Jin Hui (1995) 'The many faces of immigration entrepreneurship', in Robin Cohen (ed.) *The Cambridge survey of world migration*, Cambridge: Cambridge University Press, pp. 523–31

Chariandy, David (2006) 'Postcolonial diasporas' *Postcolonial Text*, 2(1) http://postcolonial. org/index.php/pct/article/view/440/159 (online journal with no page numbers)

Chivallon, Christine (2004) *La diaspora noire de Amériques: expériences et theories à partir de la Caraïbe*, Paris: CNRS Editions

CIA (2007) *The world factbook*, Washington: Central Intelligence Agency

Clarke, Colin *et al.* (1990) *South Asians overseas: migration and ethnicity*, Cambridge: Cambridge University Press

Clifford, James (1992) 'Traveling cultures', in Lawrence Grossberg *et al.* (eds) *Cultural studies*, New York: Routledge, pp. 96–116

Clifford, James (1994) 'Diasporas', *Current Anthropology*, 9(3), 302–38

Cohen, Abner (1971) 'Cultural strategies in the organization of trading diasporas', in Claude Meillassoux (ed.) *The development of indigenous trade and markets in West Africa*, Oxford: Oxford University Press, pp. 266–81

Cohen, Robin (1987) *The new helots: migrants in the international division of labour*, Aldershot: Gower

Cohen, Robin (1992) 'A diaspora of a diaspora? The case of the Caribbean', *Social Science Information*, 31(1), 193–203

Cohen, Robin (1994) *Frontiers of identity: the British and the Others*, London: Longman

Cohen, Robin (1996) 'Diasporas and the nation-state: from victims to challengers', *International Affairs*, 72(3), 507–20

Cohen, Robin (2007) 'Creolization and cultural globalization: the soft sounds of fugitive power', *Globalizations*, 4(3), 1–16

Cohen, Robin and Paul Kennedy (2007) *Global sociology*. Basingstoke: Palgrave

Cohen, Stanley and Laurie Taylor (1976) *Escape attempts: the theory and practice of resistance to everyday life*, London: Allen Lane

Collier, James Lincoln (1978) *The making of jazz: a comprehensive history*, London: Macmillan

Condon, Stephanie A. and Philip E. Ogden (1996) 'Questions of emigration, circulation and return: mobility between the French Caribbean and France', *International Journal of Population Geography*, 2, 35–50

Conner, Walker (1986) 'The impact of homelands upon diasporas', in Gabriel Sheffer (ed.) *Modern diasporas in international politics*, London: Croom Helm, pp. 16–45

Coward, Harold, John R. Hinnells and Raymond Brady Williams (eds) (2000) *The South Asian religious diaspora in Britain, Canada, and the United States*, Albany, NY: State University of New York Press

Craig, Susan (1992) 'Intertwining roots', *The Journal of Caribbean History*, 26(2), 215–27 (review article)

Cross, Malcolm (1995) '"Race", class formation and political interests: a comparison of Amsterdam and London', in Alec G. Hargreaves and Jeremy Leaman (eds) *Racism, ethnicity and politics in contemporary Europe*, Aldershot: Edward Elgar, pp. 47–78

Cross, Malcolm and Han Entzinger (eds) (1988) *Lost illusions: Caribbean minorities in Britain and the Netherlands*, London: Routledge

Curtin, Philip (1984) *Cross-cultural trade in world history*, Cambridge: Cambridge University Press

Dabydeen, David and Brinsley Samaroo (eds) (1987) *India and the Caribbean*, London: Hansib in association with the Centre for Caribbean Studies, University of Warwick and the London Strategic Policy Unit

Daily Gleaner (various dates) daily newspaper, Kingston, Jamaica

Datt, Krishna (1994) 'Indo-Fijian concerns', *Report on consultation on Fiji's constitutional review*, Suva, Fiji: International Alert and the School of Social and Economic Development, University of South Pacific, pp. 89–91

Dekmejian, R. Hrair (1991) 'Determinants of genocide: Armenians and Jews as case studies', in R. G. Hovannisian (ed.) *The Armenian genocide in perspective*, New Brunswick, NJ: Transaction Publishers, pp. 85–96

DeWind, Josh *et al.* (1979) 'Contract labour in US agriculture: the West Indian cane cutters in Florida', in Robin Cohen *et al.* (eds) *Peasants and proletarians: the struggles of third world workers*, London: Hutchinson, pp. 380–96

Dicken, Peter (1992) *Global shift: the internationalization of economic activity*, London: Paul Chapman Publishing (second edition)

Dickstein, Morris (1993) 'After the Cold War: culture as politics, politics as culture', *Social Research*, 60(3), 531–44

Dufoix, Stéphane (forthcoming) *Diasporas*, Berkeley: University of California Press

Dusenbery, Verne A. (1995) 'A Sikh diaspora', in Peter van der Veer (ed.) *Nation and migration: the politics of space in the South Asian diaspora*, Philadelphia: University of Pennsylvania Press, pp. 17–42

Encyclopaedia Judaica (1971) 16 volumes, with annual supplements, Jerusalem: Keter Publishing House

Endelman, M. (1991) 'The legitimization of the diaspora experience in recent Jewish historiography', *Modern Judaism*, 11(2), 195–209

Epstein, H. (1969) *Jewish labor in USA: an industrial, political and cultural history of the Jewish labor movement*, New York: Ktav

Esman, Milton J. (1994) *Ethnic politics*, Ithaca: Cornell University Press

Evans Braziel, Jana and Anita Mannur (2003) *Theorizing diaspora: a reader*, Oxford: Blackwell

Ewald, Janet J. (2000) 'Crossers of the sea: slaves, freedmen, and other migrants in the northwestern Indian Ocean, *c*. 1750–1914', *American Historical Review*, 105(1) Online version http://www.historycooperative.org/journals/ahr/105.1/ah000069.html

Falzon, Mark-Anthony (2003) '"Bombay, our cultural heart": rethinking the relation between homeland and diaspora', *Ethnic and Racial Studies*, 26(4), 602–83

Financial Times, 16 September 1994, daily newspaper, London

Fitzgerald, C. P. (1972) *China and the overseas Chinese: a study of Peking's changing policy, 1949–1970*, Cambridge: Cambridge University Press

Foner, Nancy (1979) 'West Indians in New York and London: a comparative analysis', *International Migration Review*, 13(2), 284–97

Foner, Nancy (1985) 'Race and colour: Jamaican migrants in London and New York', *International Migration Review*, 19(4), 708–27

Friedman, John (1986) 'The world city hypothesis', *Development and Change*, 17(1), 69–83

Friedmann, Daniel with Ulysses Santamara (1994) *Les enfants de la reine de Saba: les Juifs d'Éthiopie (Falachas) – histoire, exode, intégration*, Paris: Éditions Métailié

Fyfe, Christopher (1962) *A history of Sierra Leone*, London: Oxford University Press

Gabaccia, Donna (1988) *Militants and migrants: rural Sicilians become American workers*, New Brunswick, NJ: Rutgers University Press

Gabaccia, Donna (1992) 'Clase y cultura: los migrantes Italianos en los movimientos obreros en el mundo, 1876–1914, *Estudios Migratorios Latinoamericanos*, 7(22), 425–51

Gabaccia, Donna (2000) *Italy's many diasporas*, London: UCL Press

Gilman, S. (1986) *Jewish self-hatred: anti-Semitism and the hidden language of the Jews*, Baltimore: Johns Hopkins University Press

Gilroy, Paul (1987) *'There ain't no black in the Union Jack': the cultural politics of race and nation*, London: Hutchinson

Gilroy, Paul (1993a) *The black Atlantic: modernity and double consciousness*, London: Verso

Gilroy, Paul (1993b) *Small acts: thoughts on the politics of black cultures*, London: Serpent's Tail

Gittler, Joseph B. (ed.) (1981) *Jewish life in the United States: perspectives from the social sciences*, New York: New York University Press

Glick Schiller, Nina, L. Basch and C. Blanc Szanton (1995) 'From immigrant to transmigrant: theorizing transnational migration', *Anthropological Quarterly*, 68(1), 48–63.

Goitein, Solomon Dob Fritz (1967–93) *A Mediterranean society: the Jewish communities of the Arab world as portrayed in the documents of the Cairo Geniza*, 6 vols, Berkeley: University of California Press

Gold, Steven J. (2002) *The Israeli diaspora*, London: Routledge

Goldberg, David J. (2006) *The divided self: Israel and the Jewish psyche today*, London: I. B. Tauris

Goldberg, David J. and John D. Raynor (1989) *The Jewish people: their history and their religion*, Harmondsworth: Penguin

Goldberg, David Theo and Michael Krausz (eds) (1993) *Jewish identity*, Philadelphia: Temple University Press

Goldberg, J. J. (2007) 'Avraham Burg's new Zionism', www.forward.com/articles/avraham-burg-s-new-zionism accessed 2 August 2007.

Gopinath, Gayati (2005) *Impossible desire: queer diasporas and South Asian public cultures*, Durham, NC: Duke University Press

Gorny, Yosef (1994) *The state of Israel in Jewish public thought: the quest for collective identity*, Basingstoke: Macmillan

Green, Nancy L. (1995) 'The modern Jewish diaspora: Eastern European Jews in New York, London and Paris', in Dirk Hoerder and Leslie Page Moch (eds) *European migrants: global and local perspectives*, Boston: Northeastern University Press, pp. 263–81

Griffiths, David J. (2002) *Somali and Kurdish refugees in London: new identities in the diaspora*, Aldershot: Ashgate

Grunwald, M. (1936) *History of the Jews in Vienna*, Philadelphia: Jewish Publication Society of America

Guardian (various dates) daily newspaper, London

Hall, Stuart (1990) 'Cultural identity and diaspora', in Jonathan Rutherford (ed.) *Identity: community, culture, difference*, London: Lawrence & Wishart, pp. 222–37

Hall, Stuart (1991a) 'Ethnicity, identity and difference', *Radical America*, 23(4), 9–20

Hall, Stuart (1991b) 'The local and the global: globalization and ethnicity', in Anthony D. King (ed.) *Culture, globalization and the world-system: contemporary conditions for the representation of identity*, Basingstoke: Macmillan

Hall, Stuart (1995) 'Negotiating Caribbean identities', *New Left Review*, No. 209, January–February, pp. 3–14

Hamilian, Leo (1981) 'The Armenian genocide and the literary imagination', in Richard G. Hovannisian (ed.) *The Armenian genocide in perspective*, New Brunswick, NJ: Transaction, pp. 153–65

Hammerton, A. James (1979) *Emigrant gentlewomen: genteel poverty and female emigration, 1830–1914*, London: Croom Helm

Harney, Stefano (1996) *Nationalism and identity: culture and the imagination in a Caribbean diaspora*, London: Zed Books

Harris, Joseph E. (1971) *The African presence in Asia: consequences of the East African slave trade*, Evanston, IL: Northwestern University Press

Harris, Nigel (1995) *The new untouchables: immigration and the new world order*, London: I. B. Tauris

Hasan-Rokem, Galit and Alan Dundes (eds) (1986) *The wandering Jew: essays in the interpretation of a Christian legend*, Bloomington, IN: Indiana University Press

Hashimoto, Kohei (1992) 'Lebanese population movements, 1920–1939: towards a study', in Albert Hourani and Nadim Shehadi (eds) *The Lebanese in the world: a century of emigration*, London: I. B. Tauris for the Centre for Lebanese Studies, pp. 65–108

Heilman, S. (1982) 'The sociology of American Jewry: the last ten years', *Annual Review of Sociology*, 8, 135–60

Helmrich, Stefan (1992) 'Kinship, nation and Paul Gilroy's concept of diaspora', *Diaspora*, 2(2), 243–9

Helweg, Arthur W. (1979) *Sikhs in England: the development of a migrant community*, Delhi: Oxford University Press

Henderson, Jeff and Manuel Castells (eds) (1987) *Global restructuring and territorial development*, London: Sage

Herskovits, Melville J. (1937) *Life in a Haitian valley*, New York: Alfred A. Knopf

Herskovits, Melville J. (1961) *The New World Negro: selected papers in Afro-American studies*, Bloomington, IN: Indiana University Press

Herskovits, Melville J. *et al.* (1947) *Trinidad village*, New York: Alfred Knopf

Hinnells, John R. (1994) 'The modern Zoroastrian diaspora', in Judith M. Brown and Rosemary Foot (eds) *Migration: the Asian experience*, New York: St Martin's Press in association with St Antony's College, Oxford, pp. 56–82

Hinnells, John R. (2005) *The Zoroastrian diaspora: religion and migration*, Oxford: Oxford University Press

Hintjens, Helen M. (1995) *Alternatives to independence: explorations in post-colonial relations*, Aldershot: Dartmouth

Hitti, Philip K. (1974) *History of the Arabs: from the earliest times to the present*, London: Macmillan

Holt, Richard (1990) *Sport and the British: a modern history*, Oxford: Oxford University Press

Hourani, Albert (1983) *Arabic thought in the liberal age, 1798–1939,* Cambridge: Cambridge University Press

Hourani, Albert (1991) *A history of the Arab peoples*, Cambridge, MA: The Belknap Press of Harvard University Press

Hourani, Albert (1992) 'Introduction', in Albert Hourani and Nadim Shehadi (eds) *The Lebanese in the world: a century of emigration*, London: I.B. Tauris for the Centre for Lebanese Studies, pp. 3–11

Hourani, Albert and Nadim Shehadi (eds) (1992) *The Lebanese in the world: a century of emigration*, London: I. B. Tauris for the Centre for Lebanese Studies

Hourani, Guita G. and Eugene Sensinig-Dabbous (2007) *Insecurity, migration and return: the case of Lebanon following the Summer 2006 war*, Florence: Robert Schuman Centre for Advanced Studies, European University Institute

Hovanessian, Martine (1992) *Le lien communautaire: trois générations d'Armeniens*, Paris: Armand Colin

Hovannisian, Richard G. (1981) 'The historical dimensions of the Armenian question, 1878–1923', in Richard G. Hovannisian (ed.) *The Armenian genocide in perspective*, New Brunswick, NJ: Transaction, pp. 19–41

Hu-DeHart, Evelyn (1993) 'Rethinking America: the practice and politics of multiculturalism in higher education', in Becky W. Thompson and Sangeeta Tyagi (eds) *Beyond a dream deferred: multicultural education and the politics of excellence*, Minneapolis: University of Minnesota Press, pp. 3–17

Huntington, Samuel P. (2004) *Who are we? America's great debate*, London: Simon & Schuster

Hunwick, J. O. (1993) 'African slaves in the Mediterranean world: a neglected aspect of the African diaspora', in Joseph E. Harris (ed.) *Global dimensions of the African diaspora*, Washington, DC: Howard University Press, second edition, pp. 289–324

Ionescu, Dina (2007) *Engaging diasporas at development partners for home and destination countries: challenges for policymakers*, Geneva: International Organization for Migration

Israel, B. J. (1971) *The children of Israel: the Bene Israel of Bombay*, Oxford: Basil Blackwell

Issawi, Charles (1992) 'The historical background of Lebanese emigration, 1800–1914', in Albert Hourani and Nadim Shehadi (eds) *The Lebanese in the world: a century of emigration*, London: I. B. Tauris for the Centre for Lebanese Studies, pp. 13–31

Jacobson, David (1996) *Rights across borders: immigration and the decline of citizenship*, Baltimore: Johns Hopkins University Press

Kalberg, Stephen (1999) 'Max Weber', in Adam Kuper and Jessica Kuper (eds) *The social science encyclopaedia*, London: Routledge

Kalra, Virinder S., Raminder Kaur and John Hutnyk (2005) *Diaspora and hybridity*, London: Sage

Kelly, John D. (1995) '*Bhaki* and postcolonial politics: Hindu missions to Fiji', in Peter van der Veer (ed.) *Nation and migration: the politics of space in the South Asian diaspora*, Philadelphia: University of Pennsylvania Press, pp. 43–72

Kennedy, Paul (1988) *African capitalism: the struggle for ascendency*, Cambridge: Cambridge University Press

Khalidi, Walid (1984) *Before their diaspora: a photographic history of the Palestinians, 1876–1948*, Washington, DC: Institute for Palestine Studies

Khan, Aisha (1995) 'Homeland, motherland: authenticity, legitimacy and ideologies of place among Muslims in Trinidad', in Peter van der Veer (ed.) *Nation and migration: the politics of space in the South Asian diaspora*, Philadelphia: University of Pennsylvania Press, pp. 93–131

Kinealy, Christine (1995) *The great calamity: the Irish famine, 1845–52*, London: Gill & Macmillan

King, Russell, Allan M. Williams and Tony Warnes (2000) *Sunset lives: British retirement migration to the Mediterranean*, Oxford: Berg Publishers

Kirshenblatt-Gimblett, Barbara (1994) 'Spaces of dispersal', *Cultural Anthropology*, 9(3), 339–44

Klich, Ignacio (1992) '*Criollos* and Arabic speakers in Argentina: an uneasy *pas de deux*, 1888–1914', in Albert Hourani and Nadim Shehadi (eds) *The Lebanese in the world: a century of emigration*, London: I.B.Tauris for the Centre for Lebanese Studies, pp. 243–84

Knott, Kim (1991) 'Bound to change? The religions of South Asians in Britain' in Steven Vertovec (ed.) *Aspects of the South Asian diaspora*, Delhi: Oxford University Press, 1991, pp. 86–111

Koawe, Khalid (ed.) (2003) *New African diasporas*, London: Routledge

Koestler, Arthur (1976) *The thirteenth tribe: the Khazar empire and its heritage*, London: Hutchinson

Koser, Khalid (2007) 'African diasporas and post-conflict reconstruction: an Eritrean case study', in Hazel Smith and Paul Stares (eds) *Diasporas in conflict: peace-makers and peace-wreckers*, Tokyo: United Nations University Press, pp. 239–52

Koser, Khalid (ed.) (2003) *New African diasporas*, London: Routledge

Kotkin, Joel (1992) *Tribes: how race, religion and identity determine success in the new global economy*, New York: Random House

Kuper, Adam and Jessica Kuper (eds) (1999) *The social science encyclopaedia*, London: Routledge

Kurkjian, Vahan M. (1964) *A history of Armenia*, New York: Armenian General Benevolent Union of America

Kwong, Peter (1987) *The new Chinatown*, New York: Hill & Wang

Lal, Brij V., Peter Reeves and Rajesh Rai (eds) (2006) *The encyclopedia of the Indian diaspora*, Singapore: Editions Didier Millet in association with National University of Singapore

Lal, Victor (1990) 'The Fiji Indians: marooned at home', in Colin Clarke *et al.* (eds) *South Asians overseas: migration and ethnicity*, Cambridge: Cambridge University Press, pp. 113–30

Lang, David Marshall (1978) *Armenia: cradle of civilisation*, London: George Allen & Unwin

Lang, David Marshall and Christopher J. Walker (1987) *The Armenians*, London: Minority Rights Group, MRG Report No. 32, fifth edition

Lemelle, S. J. *et al.* (1994) *Imagining home: class, culture and nationalism in the African diaspora*, London: Verso

Lemon, Anthony (1990) 'The political position of Indians in South Africa', in Colin Clarke *et al.* (eds) *South Asians overseas: migration and ethnicity*, Cambridge: Cambridge University Press, pp. 131–63

Lever-Tracy, Constance, David Ip and Noel Tracy (1996) *The Chinese diaspora and Mainland China: an emerging economic synergy*, Basingstoke: Macmillan

Levin, N. (1977) *While Messiah tarried: Jewish socialist movements, 1871–1917*, New York: Schocken

Levitt, Peggy (2001) *The transnational villagers*, Berkeley: University of California Press

Levy, André and Alex Weingrod (eds) (2004) *Homelands and diasporas: holy lands and other spaces*, Stanford: Stanford University Press

Lewis, Bernard (1970) *The Arabs in history*, London: Hutchinson University Library

Lian, Kwen Fee (1995) 'Migration and the formation of Malaysia and Singapore', in Robin Cohen (ed.) *The Cambridge survey of world migration*, Cambridge: Cambridge University Press, pp. 392–6

Liebman, A. (1979) *Jews and the left*, New York: Wiley

Liebman, C. (1976) *The ambivalent American Jew*, Philadelphia: Jewish Publication Society

Liebman, Charles S. and Steven M. Cohen (1990) *Two worlds of Judaism: the Israeli and American experiences*, New Haven: Yale University Press

Lindemann, Albert S. (1993) *The Jew accused: three anti-Semitic affairs: Dreyfus, Beilis, Frank, 1884–1915*, Cambridge: Cambridge University Press

Lippman Abu-Lughod, Janet (1995) 'The displacement of the Palestinians', in Robin Cohen (ed.) *The Cambridge survey of world migration*, Cambridge: Cambridge University Press

Maalouf, Amin (1984) *The Crusades through Arab eyes*, London: Al Saqi

Magubane, Bernard Makhosezwe (1987) *The ties that bind: African-American consciousness of Africa*, Trenton, NJ: Africa World Press

Malkki, Liisa (1992) 'National geographic: the rooting of peoples and the territorialization of national identity among scholars and refugees', *Cultural Anthropology*, 7, 24–44

Marienstras, Richard (1989) 'On the notion of diaspora', in Gérard Chaliand (ed.) *Minority peoples in the age of nation-states*, London: Pluto Press

Markowitz, F. (1990) 'Plaiting the strands of Jewish identity', *Comparative Studies in Society and History*, 32(1), 181–9

Marriott, Sir John A. R. (1927) *Empire settlement*, London: Oxford University Press

Marrus, Michael R. (1980) *The politics of assimilation: the French Jewish community at the time of the Dreyfus affair*, Oxford: Clarendon Press

Marrus, Michael R. (1981) *Vichy France and the Jews*, New York: Basic Books

Marx, Karl (1959) 'The eighteenth Brumaire of Louis Napolean', in Lewis S. Feuer (ed.) *Marx and Engels: basic writings on politics and philosophy*, New York: Anchor Books, pp. 318–48 (first published 1852)

Mazrui, Ali A. (1990) *Cultural forces in world politics*, London: James Currey

McCabe, Ina Baghdiantz, Gelina Harlaftis and Ioanna Pepelasis Minoglou (eds) (2005) *Diaspora entrepreneurial networks: four centuries of history*, Oxford: Berg

McDowell, Christopher (1996) *A Tamil asylum diaspora: Sri Lankan migration, settlement and politics in Switzerland*, Oxford: Berghahn Books

McGown, Rima Berns (1999) *Muslims in the diaspora: The Somali communities of London and Toronto*, Toronto: University of Toronto Press

Melson, Robert (1992) *Revolution and genocide: on the origins of the Armenian genocide and the holocaust*, Chicago: University of Chicago Press

Mirzoeff, Nicholas (2000) *Diaspora and visual culture: representing Africans and Jews*, London: Routledge

Mishra, Vijay (2007) *The literature of the Indian diaspora: theorizing the diasporic imaginary*, London: Routledge

Mohapatra, Sanket, Dilip Ratha and Zhimei Xu (2007) *Migration and Development*, Brief 2 Development Prospects Group, Migration and Remittances Team 1, Remittance Trends, Washington, DC: World Bank

Montilus, Guerin C. (1993) 'Guinea versus Congo lands: aspects of the collective memory in Haiti', in Joseph E. Harris (ed.) *Global dimensions of the African diaspora*, Washington, DC: Howard University Press, second edition, pp. 159–66

Naff, Alixa (1992) 'Lebanese immigration into the United States: 1880 to the present', in Albert Hourani and Nadim Shehadi (eds) *The Lebanese in the world: a century of emigration*, London: I. B. Tauris for the Centre for Lebanese Studies, pp. 141–65

Nairn, Tom (1977) *The break-up of Britain: crisis and neo-nationalism*, London: Verso

Needham, Rodney (1975) 'Polythetic classification: convergence and consequences', *Man* (NS) vol. 10, pp. 349–69

Nersessian, Sirarpie Der (1969) *The Armenians*, London: Thames & Hudson

Neusner, Jacob (1985) *Israel in America: a too-comfortable exile?* Boston: Beacon

O'Sullivan, Patrick (1992–97) *The Irish world wide: history, heritage, identity*, six vols, I: *Patterns of migration*; II: *Irish in the new communities*; III: *The creative migrant*; IV: *Irish women and Irish migration*; V: *Religion and identity*; VI: *The meaning of the famine*, Leicester: Leicester University Press

Oliver, Paul (1970) *Savannah syncopators: African retentions in the blues*, London: Studio Vista

Ong, Jing Hui (1995) 'Chinese indentured labour: coolies and colonies', in Robin Cohen (ed.) *The Cambridge survey of world migration*, Cambridge: Cambridge University Press, pp. 51–6

Ottley, Roy (1948) *Black odyssey: the story of the Negro in America*, New York: Charles Scribner & Sons

Padmore, George (1972) *Pan-Africanism or communism*, New York: Doubleday (first published 1949)

Palmer, R. W. (ed.) (1990) *In search of a better life: perspectives on migration from the Caribbean*, New York: Praeger

Pan, Lynn (1991) *Sons of the yellow emperor: the story of the overseas Chinese*, London: Mandarin

Parekh, Bhikhu (1994) 'Some reflections on the Hindu diaspora', *New Community*, 20(4), 603–20

Paxton, Robert O. (2001) *Vichy France: old guard and new order*, New York: Colombia University Press

Peach, Ceri (1968) *West Indian migration to Britain: a social geography*, London: Oxford University Press

Peach, Ceri (1994) 'Three phases of South Asian emigration', in Judith M. Brown and Rosemary Foot (eds) *Migration: the Asian experience*, New York: St Martin's Press in association with St Antony's College, Oxford, pp. 38–55

Peach, Ceri (1995) 'Trends in levels of Caribbean segregation, Great Britain, 1961–91', paper presented at a Conference on Comparative History of Migration within the Caribbean and to Europe, Oxford Brookes University, Oxford, 22–4 September

Phillips, Caryl (1993) *Crossing the river*, London: Picador

Pilkington, Hilary (1998) *Migration, displacement and identity in post-Soviet Russia*, London: Routledge

Post, Ken (1978) *Arise ye starvelings: the Jamaican labour rebellion of 1938 and its aftermath*, The Hague: Martinus Nijhoff

Reich, W. (1987) 'Israel and the diaspora', *Jewish Social Studies*, 49(3–4), 326–32

Rex, John (1995) 'Ethnic identity and the nation state: the political sociology of multi-cultural societies', *Social Identities*, 1(1), 21–34

Richards, Eric (1993) 'How did poor people emigrate from the British Isles to Australia in the nineteenth century?' *Journal of British Studies*, 32(3), 250–79

Richardson, Peter (1984) 'Coolies, peasants, and proletarians: the origins of Chinese indentured labour in South African, 1904–1907', in Shula Marks and Peter Richardson (eds) *International labour migration: historical perspectives*, London: Maurice Temple Smith for the Institute of Commonwealth Studies, pp. 167–85

Richmond, Anthony H. (1994) *Global apartheid: refugees, racism and the new world order*, Toronto: Oxford University Press

Robertson, Roland (1994) 'Religion and the global field', *Social Compass*, 41(1), 121–35

Robinson, Vaughan (1995) 'The migration of East African Asians to the UK', in Robin Cohen (ed.) *The Cambridge survey of world migration*, Cambridge: Cambridge University Press, pp. 331–6

Rushdie, Salman (2006) *The Moor's last sigh*, New York: Vintage

Safran, William (1991) 'Diasporas in modern societies: myths of homeland and return', *Diaspora*, 1(1), pp. 83–99

Safran, William (2005a) 'The Jewish diaspora in a comparative and theoretical perspective', *Israel Studies*, 10(1), 37–60

Safran, William (2005b) 'The tenuous link between hostlands and homeland: the progressive dezionization of western diasporas', in Lisa Anteby-Yemeni, William Berthomière and Gabriel Sheffer (eds) *Les diasporas: 2000 ans d'histoire*, Rennes: Presse Universitaires de Rennes, pp. 193–208

Said, Edward (1991) *Orientalism: Western conceptions of the Orient*, Harmondsworth: Penguin (first published 1978)

Saroyan, William (1962) *Here comes, there goes, you know who: an autobiography*, London: Peter Davis

Sassen, Saskia (2001) *The global city*, Princeton, NJ: Princeton University Press (first published 1990)

Satzewich, Vic (2002) *The Ukrainian diaspora*, London: Routledge

Scharma, Simon (2005) *Rough crossings: Britain, the slaves and the American revolution*, London: BBC Books

Schultz, Helena Lindholm (2003) *The Palestinian diaspora: formation of identities and politics of homeland*, London: Routledge

Seagrave, Sterling (1995) *Lords of the rim: the invisible empire of the overseas Chinese*, New York: G. P. Putnam & Sons

Seeley, Sir John (1895) *The expansion of England*, Cambridge: Cambridge University Press

Segal, Aaron (1993) *An atlas of international migration*, London: Hans Zell

Segal, Ronald (1995) *The black diaspora*, London: Faber & Faber

Segal, Ronald (2001) *Islam's black slaves: the history of Africa's other black diaspora*, London: Atlantic

Selvon, Samuel (1985) *The lonely Londoners*, Harlow: Longman

Shah, Mehtab Ali (1997) *The foreign policy of Pakistan: ethnic impacts on diplomacy*, London: I.B.Tauris

Shain, Yossi (1999) *Marketing the American creed abroad: diasporas in the US and their homelands*, Cambridge: Cambridge University Press

Sharif, Regina S. (1983) *Non-Jewish Zionism: its roots in Western history*, London: Zed Books

Sheffer, Gabriel (1986) *Modern diasporas in international politics*, London: Croom Helm

Sheffer, Gabriel (2003) *Diaspora politics: at home and abroad*, Cambridge: Cambridge University Press

Shepperson, George (1993) 'African diaspora: concept and context', in Joseph E. Harris (ed.) *Global dimensions of the African diaspora*, Washington, DC: Howard University Press, second edition, pp. 41–9

Shepperson, W. S. (1957) *British emigration to North America: projects and opinions in the early Victorian period*, Oxford: Basil Blackwell

Shirreff, David (1995) *Barefeet and bandoliers: Wingate, Sandford, the Patriots and the part they played in the liberation of Ethiopia*, London: The Radcliffe Press

Shlaim, Avi (2001) *The iron wall: Israel and the Arab World*, Harmondsworth: Penguin

Shusterman, Richard (1993) 'Next year in Jerusalem: postmodern Jewish identity and the myth of return', in David Theo Goldberg and Michael Krausz (eds) *Jewish identity*, Philadephia: Temple University Press, pp. 291–308

Simms Hamilton, Ruth (1990) *Creating a paradigm and research agenda for comparative studies of the worldwide dispersion of African peoples*, East Lansing, MI: African Diaspora Research Project, Michigan State University

Singh, Gurharpal (1993) 'Review of Khushwant Singh *A history of the Sikhs. Volume 2, 1839–1988*, Delhi: Oxford University Press (second edition)', *Punjab Research Group: Newsletter of the Association for Punjab Studies in Great Britain*, 5, January, p. 13

Singh, Gurharpal and Darshan Singh Tatla (2006) *Sikhs in Britain: the making of a community*, London: Zed Books

Singh, Khushwant (1977) *A history of the Sikhs. Volume 2, 1839–1974*, Delhi: Oxford University Press (first edition)

Singh, Khushwant (1992) *My bleeding Punjab*, New Delhi: UBS Publishers

Skinner, Elliott P. (1993) 'The dialectic between diasporas and homelands', in Joseph E. Harris (ed.) *Global dimension of the African diaspora*, Washington, DC: Howard University Press, pp. 11–40 (second edition)

Smart, Ninian (1987) 'The importance of diasporas', in S. Shaked, D. Shyulman and C. G. Stroumsa (eds) *Gilgut: essays on transformation, revolution and permanence in the history of religions*, Leiden: Brill, pp. 288–97

Smith, Hazel and Paul Stares (eds) *Diasporas in conflict: peace-makers and peace-wreckers*, Tokyo: United Nations University Press

Smither, A. D. (2004) 'The business of miracle working', *Independent* (London daily newspaper) 14 August

Sökefeld, Martin (2006) 'Mobilizing in transnational space: a social movement approach to the formation of diaspora', *Global Networks*, 6 (3) pp. 265–84

Solomos, John (1989) *Race and racism in contemporary Britain*, Basingstoke: Macmillan

Soysal, Yasemin Nugoğlu (2000) 'Citizenship and identity: living in diasporas in post-war Europe?' *Ethnic and Racial Studies*, 23(1), 1–15

Suny, Roland Grigor (1993) *Looking toward Ararat: Armenia in modern history*, Bloomington, IN: Indiana University Press

Sutton, Constance R. and Susan R. Makiesky (1975) 'Migration and West Indian racial and ethnic consciousness', in Helen I. Safa and Brian M. Du Toit (eds) *Migration and development: implications for ethnic identity and political conflict*, The Hague: Mouton, pp. 113–43

Tatla, Darshan Singh (1999) *The Sikh diaspora: the search for statehood*, London: UCL Press

Thiara, Ravi (1995) 'Indian indentured workers in Mauritius, Natal and Fiji', in Robin Cohen (ed.) *The Cambridge survey of world migration*, Cambridge: Cambridge University Press, pp. 63–8

Tinker, Hugh (1974) *A new system of slavery: the export of Indian labour overseas, 1830–1920*, London: Oxford University Press for the Institute of Race Relations

Tinker, Hugh (1977) *The Banyan tree: overseas emigrants from India, Pakistan and Bangladesh*, Oxford: Oxford University Press

Tinker, Hugh (1990) 'Indians in Southeast Asia: Imperial auxiliaries', in Colin Clarke *et al.* (eds) *South Asians overseas*, Cambridge: Cambridge University Press, pp. 39–56

Tölölyan, Kachig (2000) 'Elites and institutions in the Armenian diaspora's history', *Diaspora: A Journal of Transnational Studies*, 9(1), 107–36

Tölölyan, Kachig (2002) *Redefining diasporas: old approaches, new identities: the Armenian diaspora in an international context*, Occasional paper, London: Armenian Institute.

Tölölyan, Khachig (2005) 'Restoring the logic of the sedentary to diaspora studies', in Lisa Anteby-Yemeni, William Berthomière and Gabriel Sheffer (eds) *Les diasporas: 2000 ans d'histoire*, Rennes: Presse Universitaires de Rennes, pp. 137-48

Tölölyan, Khachig (2007) 'The Armenian diaspora and the Karabagh conflict', in Hazel Smith and Paul Stares (eds) *Diasporas in conflict: peace-makers and peace-wreckers*, Tokyo: United Nations University Press, pp. 106–28.

Totoricagüena, Gloria (2004) *Basque diaspora: migration and transnational identity*, Las Vegas: Center for Basque Studies at the University of Nevada

Toynbee, Arnold (1934–61) *A study of history*, 12 vols, London: Oxford University Press

Toynbee, Arnold (ed.) (1916) *The treatment of Armenians in the Ottoman empire, 1915–16*, London: Her Majesty's Stationary Office

Toynbee, Arnold J. (1957) *A study of history*. Abridgement of vols 7–10 by D. C. Somervell, London: Oxford University Press under the auspices of the Royal Institute of International Affairs

Toynbee, Arnold with Jane Caplan (1988) *A study of history*, London: Oxford University Press (revised abridged edition, first published 1972)

Turner, Victor (1969) *The ritual process, structure and anti-structure*, London: Routledge & Kegan Paul

UNHCR (2007) *Global trends 2006*, Geneva: United Nations High Commission for Refugees, available at http://www.unhcr.org/statistics/STATISTICS/4676a71d4.pdf

van der Laan, H. L. (1975) *The Lebanese traders in Sierra Leone*, The Hague: Mouton for the Afrika-Studiecentrum, Leiden

Van Hear, Nicholas (1998) *New diasporas: the mass exodus, dispersal and regrouping of migrant communities*, London: UCL Press

Vecoli, Rudolph J. (1995) 'The Italian diaspora 1876–1976', in Robin Cohen (ed.) *The Cambridge survey of world migration*, Cambridge: Cambridge University Press, pp. 114–22

Vertovec, Steven (1995) 'Indian indentured migration to the Caribbean', in Robin Cohen (ed.) *The Cambridge survey of world migration*, Cambridge: Cambridge University Press, pp. 57–62

Vertovec, Steven (1999) 'Conceiving and researching transnationalism', *Ethnic and Racial Studies*, 22(2), 447–62

Vertovec, Steven (2000) *The Hindu diaspora: comparative patterns*, London: Routledge

Vertovec, Steven (2001) 'Religion and diaspora', Working paper, Transnational Communities Programme, University of Oxford, WPTC-01-01, http://www.transcomm.ox.ac.uk/working%20papers/Vertovec01.PDF

Vertovec, Steven and Robin Cohen (2001) 'Introduction: conceiving cosmopolitanism', in Steven Vertovec and Robin Cohen (eds) *Conceiving cosmopolitanism: theory, context and practice*, Oxford: Oxford University Press, pp. 1–22

Vertovec, Steven and Robin Cohen (eds) (1999) *Migration, diasporas and transnationalism*, Cheltenham: Edward Elgar

Visram, Rozina (1986) *Ayahs, lascars and princes: Indians in Britain, 1700–1947*, London: Pluto Press

Vital, David (1990) *The future of the Jews: a people at the cross-roads?* Cambridge, MA: Harvard University Press

Wade, Nicholas (1999) 'Group in Africa has Jewish roots, DNA indicates', *New York Times*, 9 May

Wahlbeck, Östen (1999) *Kurdish diasporas: a comparative study of Kurdish refugee communities*, Basingstoke: Palgrave Macmillan

Wakefield, Edward Gibbon (1969) *A view of the art of colonization*, New York: A. M. Kelley (first published 1849)

Waldinger, Roger (1996) 'Review of Seymour Martin Lipset and Earl Raab *Jews and the new American scene*, Cambridge, MA: Harvard University Press, 1995 in *New Community*, 22(1), 174–5

Walker, Christopher J. (1980) *Armenia: survival of a nation*, London: Croom Helm

Wang Gungwu (1991) *China and the Chinese overseas*, Singapore: Times Academic Press

Wang Gungwu (1992a) *Community and nation: China, Southeast Asia and Australia*, St Leonards, Australia: Allen & Unwin for the Asian Studies Association of Australia

Wang Gungwu (1992b) 'Sojourning: the Chinese experience in Southeast Asia', Jennifer Cushman Memorial Lecture, mimeo

Wang L. Ling-chi and Wang Gungwu (eds) *The Chinese diaspora: selected essays*, Singapore: Times Academic Press, 1998, 2 vols

Weaver, Alain Epp (n.d.) *Constantinianism, Zionism, diaspora: toward a political theology of exile and return*, Occasional Papers, Number 28, Akron, Pennsylvania: Mennonite Central Committee, http://mcc.org/respub/occasional/28.html

Weekly Gleaner (various dates) weekly newspaper, London

Weiner, Myron (1986) 'Labour migrations and incipient diasporas', in Gabriel Sheffer (ed.) *Modern diasporas in international politics*, London: Croom Helm, pp. 47–74

Werbner, Pnina (2002) 'The place which is diaspora: citizenship, religion and gender in the making of chaordic transnationalism', *Journal of Ethnic and Migration Studies*, 28(1), 119–33

Williams, Eric (1964) *Capitalism and slavery*, London: André Deutsch (first published 1944)

Wilson, Francesca M. (1959) *They came as strangers: the story of refugees to Great Britain*, London: Hamish Hamilton

Wong Siu-lun (ed) (2004) *Chinese and Indian diasporas: comparative perspectives*, Hong Kong: Centre of Asian Studies, University of Hong Kong

Woolfson, Marion (1980) *Prophets in Babylon: Jews in the Arab world*, London: Faber & Faber

Wright, Richard (1944) *American hunger*, New York: Harper & Row

Yawney, Carole D. (1995) 'The globalization of Rastafari: methodological and conceptual issues', paper presented at the annual meeting of the Society for Caribbean Studies (UK) London, 5–7 July

Zolberg, Aristide R. (1983) 'The formation of new states as a refugee generating process', *Annals of the American Academy of Political and Social Science*, 467, 24–38

Zolberg, Aristide, *et al.* (1989) *Escape from violence: conflict and the refugee crisis in the developing world*, New York: Oxford University Press

INDEX

Social Movements *A Reader*

Vincenzo Ruggiero and
Nicola Montagna, Middlesex University, UK

Routledge
Taylor & Francis Group

This timely reader plays an important role in the field of social movements, filling a
significant gap by covering a number of connected areas within social studies.
Responding to growing demand for interpretation and analysis of re-emerging social
conflicts in the developed as well as the developing world, this timely collection is the
outcome of the recent boost received by social movement studies since the spread of
contention and collective action at international level and the growth of the 'anti-
globalization' movement.

Ruggiero and Montagna have compiled key classic, as well as contemporary, works
written by distinguished international experts, from a variety of disciplines. These
address themes of conflict, social change, social movements and globalization.
Intended not only as a comprehensive introduction undergraduate and postgraduates
studying social movements, this volume is also an incredibly valuable resource for
more general modules on sociological theory, global sociology, the history of
sociological thought, contemporary social theory, international and globalization
studies.

Contents
Part 1: Conflict and Collective Action. Part 2: Hegemony and Collective Behaviour.
Part 3: Resource Mobilisation. Part 4: Social Movements and the Political Process. Part
5: New Social Movements. Part 6: New Directions. Part 7: New Global Movements

June 2008

PB: 978-0-415-44582-5: £24.99
HB: 978-0-415-44581-8 : £85.00

Routledge books are available from
all good bookshops, or can be
ordered by calling Taylor and Francis
Direct Sales on +4401264343071
(credit card orders)

Theories of Race and Racism 2e
A Reader

Les Back, University of London, UK
John Solomos, City University,
London, UK

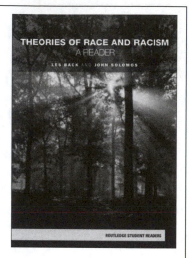

Theories of Race and Racism: A Reader is an important and innovative collection that brings together extracts from the work of scholars, both established and up and coming, who have helped to shape the study of race and racism as an historical and contemporary phenomenon.

This second edition incorporates new contributions and editorial material and allows readers to explore the changing terms of debates about the nature of race and racism in contemporary societies. All six parts are organized around the contributions made by theorists whose work has been influential in shaping theoretical debates. The various contributions have been chosen to reflect different theoretical perspectives and to help readers gain a feel for the changing terms of theoretical debate over time. As well as covering the main concerns of past and recent theoretical debates it provides a glimpse of relatively new areas of interest that are likely to attract more attention in years to come.

Contents

Part 1: Origins and Transformations Part 2: Sociology, Race and Social Theory Part 3: Racism and Anti-Semitism Part 4: Colonialism, Race and the Other Part 5: Feminism, Difference and Identity Part 6: Changing Boundaries and Spaces

July 2008

PB: 978-0-415-41254-4 : £23.99
HB: 978-0-415-41253-7 : £85.00

Routledge books are available from all good bookshops, or can be ordered by calling Taylor and Francis Direct Sales on +4401264343071 (credit card orders)